THE NATURE OF CITIES is lavishly illustrated with over 275 illustrations of plans, diagrams and photographs showing principal aspects of cities from the Stone-Age to the present.

THE NATURE OF CITIES will prove a most valuable addition to the library of any architect, engineer, town or city planner, teachers, students, municipal officials—anyone concerned with the future of our cities and humanity. 290 pages. 8 ½ x 11. Cloth bound.

Typography and jacket design by William Fleming

About the Author

Professor Hilberseimer, is a native of Karlsruhe, Germany, where he attended the Institute of Technology to study architecture and city planning. Upon completion of his studies he established himself as an independent architect and planner with activities in Berlin and other European cities.

Professor Hilberseimer has written extensively on art and architecture, housing and planning, contributing widely to many leading periodicals. He is the author of several well-known books—INTERNAZIONALE BAUKUNST (International Architecture), GROS-STADT ARCHITEKTUR (Architecture of the Metropolis), BETON ALS GESTALTER (Concrete as a Formative Element), HALLENBAUTEN (Auditoriums), written as a requested treatise for HANDBUCH DER AR-CHITEKTUR—the largest encyclopedic reference work on architecture, THE NEW CITY now out of print and THE NEW REGIONAL PATTERN.

Professor Hilberseimer taught for five years at the Bauhaus of Dessau where he founded the Department of City Planning. In 1938 he came to the United States to live. He has held the position of Professor of City Planning at the School of Architecture of the Illinois Institute of Technology in Chicago ever since.

The Nature of Cities

L. Hilberseimer

The Nature of Cities

Origin, Growth, and Decline

Pattern and Form

Planning Problems

Paul Theobald & Co.

Chicago 1955

Contents

Illustrations

A Dead and A Living City

III. Planning Problems

A Note by the Author

"The New City", published in 1944 and long out of print, may well be replaced by the present volume, "The Nature of Cities". This book deals with the same problems, but is wider in scope and more liberally illustrated.

While it was in the state of publication, some of the effects the H-bomb may have on our cities and on their spacing, were made public. This necessitated some last minute readjustments and the preparation of a diagram illustrating the probable influence on planning of these effects. The communities and city aggregates herein developed, having been planned for decentralization, met the new requirements without alteration. Only their spacing will be affected.

I wish to express my gratitude to Alfred Caldwell for his generous help. The more detailed study of the south side of Chicago was made in co-operation with Earl Bluestein, Jacques Brownson and Reginald Malcolmson. I wish also to thank various students of the Illinois Institute of Technology for their assistance in preparing some of the illustrations. I am particularly indebted to Klaus Anschuetz, Robert Jones, Joseph Krofta, David Ornstein, John Quay, David Tamminga, Ramachandrasa Vagale and Edmund Zisook.

Chicago, December, 1954

A DEAD AND A LIVING CITY

12

Preface

THE NATURE OF CITIES embodies three parallel studies. Each deals with one aspect of the city; together they form a unity. The first study deals with the city's origin, growth, and decline. It is a history of city types rather than of particular cities. The second study, on pattern and form, has to do with the two orders of planning: the geometric and the organic, which govern city types, city architecture, and city landscape. The third study considers the planning problems with which the modern city and its region are confronted in our industrial age.

The first two studies show that cities change with the changing concepts of their times. Cities are an expression of particular spiritual and material, social and political conditions, influenced and modified by the forms of production and the means of communication. The Greek city and the Roman city were both based on the work of slaves; but they differed from each other because the political and social concepts of Greece differed from those of Rome. Greek cities were small city-states; Roman cities, part of a vast empire. Medieval and Baroque cities differed from each other as well as from Greek and Roman cities. Medieval cities were based on free work and were free communities; Baroque cities were parts of growing territorial states, where manufacturing, the economic stage of production between handicraft and industry, was being developed. The cities of our industrial age have very little in common with the cities of past ages. They depend on large national states; they are based on a national economy tending to become world economy. In their extraordinary material achievement, they far surpass any cities the world has ever known.

The cities of our industrial age, however, have not yet found the pattern adequate to their potentialities, according to their function and technological development. They are a mere conglomeration of unrelated parts, each disturbing the other. They are paralyzed by insurmountable traffic and parking problems. They achieve no harmony in their component parts, no unity in their diversity. The discrepancy between what might be and what is grows ever wider. The very forces which made those cities grow seem to be now working toward their destruction.

Yet the problems of our cities and our regions could be solved. The planning methods and the planning elements we propose in these studies could work a transformation. New cities, small or large, could be built upon them. Old cities could be replanned and remade into well-functioning organisms, in which each part is related to other parts and to an harmonious whole.

Today, as in the past, cities and regions are influenced by ideas and concepts. The Medieval city was dominated by the cathedral and ruled by the church. Renaissance and Baroque cities were dominated by the palace and ruled by princes. The cities of our age are dominated by industry and commerce and ruled by interest. Some day, perhaps, cities and regions will be planned and developed according to the needs of man and ruled by reason.

1. CAHERNAMATIRECH *Stone Age settlement*

I. Origin, Growth, and Decline

The city dweller of our age can hardly imagine a world without cities. Cities seem to him as inevitable as life itself, and as eternal. Cities, however, appeared relatively late in man's long history, and they emerged only after a long struggle with the forces of nature on which man depends and of which he is also a part.

The human settlements of all ages are an expression of the societies which created them: an expression of spiritual aspirations and of material requirements. Social organization, political intention, economic means, artistic and technical ability, forms of production and consumption, means of transportation—all these are factors which determine the form and nature of man's settlements. The interaction of those forces, everywhere present, varies as one force or another tends to predominate.

Culture and civilization are the two aspects of society. Man's material progress has moved steadily forward since man's beginning. But it is highly questionable whether this material progress has always been accompanied by spiritual progress. The concept of progress, so dear to science, tends to confuse culture with civilization. They are not synonymous. Culture is the spiritual expression of a people; civilization, the material one. Civilization may advance while culture becomes sterile; and, conversely,

15

2. AICHBUEHL *Reconstruction of a Neolithic Village*

a very high cultural development may be accompanied by a low standard of civilization. Civilization without culture may become very weak, because it is cut off from the roots of its existence. But a high culture accompanied by a low civilization may be extremely productive in its unfolding. The self-elevation of man from savagery to civilization, from a life of mere accident to a planned and secure existence, took countless ages. It was a slow process, not without its periods of regression. Conquest and destruction could stop a forward march with seeming finality, might, indeed, make it necessary for mankind to retrace painfully steps already taken. But the defeated were not always exterminated. If they lived on to become serfs or slaves, they could eventually assimilate with their conquerors, transplanting seeds of their old achievements into their new setting. What

3. HOUSES ALONG A ROAD

16

4. CIRCULAR VILLAGE

5. STREET VILLAGE

had been destroyed could thus come to life again. Sometimes amalgamation of conquerors and conquered brought entirely new developments which, as a result of a special ability of the conquerors, reached higher levels than those attained before.

The age of civilization begins with the relatively peaceful development of the Neolithic period. Stone implements became more refined. Pottery and weaving emerged. Grains and fruit trees were cultivated. Animals were domesticated. The society which emerged in this era was probably a community of equals. Production was still so limited that it could satisfy only the mere needs of life. It created no surpluses on which social distinctions could be based. But people were learning to work together toward common ends. Well-established settlements, various forms of village, came into being. Life in those villages began to teach men to live, not only in harmony with themselves, but also in harmony with their neighbors and with the community to which they belonged.

This very progress led to conflicts. Fertile land was probably not abundant, and the secrets of soil fertilization and conservation were undiscovered. Yet, as wars became less frequent, population was bound to increase. Young members of the settlement were crowded out to find new land to cultivate. They could possess the living space they required only through conquest. The people they conquered had to follow the same course. These conquests, disturbing as they were, had some positive results. Since their goal was land acquisition, not the extermination of enemies, displaced populations were forced, themselves, to be on the move, and the Neolithic civilization was carried all over the Near East, North Africa, and Europe.

As the Neolithic settlements began to need defense against would-be conquerors, their structural pattern changed. The first settlers may have built isolated houses, with gardens and fields behind them, stretched sparsely along a road. Such settlements were difficult to defend and did not encourage the development of community life. When common danger loomed, necessity forced the grouping of the houses more compactly and thus brought into being various types of village. Houses tended to cluster together or be placed on both sides of a road or around a square. The circular formation around a central square proved best for defense, and the circular village appeared. Their fortification was, at first, provided by tight thorn hedges, difficult to traverse. Later palisades and ditches made stronger barriers. Then neolithic man discovered, under the spur of danger, that nature could provide even better defenses. Settlements on hills or on islands made use of natural advantages. Man began to look for these advantages. He even learned to make artificial islands in imitation of nature. Settlements of lake dwellers, built on platforms supported by posts,

6. GLASTONBURY *Reconstruction of a Lake Village*

7. LAKE OF ZURICH *Reconstruction of Lake Dwellings*

8. PLACE OF REFUGE

gave to their inhabitants the full protection of a water barrier. But the villages were still small. Aggressors in superior numbers could overwhelm and conquer them. The development of the place of refuge was the response to this continuing danger. To these fortified hills, settlers living in the dispersed villages could flee for safety in time of attack. They could take with them their animals and their movable belongings and thus preserve property as well as life. Since such a place of refuge could be built only by the common effort of those who wanted to use it, the result was a strengthening of social organization and the spirit of cooperation. The villagers, working together, learned to resist aggression and eventually to defy invaders.

Xenophon*, writing of the Drilae, a tribe in Asia Minor, pictures a place of refuge and indicates its strength. When the Drilae were attacked, Xenophone wrote, they retired to a stronghold protected by a tremendously deep ravine and almost inaccessible by road. The Greeks "were not able to take the place by assault, which was not surprising, as there was a broad ditch around it with the earth thrown up to form a rampart and with a palisade on top of the rampart and wooden towers erected at frequent intervals." The facilities of this place of refuge were so effective that a primitive tribe could resist the onslaught of an organized army of professional soldiers. Those professionals, Xenophon adds, even found it difficult to retreat from the place.

* Xenophon: *The Persian Expedition*

20

A place of refuge preserved the lives of the people, their animals and some of their movable belongings. But it did not keep houses and villages from destruction. Invaders could burn and pillage and leave to the discouraged villagers the task of rebuilding from ashes. It seems probable that, in places of recurrent attack, people began to desert their villages and to settle on their places of refuge. This meant that the fortified places had to be extended to provide space for more permanent settlements. Such settlements developed in time into towns and even came to form the nuclei of cities. The hill towns of Italy bear out this assumption. Prehistoric Athens was located on the hill of the Acropolis; prehistoric Rome on the Palatine Hill. In all probability these settlements stood on former places of refuge established as early as Neolithic times.

The Neolithic people, who achieved so much in agriculture, also created the village. Like many other objects of the Neolithic age, the village pattern survived its creators and still fulfills its original function in some of the so-called backward countries even to our day.

The settlement structure of the Neolithic Age remained almost unchanged as men laid aside stone tools for the newly discovered and more efficient copper. With the coming of the Bronze Age, however, advancing technology brought changes in the pattern, both economic and technical. Villages turned into towns; some destined to become cities; a few the capitals of great empires.

9. ITALIAN HILLTOWN

What made this transformation possible? Where did it take place? In all probability, man's first cities arose at the southeastern end of the area which Breasted calls "the fertile crescent," which stretches from the southeastern Mediterranean to the Persian Gulf. Toward the north and east this crescent is bordered by highlands and mountain ranges. Its inside rim is formed by the northern extension of the Arabian Desert. The history of this region was characterized by unceasing conflict between settled peasants and the wandering nomads who entered the fertile crescent from either side, conquered the settled inhabitants, and were themselves, in turn, conquered by new invaders. A new element appeared in these recurring conquests. The new conquerors wanted, not only the land, but also the labor of the people who tilled it. The nomads, attracted by the richness of the fertile crescent, were superior because of their mobility. The soil-rooted peasants became serfs of their conquering masters, forced to tend and till the fields for them.

Results of this unmutual contact between peasants and nomads were significant, positively as well as negatively. Conquest inflicted heavy burdens on the peasant, but it worked to the advantage of humanity. Eventually it benefitted even its peasant victims. Through the interaction of settled and soil-bound peasant and mobile, restless nomad, a higher society emerged, more differentiated in character and better integrated economically and politically. The new rulers discovered the potentialities of the country and the secret of increasing production on the conquered land. This not only made their own support possible but helped also in the realization of their political and religious aims.

There was rich fertile soil, water, and sunshine in abundance. What was needed was the integration of those natural resources and a more effective way of production. Water of the rivers overflowed the land in some places, left others dry and arid. Dikes were needed to stem the overflow; canals, to carry water to thirsty areas. Vast irrigation systems had to be established. The canals, developed for water control, provided also means of transportation. To make production more effective, it was necessary to organize it. The hoe had to be replaced by the plough; plot cultivation by agriculture. Stockbreeding developed to provide the oxen needed to draw the plough. How did the plough come into existence? Was it a technical invention only; or did it derive from religious symbol or cosmic concept? Was its practical use a technical application only? Some believe that the plough is a phallic symbol, and that ploughing itself is an imitation of what Freudians call "the primeval scene." Some believe that the use of draught animals is also based on a religious concept, that the chariots in which the gods rode along the Milky Way furnished the prototype of the wagon as well as of the plough. Images of such chariots were placed as holy vessels on altars to symbolize the presence of the gods.

As the culture of the hoe gave way to that of the plough, this magic ideology carried into the fields the idea of holiness. The hoe had been a woman's tool. The plough, originally a priestly vessel, could obviously be properly handled only by a man. The new tool made it possible to grow grain on a scale large enough, eventually, to feed the masses of the growing cities. It also profoundly altered the status of woman in society. It was, in all probability, one of the factors in the social change from the matriarchate to the patriarchate.* The use of the plough made agriculture possible; provided food for an increasing population; made life more stable; and brought about a division of labor. Craftsmen and merchants appeared in the developing society. Caravans and river boats made possible the exchange of surplus products. Timber and stone for buildings, copper and lead and precious metals and stones for the adornment of temples and palaces could then be imported. The new merchants developed the trade; the craftsmen found employment in working these materials. Gradually craftsmanship rose to creative art. Meanwhile living conditions improved. Larger settlements became possible. Society became more complex and more differentiated. The city stands as symbol of this development.

The despotic states arising from victory coordinated, politically and economically, an ever-increasing territory, and came eventually to comprise a whole coastal region, an entire river valley. Large dominions were thus established in the regions of the Euphrates and Tigris, the Nile, the Ganges and Indes, the Hoang-Ho and Yangtze-kiang, and other great rivers. The organization required for this development must have been tremendous. Swamps had to be drained and made useful. Irrigation systems had to be planned and built. Dams, canals, tanks and reservoirs had to be constructed. Only an autocratic system could accomplish this task and attain and secure permanent stable living conditions.

The tremendous technical tasks required the services of many workers, and these workers had to be employed without regard to their personal fates. The caste system, serfdom and slavery, were a necessity for those early states. All were built upon a wide stratum of a subject people, dominated and ruled by their conquerors. Slave and masters, however, each contributed to the building. As Paul Aman puts it:

"But the conquerors—king, priest, warrior—were also slaves to their calling. The life of the ruler, as well as that of all members of the state, depended upon a complicated mastery which had to be maintained even if it meant sacrificing all natural values of life. The problematic nature of civilization is thus shown in its early beginning."**

---

* Hahn, Edward: *Von der Hacke sum Pflug Leipzig*, 1914
** Aman, Paul: *Tradition and Weltkrise*. Berlin, 1934

10. UR, TEMPLE PRECINCT

The Sumerians were probably the founders of the first small city kingdoms and temple states. These were fortified cities surrounded by the agricultural land which supported them. One of them was Ur,* which eventually gained the leadership of Sumer. Originally, Ur was a Neolithic village on one of the river islands of the Euphrates at the southeast end of the fertile crescent. Its settlers lived by cultivating the rich earth. When their huts of mud bricks fell into decay, as they often did, the settlers simply built new huts on top of those which had collapsed. In the course of time, on the once low village site, a small hill arose with a village on top of it. This rising of a hill of decayed mud huts may have been the only happening in Ur's early history.

All of a sudden things began to change. A new people moved into the valley: the Sumerians. We do not know when they came, nor where they came from. But we do know that they conquered Ur, took possession of its hill and its arable land, and drove the old inhabitants to the lands below the hill where they were forced to till the fields for their new masters.

The Sumerians were of superior ability. They fortified the hill for their safety. They erected permanent buildings of burnt brick—temples for their gods and houses for themselves. Ur became in time a prospering city. The temples of the Ziggurat are an expression of that prosperity. Remains in the tombs of kings reveal a highly developed culture and refinement of life. Ur's two harbors suggest that it may have been a successful trade city. It is quite possible that increases in the arable land were also achieved. The population was divided into the people who lived in the city and the serfs who tilled the land and lived in villages in the fields.

* Woolley, C. Leonard: *Ur of the Chaldees.* London, 1929

When Ur was already a leading city of the united kingdom of Sumer and Akkad, a cultural and commercial center which extended its influence as far north as the Assyrian capital of Assur at the Tigris, Babylon was still a village, whose future greatness no one could foresee. Babylon's early development was not unlike that of Ur. The Amorites, entering the Euphrates Valley, conquered the Babylonian plain and made Babylon their capital city. Copper was being replaced by bronze at that time; iron was already known, though still too scarce for common use. The Ammonites made use of new technological means to produce wool and leather and manufactured woolen goods. Hammurabi made Babylon a political and commercial center. But after his death the area was raided by the Hittites from the northwest and eventually taken over by the Kassites from the northeast. The Kassite conquest ended Babylon's first civilization. The city vanished.

But Babylon was reborn. The Chaldeans, who conquered the whole of the fertile crescent and ruled over it, made Babylon their capital and rebuilt it. To express their power and to impress upon their subjects their right to rule, they adorned their city with monumental buildings, temples, towers, and palaces. Herodotus*, who in all probability saw Babylon, describes in his history the monumental city of Nebuchadnezzar. We glimpse its greatness also in the reconstruction made by its excavator, R. Koldewey.**

Babylon stood on a broad fertile plain where the Euphrates comes close to the Tigris. The two great rivers were connected at this point by a canal and were crossed by a road from the east leading westward to Damascus and thence, along the Jordan valley, to Egypt. Herodotus describes Babylon's shape as a square, and this is true for the older part of the city. Its shape was probably a reflection of a religious-astronomical belief. There is a square constellation of stars which the Babylonians called "the field" and which they imagined to be the agricultural land of the gods. The city of Babylon was supposed to be the projection upon earth of that celestial field.

But even at the time of Herodotus, Babylon was a rectangle rather than a true square. It had been extended across the river to the west, and its parts were connected by a bridge, the first passenger bridge of which we have any record. The city was surrounded by a broad deep moat, filled with water. Behind this moat rose a wall of considerable height and width. Nebuchadnezzar built a second wall very close to the first one around the older part of the city. The city's main fortress stood at the north of the area between the river and the procession street. South of it were the temples and the great temple tower, the Ziggurat. Secondary

---

* Herodotus: *History*
** Koldewey, R.: *Excavation at Babylon,* 1914

11. BABYLON OF NEBUCHADNEZZAR *Reconstruction*

fortresses stood in the center of each city division, according to Herodotus. He described the houses as being usually three or four stories high; the streets as all straight, the principal ones running parallel to the river, and the others crossing the main avenues at right angles. Outside the city walls, Herodotus observed suburban settlements, but these may have been the villages in which lived the people tilling the land for landlords living within the city.

Herodotus was deeply impressed with Babylon. "In magnificence there is no other city that approaches it," he remarked. The Babylon of his day belonged to Persia, then master of the largest empire ever established in the Near East. The Persians had made Parsagadae their capital and used Babylon only as an occasional residence. The Persian kings, in order to prove their true succession to the vanished and vanquished kings they replaced, resided in Babylon in the winter; in the Elamite city of Susa and Ecbatan, the Medean city, in the summer. Babylon retained also the importance as a commercial center to which its location destined it.

This established commercial importance was challenged, however, when Seleucus, one of the principal heirs of Alexander the Great, took possession of most of Alexander's Asiatic empire. The new city of Seleucia, which he founded as capital of his empire, was located on the western bank of the Tigris, northeast of Babylon. Seleucia grew at the expense of Babylon. It had the same advantageous traffic position as the older city, and it had the added advantage of being the center of a great empire.

Babylon, thus challenged by its newer rival, was reduced to impotence by positive destructive action. Seleucus wanted his new capital to be as large and important as possible to give adequate expression to the greatness of his power. Therefore, he populated Seleucia with the forced migration of a great part of Babylon's people. And he used the older city as source of building material for the new. Bricks of Babylon's fortification and buildings were used for Seleucia's buildings and fortifications.* Babylon was still a city, but, inevitably, a declining one.

At the time of the Roman emperor Hadrian, Babylon had reached its lowest stage. It had become again, as it had been two thousand years before, an insignificant village. The prophecy of Isaiah had been fulfilled: "And Babylon, the glory of Kingdoms, the beauty of the Chaldees, shall be as when God overthrew Sodom and Gomorrah. It shall never be inhabited, neither shall it be dwelt in from generation to generation; neither shall the Arabian pitch tents there; neither shall the shepherds make their fold there.

"But wild beasts of the desert shall lie there; and their houses shall be full of doleful creatures; and owls shall dwell there, and Satyrs shall dance

---

* Streck, Maximilian: *Seleucia and Ktesiphon*. Leipzig, 1917

there, and the wild beasts of the islands shall cry in their desolate houses, and dragons in their pleasant palaces; and her time is near to come, and her days shall not be prolonged."

There is tragedy in the death of a proud city.

Seleucia, Babylon's successful rival, did not long remain the capital of the Seleucids. Gradually their empire gravitated toward the west; then their capital had to be in the west also. Antioch on the Orontes became the new capital; Seleucia was reduced to the status of second city of the empire. But Seleucia became more important commercially as it lost political prestige. Its favorable location, at the crossing point of land and river traffic, made it, as it had once made Babylon, one of the chief commercial cities of antiquity and the principal market of the Asiatic caravan traffic. It grew into a large city, inhabited by a mixed population of Greeks, Macedonians, Babylonians, and Jews, in which the Greeks came to dominate.

The moving of the capital to Antioch proved disastrous to the empire of the Seleucids. When the Arsacids, ruling family of the Parthians, conquered the western part of the Seleucid empire, they made Ctesiphon, on the eastern bank of the Tigris, opposite Seleucia, their capital. Ctesiphon had existed before the Parthian conquest as a small settlement and a place where goods brought by caravans from the East were relayed to the market of Seleucia. Its new position as Parthian capital did not, at first, affect Seleucia's commercial position.

Why did the Arsacids not make the rich and prosperous Greek city of Seleucia their capital? Did they mistrust its people? Or was their aim, as Strabo suggests,* to "spare the Seleucians the burdens of furnishing quarters for the Scythian soldiery" consisting of rough nomads? Or was the choice of Ctesiphon an expression of the Asiatic tradition that new rulers must always found new capitals? Perhaps the new rulers saw an advantage in keeping themselves independent from the traders of Seleucia. Seleucia was then a large market from which they could draw revenues. This was not an unheard-of arrangement. The twin city of Kura, the former capital of Borna west of Lake Tchad in Africa, also had its great market outside the city limits toward the west, in order to keep the city free from the influence of the traders. Ctesiphon was a military camp, a fortress protecting the seat of the ruler, and part of its function was to keep the Seleucians at bay.

The Romans, through their oriental politics, came into conflict with the Parthians. Seleucia, like other conquered Greek cities, saw in Rome a

---

* Strabo: *Geography*

deliverer from hated Parthian rule. N. Licinius Crassus, with Pompey and Caesar a member of the triumvirate, tried to liberate those Greek cities. But his army was ambushed, the battle lost; and Crassus caused himself to be stabbed to death by his shield bearer.

The Roman-Parthian struggle destroyed Seleucia at last. The city was sacked and burned by the soldiers of Aridus Cassius, the legate of the Emperor L. Verus. Most of its 400,000 inhabitants were killed, the rest sold into slavery. The Roman, who professed desire to defend Hellenism, greatly weakened his position in the Near East through this pillage of Seleucia.

Less than a century later, a new power arose in that region. New Persia restored its national life under the leadership of the Sassanid kings, overthrew the Parthians and conquered the whole of the fertile crescent. Ctesiphon, which had fallen heir to Seleucia's trading position, became their residence, and remained, until the rise of Islam, a leading city and the capital of a great empire. The ruins of the palace of the Sassanid kings still exist. Its wide-spanned impressive hall symbolized the greatness of its builders. That this hall has come down to us even in ruins may be due to the fact that the Moslem Arabs, who terminated the Sassanid rule, found it useful as a place of worship.

When the Sassanid empire had existed for more than four hundred years, Mohammed, born in Mecca in Arabia, became the prophet of a new religion: Islam. This religion was spiritual in origin, but forceful in action.

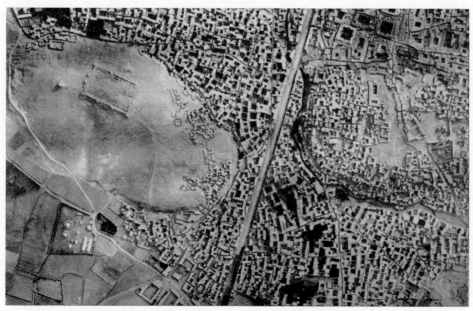

12. THE MOUND OF ECBATANA *below present Hamadan*

The courage of the converted barbarian Arabs in combination with their religious zeal made the new movement invincible. The Islamic forces took Egypt and Syria from the feeble Byzantine empire; Mesopotamia from the Sassanids. A great new oriental empire came into being, in which the usual passivity of the oriental had been converted into dynamic activity. In a relatively short time, the established structure of the countries surrounding the Mediterranean had collapsed and the new Islamic empire had swept from India, along North Africa, and, eventually, into Spain. Baghdad, not very far north of Ctesiphon, was founded as the capital of the new empire and the seat of the Caliphs, its rulers. As Baghdad succeeded Ctesiphon as a ruling city, it inherited also its flourishing trade. Ctesiphon declined and Baghdad became the leading city of the East, the political center of the Moslem empire as Mecca was its religious center. The rise of Islam and its political consequences terminated the Greek and Roman influence which had so long prevailed in those regions. An upheaval had thrust out an intrusive civilization. Arnold Toynbee* describes this upheaval: "Confronted with this challenge, the Syrian society made a number of attempts to respond, and these attempts all had a common feature. In every instance, the anti-Hellenic reaction took a religious movement for its vehicle. Nevertheless, there was a fundamental difference between the first four of these reactions and the last one. The Zoroastrain, the Jewish, the Nestorian, and the Monophysite reactions were failures. The Islamic reaction was a success."

Within the relatively small area between the Euphrates and the Tigris, where these rivers come close together, great and prosperous cities arose during the milleniums. One after another they rose and fell. As early as the Sumeric times, city states were fighting to subdue each other. Later, as larger states developed, they too fought each other with the same aim. Babylon, twice founded, succeeded itself and was succeeded by Seleucia. Seleucia was succeeded by Ctesiphon; Ctesiphon by Baghdad. The rise of each new city meant the decline of the old one. People of the deposed cities were sometimes killed or sold into slavery. More often they were transplanted to the new city. The older city always provided the building material for the new. The bricks made for Babylon were used to build Seleucia, Ctesiphon, and eventually Baghdad.

Babylon, oldest of these cities, was also the most famous. In the minds of people, it had always existed. In ancient times it was identified with Seleucia. Medieval travelers identified it with Baghdad, sometimes called Baghdad, Babylon.

---

* Toynbee, Arnold J.: *A Study of History*. New York and London, 1947

13. PERSEPOLIS

All these cities originated with the founding of new states and empires after conquest. Quite different is the origin of Ecbatana, the Medean capital. Here the city was the foundation for the state. Before Ecbatana was founded, the Medes lived in scattered villages without any central authority. Lawlessness prevailed throughout the land. To rid themselves of this disorder, the Medes elected a king—and elected him unanimously. The king, upon his elevation, "required a palace to be built for him suitable to his rank, and a guard to be given to him for his person. The Medes complied and built him a strong and large palace on a spot which he himself pointed out, and likewise gave him the liberty to choose himself a body guard from the whole nation. Thus settled upon the throne, he further required them to build a single great city, and disregarding the petty towns in which they had formerly dwelt, make the new capital the object of their chief attention. The Medes were again obedient and built the city now called Ecbatana, the walls of which are of great size and strength, rising in circles, one within the other. The plan of the place is, that each of the walls should out-top the one beyond it by the battlements. The nature of the ground, which is a gentle hill, favours this arrangement in some degree, but it was mainly effected by art. The number of the circles is seven. The royal palace and the treasuries standing within the last. The circuit of the outer wall is very nearly the same as that of Athens. Thus Deioces [the name of the king] collected the Medes into a nation and ruled over them alone."*

* Herodotus: *History*

31

After a long reign Deioces was succeeded by his son Phraortes, who attacked the Persians and brought them under his rule. He was then the king of two nations and powerful enough to think about conquering all Asia. But Cyrus, son of a Medean princess and a Persian nobleman, eventually subdued the Medes, made the Persians the ruling class, and established himself as the ruler of Asia. His successors extended the empire, consolidated their conquests, and became kings of kings.

Persepolis, the residence of the Persian kings, represents a new city type. It was a palace-city; and it was no longer fortified. The palaces, built by different kings, were on a large artificial terrace. Persepolis was a city for the king, his court, his nobles and his administration. The people to serve that city were settled below the terrace. Alexander destroyed the palaces to avenge the destruction of Athens by the Persians one hundred and fifty years earlier. The ruins of the city still reveal its past greatness.

While the Persian kings were building their palaces at Persepolis, kings of Egypt were building themselves cities. More stable conditions in their land permitted the royal city to develop much earlier. When a king ascended the throne of Egypt, he erected a new palace and a new pyramid, his future tomb. And he founded also a new city for his court and administration. Behind this custom and practice was probably a magic concept, expressed in ancient rituals derived from Animism, which caused primitive man to shun all the belongings of a dead man. When a king, who was

14. EGYPT *Pyramids*

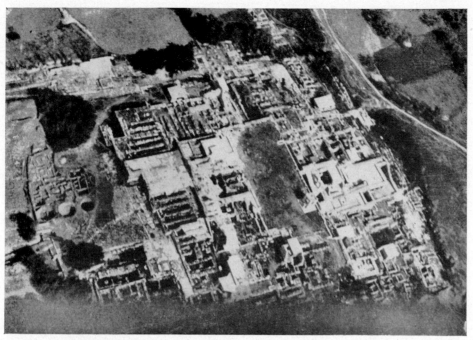

15. KNOSSOS *Palace of King Minos*

considered godlike, died, it was only natural that his palace-city should be abandoned and left to decay. Those royal cities of Egypt have entirely disappeared. Only their pyramids, the tombs of the dead kings, have survived. The long row of Pyramids south of the Great Pyramid of Khafre are the only remains of once royal cities. The Nile's yearly floods have borne away the rest. The royal cities of Egypt are an expression of absolutism. It is not surprising that, when absolutism appeared again in Europe, the royal-city type was reborn.

The plain of the rivers Euphrates and Tigris is vastly different, in geographic structure and topographical formation, from the Greek mainland and the islands of the Aegean Sea. In contrast to the uniformity and evenness of the plain of the two rivers, Greece's geographical structure and topography presents endless variety. There are rivers and valleys, mountains and plains. There are bays and inlets. There is the sea itself, with its myriad islands. Since the Gulf of Corinth cuts the Greek mainland into two parts, almost every place of any importance can have more or less direct access to the Sea. Small fertile plains are isolated and protected by surrounding mountains, and thus a great variety of local developments becomes possible. No large empire could be established in this setting, but small kingdoms and, later, city states could grow up, independent of each other but united through a common language and common cultural aims. The character of the country well matched the Greek concept of life, may have, indeed, helped to form their preference for small, independent communities.

Western civilization developed first, not on the Greek mainland, but on the islands of the Aegean Sea. Aegean civilization preceded Greek civilization, going back to the Neolithicum and developing parallel with the civilizations of Egypt and the Near East. All these civilizations influenced each other, but each had its own aims and each its unique development. The Aegean Sea, with its countless islands, is like a lake. Its southern end is "closed" by a chain of islands of which Crete is the largest. Midway between Europe, Asia, and Africa, Crete forms a natural link between three continents. It was inevitable that it should become a main trading center between Egypt and the Orient and Europe. Even in ancient times, travel between the Aegean islands and these lands was not very difficult. Though his ship was small, the sailor could feel a measure of confidence and security. Some land was always within sight. He could always count on a harbor for the night.

Those favorable conditions, however, had some distinctly unfavorable aspects. The character of the Sea and its islands encouraged piracy to flourish. The early development of the Aegean was as much influenced by the nomads of the sea as that of the fertile crescent by the nomads of the desert.

Thucydides* describes the activities of the Aegean pirates: "In early times the Hellenes and the Barbarians of the coast and islands, as communication by sea became more common, were tempted to turn pirates, under the conduct of their most powerful man; the motives being to serve their own cupidity and to support the needy. They would fall upon a town unprotected by walls, and consisting of a mere collection of villages, and would plunder it; indeed, this came to be the main source of their livelihood, no disgrace being yet attached to such achievement, but even some glory. The same prevailed also by land."

Homer** also considered the pirate raids quite legal and right. His most famous hero Odysseus calls himself "a sacker of cities" and makes the meaning of the phrase very clear when he tells of his exploits at Ismarus, the city of the Cicones: "I reached this place and destroyed the men who held it. Their wives and the rich plunder that we took from the town we divided so that no one should go short of his proper share."

Minos of Crete was able to establish a navy to defeat the pirates and to make himself master of the Aegean Sea. Was Minos, Jacob Burckhardt asks, himself a pirate?*** He could have been. He certainly must have been very powerful. The sea kingdom he founded was based on a system of feudalism and commercial exploitation.

---

* Thucydides: *The Peloponnesian War*
** Homer: *The Odyssey*
*** Bruckhardt, Jacob: *Griechische Kultur geschichte*

16. MYCENAE

To strengthen his kingdom and to secure its trade, Minos established outposts, selecting their sites for their strategic possibilities, but also with due
regard for the fertility of the soil on which they must depend for support.
These fortress-castles towered over fruitful plains. Most famous are those
of the Argive Plain. Here the castles of Mycenea, Tiryns, and Midea were
so located as to cover the passes leading to the plain, while Larisa, on top
of a free standing hill, dominated the whole area.

17. TIRYNS

18. LARISSA—ARGOS

Minos may have sent his sons, relatives, or captains to command such outposts. Certainly, he needed able men there, to rule over the people and to keep order in the domain. For his own residence, he chose Knossos, located at the north side of Crete, inland but close to the harbor from which the trade in the Aegean sea could be controlled. On the southern side of the island, he founded Phaestos, possibly as his second residence. The harbors of Phaestos served the trade with Egypt.

These settlements of Minos possessed the characteristics common to all feudalistic settlements. The castles or palaces of the rulers in a dominating position on their large estates; the surrounding villages in which the subject people, often reduced to serfdom, lived to till the fields for their masters and to mingle with the people of the castles only when danger loomed and they were summoned to help defend the stronghold. Such settlements were economically dependent on agriculture. Some of the Aegean castles and palaces, at least their heavy fortification walls and foundations, have defied time. But the villages disappeared.

The sea kingdom of Minos, unlike most feudal states, was, however, based on trade as well as agriculture. Originally that trade may have dealt with the exchange of raw materials for manufactured goods of more advanced countries. It is quite possible that the Aegeans imported and distributed iron discovered and processed by the Hittites into the world around the Mediterranean. The fact of this trade base made necessary settlements of a different character from the fortress outpost with its villages.

Organized trade requires harbor facilities, wharves and shipyards, warehouses and houses for the people working there and for the sailors between voyages. When the Aegean civilization advanced to the point where it could produce goods wanted everywhere, shops and settlements for workers and craftsmen must have been established. We may assume that such settlements were in the possession of the king or the ruling class, since trade was a royal prerogative.

We know nothing about the settlements Crete developed for its harbor workers and for its craftsmen. They may have been similar to a known Egyptian workman's settlement at Kahun, built to provide houses for the workers on the pyramid. The pattern of any such settlement would be modified, of course, according to the topography of its site.

Excavation of the Cretan settlement of Gournia has revealed houses with stone foundations grouped close together around a palace. Since Gournia is close to the sea, perhaps this was a settlement of traders or merchants. There may have been similar settlements connected with other Cretan palaces. At Knossos larger houses were discovered close to the Palace, built, it may be, for nobles who had to live close to the court.

The palaces of Crete, unlike those of the Greek mainland, were not fortified. This indicates that the power of the Aegean kings must have been very great and their fleet very efficient. Those palaces differ widely in size, but they all have common characteristics. All are built around a rectangular court. All show the tendency to relate the enclosed space to the open space of the landscape.

Real cities did not exist in the Aegean world. None of its settlements con-

19. GOURNIA

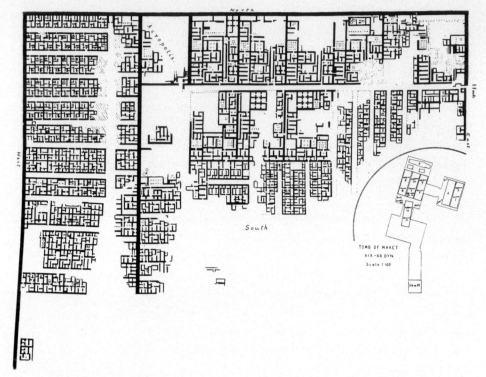

20. KAHUN

stituted a city. They were never more than parts of cities, not yet integrated into a whole, with unified political and economical life and aims of its own.

The great artistic abilities of the Aegeans and the work they created were unknown until our time. What Schliemann excavated at Troy, Tiryns and Mycenea; what Evans discovered at Knossos, astonished the whole world. At last we knew that Homer's works were not poet's fantasies but poetic descriptions of a world which once existed. The cultural remains of the Aegean civilization are like the missing link between the cultural development before the Greeks and that of the Greeks themselves.

When the Aegean civilization was at its peak, the Greeks, coming from the north, entered the Greek mainland. "The country now called Hellas," Thucydides* wrote, "had no settled population; on the contrary, migrations were of frequent occurrence, the several tribes readily abandoning their homes under pressure of superior numbers. Without commerce, without freedom of communication either by land or sea, cultivating no more of their territory than the exigencies of life required, destitute of capital, never planting their land (for they could not tell when an invader

---

* Thucydides: *The Peloponnesian War*

might not come and take it all away, and when he did come they had no walls to stop him), thinking that the necessities of daily sustenance could be supplied at one place as well as another. They cared little for shifting the habitation, and consequently neither built large cities nor attained to any other form of greatness. The richest soils were always most subject to this change of masters. The goodness of the land favored the aggrandisement of particular individuals, and thus created faction which proved a fertile source of ruin. It also invited invasion."

As a result of those successive migrations, new powers crystallized, new kingdoms arose. This process had, in all probability, an adverse, not to say destructive, effect upon the settlements of the Aegeans and their cultural achievements. We may assume that those new powers took possession of the Aegean fortified castles and established themselves there by right of conquest.

Crete was finally conquered at an unknown time and by an unknown people. Its centers of culture and its palaces were destroyed. The Aegean civilization came to an end. The kings of Crete must have tried to cover their possessions on the mainland, and, in so doing, provoked new conflicts. As soon as the new rulers in Greece were powerful enough and had a navy of their own, they attacked Crete, defeated her, and established themselves on that island and, eventually, on all the islands of the Aegean Sea. Troy may, quite possibly, have been the last stronghold of the Aegeans to resist Greek aggression; and the war against Troy, the last of many Aegean wars. Troy was attacked by the Achaeans or, as Homer occasionally calls them, Argives and Danaans. After long siege, Troy was utterly destroyed.

The Greeks were destroyers but also creators. Under their touch, in the course of time, an entirely new settlement development took place everywhere in the Greek world. It reached final expression in the free city. Greek city states, as they came into being, were based on slavery, but they provided for their citizens opportunity for a rich and vigorous individual life. The life which these Greeks created—a life of freedom within the limits of the restrictions of society—was an achievement which, ever since, has continued to stir the imagination of man.

Greece developed no large cities. Its ever-varying landscape, by its very formation, fostered the creation and maintenance of small states, conceived on the human scale in which the rich potentialities of the Greek spirit might unfold in utmost variety. The great cultural achievements of Greece may be due in part to the physical smallness of her cities. The smallness of the scale had political implications, too. It made it possible for each citizen to take his active part in the life of his city.

As both Plato* and Aristotle** indicate, the Greeks had definite ideas about their city states and a clear sense of direction as they worked to make them the embodiment of their ideals. They thought clearly, too, about the relation of the city to its territory, about its living space and the ways in which the citizen could provide for his livelihood.

A state, Aristotle wrote, "begins to exist when it has attained a population sufficient for a good life in the political community. As to the size of the state, there is a limit, as there is to other things, plants, animals, implements; for none of these retain their natural power when they are too large or too small—for example, a ship which is only a span long will not be a ship at all, nor a ship a quarter of a mile long. If the citizens of the state are to judge and to distribute offices according to merit, then they must know each other's character. When they do not possess this knowledge, both the election to offices and the decision of law suits will go wrong. Clearly then the best limit of the population of a state is the largest number which suffices for the purpose of life and can be taken in at a single view."

Aristotle does not give the exact figure he considered appropriate, but he may have agreed with Hippodamus of Miletus, philosopher and city planner, whose ideal state consisted of 10,000 citizens, Aristotle mentions Hippodamus and was certainly acquainted with his work. Aristotle, however, recognized other considerations influencing the size of a city. It should be small enough, he thought, so that every citizen could hear the speaker on the Agora; large enough to provide as many hoplites as any neighboring city with which it might come into conflict. It had to be prepared against aggression.

Plato also believed that a city should be neither too large nor too small. He concludes his discussion about the size of the state by saying, "Our rulers will find the best principle for determining the size of the state and the proportionate amount of territory beyond which they will not go: the state should be allowed to grow only so far as it can increase in size without loss of unity."

Both Plato and Aristotle accepted the institution of slavery as a necessity. Aristotle draws a distinction between members of a state and its servants. He excludes from citizenship also merchants, traders, and husbandmen. Husbandmen, he believes, will of necessity be slaves or barbarian Perioeci. The distinction between a ruling class and a subject class seemed to him natural and right.

---

* Plato: *Republic*
** Aristotle: *Politics*

Aristotle's measure of the physical size of his ideal territory was the need of its people. It should be of such size, he said, "as may enable the inhabitants to live at once temperately and liberally in the enjoyment of leisure. It should be a territory which is all-producing, for to have all things and to want nothing is sufficiency. Moreover, it is necessary that they should import from abroad what is not found in their own country and that they should export what they have in excess; for a city ought to be a market, not indeed for others, but for herself."

Regarding the location of the city, Aristotle remarks, "If we could have what we wish, it should be well situated in regard both to sea and land. It should be a convenient place for the production of the whole country. It should be difficult of access to the enemy and easy of egress to the inhabitants."

Aristotle considered also the health needs of his city and decided that wind and water were the most important factors in assuring civic well-being. Cities which lie toward the east and are blown upon by east winds are the healthiest, he thinks. Next come those sheltered from the north wind, for they have milder winters. "There should be a natural abundance of springs and fountains in the towns, or, if there is a deficiency of them, great reservoirs may be established for the collection of rain water, such as will not fail when the inhabitants are cut off from the country by war."

Aristotle agreed with Hippodamus that cities should be planned with streets regularly laid out. However, he makes also this interesting observation: "For security in war the antiquated mode of building, which made it difficult for strangers to get out of a town and for assailents to find the way in, is preferable. The whole town should not be laid out in straight lines, but only certain quarters and regions; thus security and beauty will be combined."

Before the Greeks established cities, the various clans lived in villages and were ruled over by chieftains who were called kings. The power of the kings was limited in peace time, increased sharply when war came. The people of those early villages may have built themselves places of refuge as they presumably had done in the countries from which they originally came.

Perhaps the dangers they were exposed to because of the prevailing piracy on land and sea forced them to take further steps, to draw together into one larger place, a fortified city strong enough to protect them against sudden raids. In such a stronghold life could be lived with some sense of security. Such an explanation seems rational, but it may well be only part of the story. There may have been at work other forces than necessity, forces not material in nature. The development of the Greek city may have been, in large part, the expression of Greek creative ability and comprehensive sense of harmony. There may have been an urge to create a new way of life, a spiritual impulse which spurred the Greeks on to transcend mere material necessity. The *demos* may have gained consciousness and manifested itself with the creation of the Agora, the symbol of the Polis, the center of its political life.

It was believed that the Agora was also a market place. This is not true. There were markets in Greek cities, but not on the Agora. The Agora was a political meeting place for the discussion of public affairs and a gathering place for the free men of the city. From it, Aristotle remarks, "all trade should be excluded and no mechanic, husbandman, or any such person allowed to enter unless he be summoned by the magistrates."

What brought the Polis into existence we do not know exactly. Its origin is still hidden behind a veil of mystery. No one has yet been able fully to penetrate that secret.

So far as we know, the Polis was the result of the process of synoecism: the condensation of a clan into a city. In its territory no other independent community was allowed to exist. Synoecism involved a corporate decision to live together politically which had as its corollary the abolition of local governments in favor of one. The seat of the new unified government might be at a place selected from among those already in existence; or it might be newly founded as the center for the government which had just come into being. Here was the Agora, the government offices, the gymnasiums, the theater, the fountain with flowing water. People might still be allowed to live in their old villages, but their rights and obligations now had to be exercised in the Polis.

For many, synoecism must have been an unhappy experience. They had to abandon old inherited estates and, worst of all, the graves of their ancestors and the cults connected with them. Perhaps, in some cases, the process of synoecism had been forced by a small powerful group, by a king with imagination about the future. Possibly human sacrifices were sometimes connected with the process, the victims being afterwards adored as the Tyche of the Polis.

The creation of the Polis was always a decisive experience in the life of its people; its maintenance and ever-present obligation. The Polis was more than a city. It was regarded as something higher than life itself, something to which life had to be subordinated. Not to be a citizen of a polis was considered a grave misfortune. To be deprived of citizenship was punishment second only to death. The polis was conscious of its power over the lives of its citizens; the citizens accepted this power freely and proudly.

When Socrates, condemned to death, refused the offer of his friends to

21. THEBES

help him escape to some other city, his decision was based on his concept of the polis and its right. In the Crito,* he makes the laws of Athens speak: "If we mean to kill you," they say, "because we think it just, must you do your best to kill us in your turn? Can you claim that you have a right to do this, you the lover of virtue. Is this your wisdom, not to know that above father and mother and forefathers stands our country, dearer and holier than they, more sacred, and held in more honor by God and men of understanding? That you ought to reverence her, and submit to her and work for her when she is in need, for your country more than your father, and either win her consent or obey her will and suffer what she bids you suffer, and hold your peace; be it imprisonment, or blows, or wounds in war or death—it must be borne, and it is right it should be borne; there must be no yielding, no running away, no deserting of one's past: in war and in the law courts and everywhere we must do what our city bids us do and our country, or else convince her where justice lies. For it is not lawful to use force against father or mother, and still less against our fatherland." "What shall we say to this, Crito?" Socrates demands, "that the laws speak the truth or not?" And Crito can only answer, "I believe they do."

The Polis is the peculiar product of the Greek spirit, an expression of its essential activity. It is based on the participation of every citizen. Life in the Polis became, to the Greek, the only form of human existence worth living, the only life adequate to the aims of Greece. Life in villages was

* Plato: *Crito*

43

regarded as beneath human dignity. Villages had no agora, no government offices; therefore no political activity could develop in them. They had no gymnasium nor theater; therefore no cultural life was possible. The dissolution of a polis, the leading back of the citizens to their original villages was a severe punishment sometimes inflicted upon a city. Such a fate, for instance, fell upon Mantinea after that city surrendered to Agesipolis, the Spartan king. It was broken into its five constituent villages. "Those who originally belonged to the village of Mantinea remained on the site of the city. The rest had to pull down their houses and move each to the village where his property was. The loss of civil life meant to a Greek the loss of all his higher interests."*

Greece had many cities, but few of them gained more than local fame. Some rose to prominence through conquest, others through industry or a favorable trade location. It may well have been that most Greek cities were content merely to be independent and to provide a good life for their citizens. But independence was always in danger. Intentions of neighbors could not always be trusted. Thebes, for instance, tried to unify the whole of Boetia and eventually succeeded. But not without making Athens her enemy. Corinth, by the very nature of her location, gained importance as a trading center, and also came in conflict with Athens. Acro-Corinth, the acropolis of the city, had a commanding position on the Isthmus. Since the Isthmus was the link between northern and southern Greece, Corinth held the key to the Peloponnesus. Moreover, two important trade routes crossed each other at Corinth: a road running north and south and a waterway running east and west. Corinth was inevitably, therefore, a market place. The city grew rich and prosperous, founded colonies of which Syracuse became the most famous. Like Thebes, Corinth looked with jealousy on the growing power and commercial success of Athens. The policies of the Corinthians toward this rival and also toward Sparta changed with changing events. Envy of Athens mounted to such a pitch eventually that, when the Peloponnesian War was over, Corinth insisted that Athens must be annihilated, a proposal which Sparta rejected. Thebes and Corinth both were to learn themselves what annihilation meant: Thebes when she rebelled unsuccessfully against Macedonia after the death of Philip; Corinth when she rebelled against the Romans. Both cities were burned to the ground, their people sold into slavery. Both cities were later rebuilt. Athens and other Greek cities helped to reestablish Thebes, but the new city occupied the Cadmeia only, its former acropolis. Julius Caesar, recognizing the important advantages of its location, rebuilt Corinth as a Roman colony.

---

* Bury, J. B.: *A History of Greece*

22. SPARTA *Site of the Ancient City*

Sparta and Athens were the leading cities of Greece, and they differed from each other in every possible aspect. They differed in their political concepts; they differed also in their means of subsistence. Sparta lived by exploiting its subdued people; Athens, by industry and commerce. But both cities shared a common aim: to achieve hegemony over Greece.

The conquest of Laconia, the southeastern part of the Peloponnesus, by Doric tribes ended the Doric Wandering, the migration into Greece from the north. The pressure from outside ceased, and eventually an inner equilibrium was established. New states emerged. The most powerful of them was Sparta.

The Spartans were few in number but powerful through the efficiency of their military organization. Their state was based on conquest and they strove to be conquerors all the time. Their military organization was the source of their success and the reason for their strength. Conservative in character, they might change their constitution, but they would never change their military organization. They lived a kind of barrack life, had common meals. They did not work, but they were always on the alert. Watchfulness was important if only to keep subjected peoples submissive. The Spartan devoted his whole life to service of the state.

The two kings who headed Sparta were related to the military organization. They had power only in time of war. They represented a survival from the heroic age of Greece, their functions being reminiscent of the old kingships of the time of the Doric Wandering. This suggests that the

Spartans may have originated when two bands of warriors, each with its own king-leader, joined forces. Five Ephors controlled the kings of Sparta, and the power of Ephors increased as that of the kings declined. The Ephors, Bury believes, "must have won that power in a conflict between the nobility who governed in conjunction with the kings, and the people who had no share in the government. In that struggle, the kings represented the cause of the nobility, while the Ephors were the representatives of the people."*

The Spartans took possession of and settled in the rich valley of the Eurotas, surrounded by high mountain ranges. From there, they penetrated almost the whole of the Peloponnesus and established hegemony over it. They considered themselves a master race, kept their blood pure, did not mix with the inhabitants who were, in differing degrees, their subjects. Some of the people of the Peleponnesus accepted the supremacy of the Spartans and became their allies.

The other two groups were: the Perioeci who were relatively free peasants and had to serve in the army; and the conquered people who became helots, had no rights, and were required to work and till the land for their Spartan masters.

When the Spartans increased in number, a pressing land problem arose. To solve it, Sparta undertook the conquest of Messenia, the country beyond Mount Taygetos. Subjection of the people of Messenia required long wars, but Sparta was at last successful. New land and new helots to work the lands were acquired by the conquerors. The Spartans solved their economic problems in this way, but they did so at the cost of never-ending danger. They had always to be prepared to put down a rebellion of the helots. The permanent army life of the Spartans became, in time, a stern economic necessity.

Only noble families owned land. To provide equality and economic independence for the common people of Sparta, the land was divided into lots and each Spartan was assigned a lot or, more accurately, was allowed the use of it. The land passed from father to son, but it remained always under the ownership of the state and could not, therefore, be subdivided or sold. The helots who tilled the land belonged also to the state. They were required to deliver to their masters a certain amount of produce; they might keep for their own use any surplus beyond that amount.

Sparta, the Spartan capital, was located between the two rivers, the Eurotas and its tributary, close to the mountains in the north of Laconia. Originally it had been an army camp, well protected by those rivers and the moun-

---

* Bury, J. B.: *A History of Greece.* New York

tains. Out of this camp the city grew. Its acropolis, with the temple of Athena, stood on a promontory. Below it was a large theater, and farther down toward the plain was the city itself. One would expect that the military Spartans would make their capital a fortified city. But Sparta was never fortified, at least not until Roman times. The city was protected by its men or, as Lycurgus is quoted to have expressed it, "The city is well fortified which has a wall of men instead of stone."*

Villages were the original type of Spartan settlements, and Sparta was formed by the unification of five villages which, to some degree, always retained their identity. Each village was headed by one of the five Ephors. Sparta was never a city like Athens, Corinth, or Thebes. It always kept its village character; it was always a city of houses connected with gardens. It was, as Homer called it, a "broad" city, covering a space much larger than that of more populous Athens. "If Sparta," remarked Thucydides, "were to become desolate, and the temples and the foundation of the public buildings were left . . . as time went on there would be a strong disposition with posterity to refuse to accept her fame as a true exponent of her power. And yet they (the Spartans) occupy two-fifths of Peloponnese and lead the whole, not to speak of their numerous allies without. Still, as the city is neither built in a compact form nor adorned with magnificent temples and public edifices, but composed of villages after the old fashion of Hellas, there would be an impression of inadequacy. Whereas, if Athens were to suffer the same misfortune, I suppose that any inference from appearance presented to the eye would make her power to have been twice as great as it is."**

What Thucydides predicted, history proved. When, in the course of time, both cities became desolated, Sparta vanished entirely, leaving no trace, but the Acropolis of Athens still bears witness to the former grandeur of a great city.

Athens and Sparta were both selfish cities, always keeping their own interests uppermost in mind. When Athens succeeded in building up her empire, she was hated for her success. When Sparta conquered and enslaved her fellow Greeks, she was greatly admired for her military strength. Athens had all the vices; Sparta all the virtues. But when Athens met defeat in the Peloponnesian war, the Greeks found that they had only changed their masters. Sparta claimed her intention of restoring the independence of the Greek cities. But such proclamations proved to be only camouflage for Sparta's real aim—the establishment of her own hegemony. Brasidas the Spartan, speaking to the citizens of Acanthus, said so frankly. "I shall take the Gods and the heroes of your country to witness that I came for

---

* Plutarch: *Lives.* Lycurgus
** Thucydides: *The Peloponnesian War*

your good and was rejected, and shall do my best to compel you by laying waste your land. I shall do so without scruple, being justified by the necessity which constrains me, first to prevent the Lacedaemonians from being damaged by you, their friends—and secondly, to prevent the Hellenes from being hindered by you in shaking off their servitude."*

The Athenians always considered themselves the autochthonous population of Attica. As a matter of fact, all the Greeks were relatively new comers in the area. Herodotus** makes a modified claim to Athenian priority when he calls them "the more ancient natives in Greece, the only Greeks who have never changed their abode." Thucydides* also comments on Athenian stability. It was due, he said, to the fact that Attica's soil was so poor that did not tempt invaders, and therefore the settlers there enjoyed, "from a very remote period, freedom from faction," and the area "never changed its inhabitants."

We now know that the settling of Attica took place in very ancient times. There may have been Neolithic settlements, villages whose people tilled the soil and used the commanding hill of the Acropolis as their place of refuge. The Acropolis lies four miles from the sea, and it was girded by two small streams which were, in that day, large enough to give added protection. Quite probably, Attica, like the Argivian Plain, came into the possession of the Aegeans, who made the Acropolis the fortress from which they ruled the subject population. When the Greeks conquered Attica and made it their home, they settled in villages and the Acropolis again may have become a place of refuge, then, later, the seat of kings. Thucydides writes: "Under Cecrops and the first kings down to the reign of Theseus, Athica had always consisted of a number of independent townships, each with its own townhall and magistrates. Except in times of danger, the king of Athens was not consulted; in ordinary cases they carried on their government and settled their affairs without his interference. . . . In Theseus, however, they had a king of equal intelligence and power, and one of the chief features in his organization of the country was to abolish the council chambers and magistrates of the petty cities, and to merge them in the single council chamber and town hall of the present capital. Individuals might still enjoy their private property just as before, but they were henceforth compelled to have only one political center, viz. Athens, which thus counted all the inhabitants of Attica among her citizens, so that when Theseus died he left a great state behind him. Indeed, from him dates the Synoecia, or Feast of Union."*

Unlike Sparta, Athens opened its gates freely to other Greeks. Victims

---

* Thucydides: *The Peloponnesian War*
** Herodotus: *History*

48

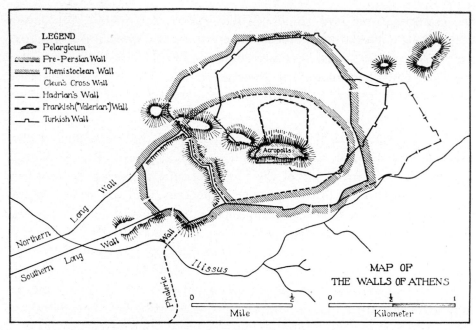

LEGEND
Pelargicum
Pre-Persian Wall
Themistoclean Wall
Cleun's Cross Wall
Hadrian's Wall
Frankish ("Valerian") Wall
Turkish Wall

Acropolis

Northern Long Wall
Southern Long Wall
Phaleric Wall
Ilissus

MAP OF
THE WALLS OF ATHENS

Mile
Kilometer

23. THE WALLS OF ATHENS

of faction and war from all of Hellas found there not only a retreat but also an opportunity to become Athenian citizens. This may explain the unique character of Athens, its cosmopolitanism, its industrial and trade activities. It may explain also the striving for power which led, at last, to the city's tragic end.

Before the Synoecism of Theseus, Athens consisted of the fortified Acropolis and a single district beneath it toward the south. As it became the capital of Attica, the city began to grow, both in population and in extent. New districts toward the west, the east, and the north gradually turned it into a circular, wheel-shaped city, with the Acropolis in its center. It was a city without walls. The old walled-in city which long ago had looked to a fortress Acropolis had been replaced by a new city for which the Acropolis was no longer a stronghold but the sacred abode of the gods.

The population pressures in Greece increased with increasing prosperity. It became impossible for the city state to feed its people upon its limited area. Many of the city states solved this problem by colonization, by taking new living space beyond their own borders. Sparta solved it by conquest and the enslavement of conquered peoples. Ingenious Athens found her own solution in the development of industry and trade which enabled her to exchange industrial products for necessary food. This resulted in changes in the social as well as the economic structure of Athenian life. There came to be in the city four distinct classes: the nobles, the peasants, the craftsmen and merchants, and the non-citizens—metics and slaves. Some of the nobles still lived on their country estates; most of the peasants, on their farms. Craftsmen and merchants lived in the city; the potters, for example, had their quarters at the Kerameikos. The non-citizen group worked on the estates of the nobles or in the workshops of the craftsmen.

The rise of manufacturing and trade undermined the importance of the aristocracy. Industrious merchants and craftsmen, gaining wealth, gained also political power. Some of the nobles became interested in the new sources of wealth which trade and manufacturing had uncovered. Social distinction based on wealth began to supersede distinction based on birth. Aristocracy gave way to timocracy. The problems created by this transformation were very serious. Ironically, growth and progress resulted in internal conflict, discontent, and poverty. The old agricultural economy was disturbed by the increasing importance of the new economy of trade and manufacturing. Money, the measure of wealth, became an end in itself. The rich few became richer and also more oppressive in their dealings with the small farmer and the craftsman. Farmers were forced to mortgage their farms to meet the new competition. Craftsmen had to borrow money to make improvements necessary for new types of production. The rate of interest was high; the laws harsh. If they could not fulfill their obligations, farmers lost their farms, craftsmen their independence. Insolvent debtors, both farmer and craftsman, could eventually be sold into slavery. The leaders of the city did nothing to better such conditions. Most of them merely tried to take full advantage of them.

Solon, the great statesman and law giver of Athens, tried to bring order out of the prevailing disorder. He recognized four groups of the population, graded according to wealth, each possessing certain rights and duties to correspond with those rights. Only the nobles could hold high office; the lowest class had at least the right to vote. Solon also established the principle that it is the duty of the community to provide for its invalids and its poor. He cancelled all debts, and passed a law forbidding debtors to be sold into slavery. "He fixed a limit for the measure of land which could be owned by a single person, so as to prevent the growth of dangerously large estates. And he forbade the exportation of Attic products, except oil. For it had been found that too much corn (wheat) was carried to foreign markets, where the prices were higher, that an insufficient supply remained for the population of Attica. It is to be observed, that, at this time, the Athenians had not yet begun to import Pontic corn."*
The results of Solon's reforms were sadly disappointing. The people called

---

* Bury, J. B.: *A History of Greece*. New York

upon to make sacrifices complained that they sacrificed too much. Those who gained grumbled that they did not gain enough. Solon, a merchant himself, had made the mistake of basing his reforms too much on the already passing economy of agricultural self-sufficiency. That economy could no longer support the increased population. But Athens was already moving toward a new economic concept: the exchange of specified agricultural and manufactured produce for food from overseas. An economic improvement was under way which eventually would make possible the support of the whole population.

It was a time of transition. Its very creativity caused dangerous troubles. Aristocracy had been both weakened and corrupted; democracy was not yet strong. Party strife complicated the situation. Tyranny, which Solon had tried hard to avoid, now became reality. It was Pisistratus who took political advantage of the prevailing economic and social disorder. He had gained great popularity through his conquest of Nisaea, the port of Megara, and his subsequent conquest of Salamis. He used this popularity to establish himself as tyrant of Athens. His sons continued the Pisistratean rule.

Pisistrates changed the physical structure of Athens, as Solon never changed it. He and the tyrants who succeeded him constructed a network of roads to connect outlying settlements with Athens. They built an aqueduct to supply the city with water. They made the Acropolis a citadel again, using its fortifications for their protection and building their palace within its walls. On the Acropolis they also surrounded the temple of Athena, the Hecatompedon, with colonades, and built the old Propylaca, the entrance gate. Possibly they had great plans for the city too. They pulled down the wall erected during the VII century to make extension of the city possible. Since they built nothing in its place, Athens became an open, defenseless city, and was to remain so for more than half a century.

The Athenians may not have enjoyed the rule of the Pisistradids. Nevertheless, these tyrants had imagination to see the coming of the Athenian empire and to work for it. It was they who established the Athenian navy. But they left to Miltiades, who came to power after their defeat, the important achievement of gaining the Thracian Chersonese which assured the wheat supply for Athens' growing population.

When the Ionian cities of Asia Minor revolted against the Persians, Athens, supporting the rebels, won the deep enmity of Persia. Persia's first attempt at vengeance ended in defeat. But ten years later, a second invasion of Attica razed Athens to the ground. The old Athens disappeared. Again the tide of battle turned. Themistocles defeated the Persian navy at Salamis; the united armies of Sparta and Athens defeated the Persian army at Plataea, the Athenian fleet won a victory at the Hellespont.

Greece and the Ionians in Asia Minor were free at last from the Persian menace. Athens could move forward in her political and commercial expansion. The Athenian empire became a reality.

Athens, the city, no longer existed. It had been reduced to ashes in the Persian wars. Should it be built again on its old site? Should the capital of the new empire be placed closer to the sea? Many urged the second course as befitting the sea power Athens was fast becoming. Tradition, however, resisted such innovation. Athens and its sacred Acropolis were rebuilt. A new harbor city, the Piraeus, was planned. Themistocles began and Pericles finished this great undertaking. In spite of protests from Sparta, the new Athens was soon fortified again by a wall. This wall enclosed a space nearly twice as large as the old city, including city extensions toward the north and the southwest and the settlements which had grown up outside the old wall demolished by the Pisistradids.

The original harbor of Athens, merely a place where ships could ride at anchor, had been located at the north shore of the bay of Phalerum. Themistocles, seeking more adequate harbor facilities for a great fleet, found them on the Piraean peninsula. Three natural harbors here were strategically fitted to serve a naval station. Two smaller harbors, Munychia and Zea, became the harbors for the warships. They were fortified and moles were built in connection with the fortifications. Shelters for the ships were also provided. The large harbor at the west side of the pen-

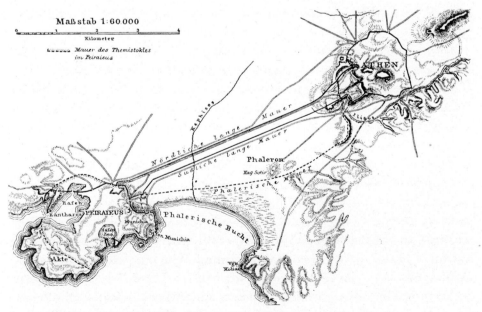

24. ATHENS AND PIRAEUS, *with the Long Walls Connecting Them*

insula became the port for merchant vessels. It too was fortified and protected against the sea by moles. Piraeus, harbor city of Athens, rose on the peninsula between the harbors. It was built under Pericles after a plan by Hippodamus.

Athens now comprised two cities, dependent on each other but separated by a distance of four miles. If war came, a strong enemy army could cut communications between them. Athens would then be without food supply and could be forced to surrender. To meet this danger, the two cities were connected by the so-called long walls. These were costly to build and difficult to defend, but they made the two cities one defense unit. The space between the walls could provide shelter for the people of Attica in time of danger. It was so used during the Peloponnesian War.

All Greek cities felt it a religious obligation to rebuild the temples destroyed during the war with Persia. Nowhere, however, was this rebuilding done with greater splendor than in Athens under Pericles. The Acropolis had again become, not a fortress, but a sacred precinct, devoted to the gods and their temples. Those temples, built of marble and adorned with sculpture, are a magnificent expression of the artistic culture of classic Athens.

Athenian sea power had liberated the Greek cities of Asia Minor and the islands of the Aegean Sea. It was, therefore, appropriate that Athens should assume leadership in the Delian league, established to maintain the independence of these cities. The league was technically a federation; in fact, it became the Athenian empire. Cities who did not voluntarily join the league could be forced to become members. Member cities who wanted to withdraw found that such withdrawal might be prevented by force.

The cities which made up the Delian League were all, in one way or another, dependent on Athens. Some even had to give up their own sovereignty. But the panhellenistic tendencies of Athens were in constant conflict with the Greek passion for unresrticted freedom. The necessary unity was not achieved. When Athens entered the western Mediterranean, the domain of Corinth, the Athenian traders began to out-distance the Corinthians, conflict became unavoidable. Conflict with Corinth eventually led to the Peloponnesian War in which Athens, after exerting all her strength, was defeated, forced to tear down her long walls, to demolish her harbors, and to turn her fleet over to Sparta. Internal strife increased the disorder caused by war. Athens recovered, eventually, but she never regained her former importance. Conflict with the Macedonians put further strains upon her. Then the Romans became the threat. Athens took sides with Mithradates, and, defeated, faced disaster second only to that brought by the Persian victory. Politically Athens lost all impor-

25. ANCIENT ATHENS

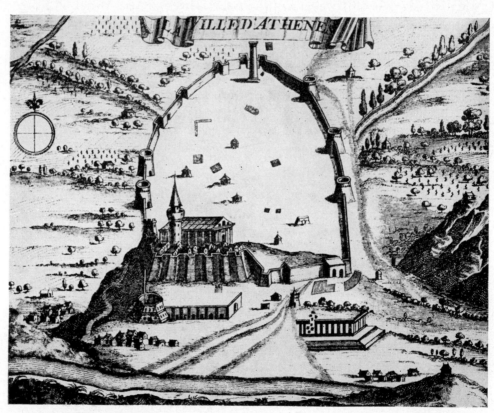

26. MEDIEVAL ATHENS

tance. Some Roman emperors, however, looked with favor on the city. Hadrian was one. In his time, Athens extended its city area toward the east, and Hadrian adorned this new part with magnificent public buildings. What Athens had created in the time of her greatness now became the source of the city's livelihood. Visitors from all over the known world came to gaze upon her works of art and architecture. Athens became a center of learning. To be educated in one of her schools was a mark of distinction. Politically dead, Athens exercised for a time great spiritual influence. Then Constantinople became the capital of the Eastern Empire and Athens lost even her intellectual prestige. Under Justinian, her philosophical schools were closed. Athens then slowly decayed as a city.

For most Greek cities colonization was the method used to solve population problems. Instead of adopting Sparta's plan of conquest or Athens' plan of developing manufacture and trade, these cities dealt with surplus population by sending some of their people elsewhere. The Thereans, for example, in a time when their food problem was rendered more acute by famine, used lottery to select colonizers. Brothers drew lots to determine which must emigrate. The colonizers thus selected met with great misfortunes. But when they tried to come home, their kinsmen met them with showers of missiles and would not let them come near the shore. They had to set sail again, and, eventually, guided by the Libyans, the forced exiles founded Cyrene in North Africa.

Colonization developed also from causes other than famine. Political discontent caused by the concentration of land in the hands of the aristocracy, the suppression of the common people and the consequent internal strife sent many discontented men in search of new homelands. Military defeat had the same result. Yet when the Persians subdued all the Greek cities in Asia Minor only two of them, Phocaea and Teos, preferred exile to submission.

To establish colonies on barbaric shores was not easy. It was possible only because the Greeks were far superior to the barbarians they encountered. Those barbarians were not able to recognize the potentialities of their countries, or to develop the potentialities they did recognize. The Greeks, on the other hand, by experience and tradition, had a clear conception of a city and its area of sustenance. They knew how a city should be located and what was required to provide the necessities of its life. They knew that a city should be easily accessible and easily defended, that it should have a natural harbor to make possible intercourse with other cities and the exchange of goods with them.

Homer in the Odyssey vividly describes an island he considered a suitable site for a city. He explains clearly why the natives were not able to build that city. ". . . we came to the land of the Cyclopes, a fierce, uncivilized people, who never lift a hand to plant or plough but put their trust in Providence. All the crops they require spring up unsown and untilled, wheat and barley and the vines whose generous clusters give them wine when ripened for them by timely rains. The Cyclopes have no assemblies for the making of laws, nor any settled customs, but live in hollow caverns in the mountain heights, where each man is law giver to his children and his wives, and nobody cares a lot for his neighbors.

"Not very far from the harbour on their coast and not so near either, there lies a luxuriant island covered with wood which is the home of innumerable goats. . . Used neither for grazing nor for ploughing, it lies forever unsown and untilled; and this land where no man goes makes a happy pasture for the bleating goats. I must explain that the Cyclopes have nothing like our ships with their crimson prow; nor have they any shipwrights to build merchant men that could serve their needs of plying to foreign ports in the course of that overseas traffic which ships have established between nations. Such craftsmen would have turned the island into a fine colony for the Cyclopes. For it is by no means a poor country, but capable of yielding any crop in due season. Along the shore of the grey sea there are soft water meadows where the vine would never wither, and there is plenty of land level enough for the plough, where they could count on cutting a deep crop at every harvest time, for the soil below the surface is exceedingly rich. Also it has a safe harbor in which there is no occasion to tie up at all. You need neither cast anchor nor make fast with hawsers: all your crew have to do is to beach their boat and wait till the spirit moves them and the light wind blows. Finally at the head of the harbor there is a stream of fresh water running out of a cave in a grove of poplar trees."

Travelers like Odysseus may have directed early emigrants in their search for new land on which to settle. Soon, however, the choice of the site for a prospective colony was taken out of the hands of the imigrants. To avoid interference and, eventually, hostilities between colonies, some regulation was needed. The Delphic Oracle assumed this regulatory function, with all the authority derived from its religious importance. New colonies might not be founded without consulting the Oracle. The priests through whom the Oracle spoke must have had a thorough knowledge of geography, topography, and ethnology. For the soundness of the oracular advice was attested by the rewards the colonists bestowed in gratitude upon the Oracle which had guided them so wisely and auspiciously.

Greek success in colonization was based on their thorough knowledge of their world and the people who lived in it. It was based also on their unique sense of social organization. They had the ability to make laws and the discipline to obey them. They were at once daring and conservative, proud of their habits and customs, regarding themselves as distinct from and superior to all others. Nicias, the Athenian general, addressing his defeated army at Syracuse, spoke in this spirit:* ". . . you are yourselves at once a city, wherever you sit down . . . men make the city and not walls and ships without men in them." Xenephon,** leading his army back from Persia after the death of Cyrus, expressed the Greek drive toward colonization and the Greek concept of the city. When he considered that they were in the Euxine, he writes, where such a powerful force (as his army) could never have been assembled without enormous expense, he thought what a fine thing it would be to found a city there and so gain more territory and power for Greece. It would be a great city, he mused, as he reckoned up the number of Greeks and of the people living around the Euxine.

In founding their colonies, the Greeks had to reckon with the natives of the lands they chose for their settlements. It is hard to find out how those natives reacted toward the Greeks who took away from them something whose value they were not always able to recognize. They may have been submissive or aggressive, according to particular circumstances. They undeniably received great benefits from their contact with the Greeks. They acquired things they had never dreamed of and gained knowledge of an advanced civilization. They learned about the land, how to drain it and how to cultivate it efficiently. They learned about different kinds of industry and production; about the use of resources and how to enrich their lives. As the Greeks usually settled on the coast, they affected the hinterland only indirectly. The native population may have not been dense enough to create real pressure. Naturally the new colonial cities became markets, advantageous both for the natives and for the Greeks, where natural products could be exchanged for processed and manufactured goods.

Peaceful conditions seem to have prevailed between colonists and natives on most shores where the Greeks settled. The colonists did, however, sometimes get into trouble. The settlers of Byzantium were subject to steady attacks by the Thracians, whose aggressiveness may have caused the Calcedonians to settle on the opposite shore. The Phoceans who settled at Atalia in Corsica came into conflict with the Phoenicians, who claimed the island as theirs and nearly annihilated the Phocean fleet. The colony on the island of Lipara, where people from Cnidos and Rhodos settled, had continuous fights with pirates. Some Greek settlers, unable to cope with marauders, turned pirates themselves.

---

* Thucydides: *The Peloponnesian War*
** Xenophon: *The Persian Expedition*

27. AMASTRIS

The Greeks prevented the Phonoecians from settling on the islands and shores of the Aegean Sea, and by so doing, cut them off also from the Euxine Sea, whose shores the Phonoecians had exploited for centuries. In contrast with the Aegean Sea, with its many islands, where land is almost always in sight, the Euxine Sea seemed to the Greeks like a boundless ocean, full of danger. But it attracted their adventurous spirit. When they navigated its shores, they saw what they had never seen before: the rich and fertile fields and pastureland and cattle of the north and the southern mountains, rich in metal and forests.

Miletus was the leading city in the colonization of those vast shores of the Euxine Sea. Its merchants exchanged its natural products for the manufactured goods of Miletus. The Greeks founded cities also. Amastris,* on the southern shore of the Euxine Sea, was one of many colonial cities. Its site exhibits all the features the Greeks desired for a city location. It consists of a rocky peninsula connected with the mainland by a narrow isthmus, easy to defend, and so formed as to provide two harbors, small but secure, between the peninsula and the mainland.

In parts of the western Mediterranean, the Greeks encountered already organized communities. The Etruscans as well as the Latins kept them from settling in their respective countries, as the Greeks had themselves prevented the Phoenicians from landing on theirs.

Cyme was one of the oldest Greek settlements on Italian soil. It was also the settlement farthest north. With Neapolis and Poseidonia (Paestum)

---

* The name derived from Amastris, the niece of Darius Codomanus, who refounded the city after its destruction.

28. SYRACUSE *The Island of Ortygia*

29. SELINUS *Reconstruction*

it formed the northern group of Greek settlements in Italy. South of this group, the shores were all settled with Greek colonies. These, with the colonies of Sicily, were called Magna Graecia.

Poseidonia was founded by Sybaris at the Tyrrhenian Sea. Located on a plain between the mountains and the sea, it was famous for its temples, especially for the temple of Poseidon which, in its heaviness, exhibits the spirit of early Doric architecture. Poseidonia flourished as an agricultural and trade city. Two hundred years after its founding, the Lucanians, native population of the area, took possession of it and suppressed the Greek colonists. Later it became a Roman city, the colony Paestum. It was, however, a malaria-infested spot, and eventually it fell into decay.

The Phoenicians had preceeded the Greeks as settlers on Sicily. Their settlements were, for the most part, at the western end of the island, and the Greeks were able to occupy the better sites where the people, evidently, had been able to offer successful resistance to the Phoenicians. One of these sites was Syracuse.

Syracuse was founded by the Corinthians at the southeastern part of Sicily, on the island of Ortygia close to the shore. One of the oldest Greek colonies in Sicily, it was destined to become its leading city and one of the most important cities of the Hellenic world. Its two natural harbors, a small one at the north side of the island and a larger one at the west of it, gave Syracuse opportunity to develop as a trading center.

The native population at Syracuse was reduced to serfdom and forced, after the Spartan tradition, to cultivate the soil for their Corinthian masters. The settlement grew rapidly and was soon able to found colonies of its own. When the island was connected with the mainland, the growing city could be extended on the slopes of the mountain.

Syracuse came into conflict with Carthage, rose to supremacy when she defeated her rival at Himera. The Athenians laid siege to the city during the Peloponnesian War, but their forces were defeated and annihilated. Then, during the first Punic War, the city was taken by the Romans, plundered, and reduced to the status of a provincial town. Today the old city occupies only its original small site, the island of Ortygia.

The farthest west of the Greek colonies was Selinus, on the southwest coast of Sicily, founded by people from Megara. Its oldest part stood on a precipice above the sea. Its layout is remarkable for simplicity. One main street is crossed at right angles by side streets, the size of the blocks being determined by the plans of the houses which, in their simplicity, contrasted with the splendid community buildings and temples. Later the city had to be extended, first toward the north, then behind the older part of the city, and finally on the gently sloping hillside toward the east and the harbor and on the western slope toward the river. Outside the city and separated from it by a marshy valley was a sacred precinct.

Selinus, by its very location, was subject to Carthaginian attack. Eventually the city was conquered and most of its inhabitants killed or taken prisoner. During the first Punic War, Selinus was utterly destroyed. It has remained ever since a deserted place.

While the Greek city states weakened each other in their fight for hegemony only to fall victim to the concentrated power of Macedonia, Rome slowly gained hegemony over Latium, became supreme in Italy and the whole Mediterranean world, and eventually extended her boundaries of empire from the Euphrates to the Atlantic.

What was the reason for such an extraordinary political achievement? Was it that Rome's commanding position in the center of the Mediterranean was always vulnerable to attack and the Romans, therefore, always forced to hold themselves ready for any challenge? Was it the spirit of Rome's people: the vitality developed in internal conflict between conservative aristocrat and peasant and progressive industrialist and merchant? That conflict, forever increasing, may have kept this vitality alive by the more and more complex activities it fostered. Was the secret of Rome's greatness in the strength developed as she threw back invading Greeks, Phoenicians, Etruscans? Or was it that the time was ripe for the unification and integration of the world which alone would make possible the survival of civilization?

There are no clear answers to those questions. In the life of a city as in the life of a man the most essential qualities are often indiscernible and hidden in impenetrable darkness.

Because Italy is a peninsula, located at the center of the Mediterranean, it could develop both land and sea power. The geographical and topographical structure of the peninsula is very simple. A mountain system, branching off toward the south from the west Alps, runs across the peninsula and then south, parallel to the shore lines of the seas. These mountain ranges, the Apennines, divide the peninsula into two halves. At either side, the mountains diminish into lower hills sloping toward a more or less extended plain along the shore with some small hills rising above it. Even without the great river valley of the Po, which originally did not belong to Italy proper, here was a land well fitted for human habitation.

In the middle of the west side of the peninsula, between the mountains and the sea, south and southeast of the river Tiber and around the Alban mountains, lies Latium. Here the Latins, who entered Italy from the north, made their settlement. Like their neighbors, they cultivated the plains and pastured their herds on the uplands. The land they worked was not very fertile. The most important Latin settlement, probably their religious and governmental center, the leading city of their federation, and their main stronghold, was Alba Longa. This city stood on Mount Alban, along the ridge bordering Lake Albano. Around it, in the plain, lay the villages of the Latins, surrounded by their fields.

Rome was originally only a village founded by Alba Longa. Like Athens, Rome was placed on a river at some distance from the sea. Ships could sail up the Tiber to its site. There is an island here, the water around it shallow enough for easy fording. The river formed the boundary between Latium and Etruria. Since Etruria was more advanced than Latium, it offered manufactured goods which the Latins were glad to exchange for their food and raw materials. Rome became the natural market place for such exchanges. And, since the Etrurians were hostile to the Latins, it was natural also that Rome, the border town, should become an important outlying defense post.

The advantages of Rome's location were offset by some disadvantages. Her territory was less fertile than other parts of Latium. Her river frequently overflowed its banks. The natural drainage was so imperfect that, in rainy seasons, water rushing from the hills converted lowlands into marshes which bred discomfort and disease. Rome's people, however, turned even such handicaps into advantages. To avoid the fever marshes, the peasants were forced to build their settlements on the more airy and salubrious hills. The integrated community which thus developed was an advance over the typical Latin pattern. Proximity to the sea encouraged the development of trade; and trade stimulated new activities in agriculture and industry. Rome must have early drawn a numerous non-agricultural population, as foreigners and Latins alike saw opportunities in the already crowded and still growing community.

Were there, as legend insists, seven villages (*septem pagi*) on the seven hills of Rome? We do not know. But we do know that the settlements on the Palatine and the Quirinal were superior to the others; they were all more or less fortified and formed independent communities. We know also that three communities were united by Synoecism and the settlement on the Palatine hill, *Roma quadrata,* became the seat of the Roman community and was surrounded by a wall. Synoecism, as we have already noted, did not require that all citizens actually settle in one place. Each of the three original communities retained possession of one-third of the common domain. The people continued to live on their land or in their respective settlements. Synoecism meant that henceforth there should be one city center, one council house and one comitium for the whole community, one place where citizens assembled to exercise their rights. This center was *Roma quadrata* on the Palatine.

Rome was not, as the saying goes, built in one day. But it is wholly possible that it was created as a community in one day by this act of Synoecism. Plutarch* relates the legendary story of the religious rites which founded the city on the Palatine. Romulus, he says: "set to building his city, and sent four men out of Tuscany who directed him by sacred usages and written rules in all the ceremonies to be observed, as in a religious rite. First, they dug a round trench about that which is now the comitium or court of assembly, and into it solemnly threw the first fruits of all things either good by custom or necessary by nature; lastly, every man taking a small piece of earth of the country from whence he came, they all threw in promiscuously together. This trench they call, as they do the heavens, *Mundus,* making which their center, they described the city in a circle around it. Then the founder fitted to a plough a brazen ploughshare, and, yoking together a bull and a cow, drove himself a deep line or furrow around the bounds; while the business of those that followed after was to see that whatever earth was thrown up should be turned all inwards toward the city, and not to let any clod lie outside. With this line they described the wall, and called it, by a contraction, Pomoerium, that is *postmurum,* after or beside the wall; and where they designed to make a gate, there they took out the share, carried the plough over and left a space; for which reason they consider the whole wall holy, except where the gates are; for had they adjudged them also sacred, they could not, without offense to religion, have given free ingress and egress for the necessaries of human life, some of which are in themselves unclean."

Rome, like Athens, welcomed strangers, opened its gates to immigrants, and by law incorporated them into the body of citizens. Sabines and Etruscans were attracted to Rome and settled there, contributing their industry to the industrial and mercantile progress of their adopted city. Rome was full of busy workshops. Soon she produced nearly everything she needed for herself and for the other communities of Latium. Eventually her people learned to build ships and to carry on trade, like the Etruscans, Greeks, and Carthaginians. At Ostia, at the mouth of the river Tiber, they established salt works, built a harbor, and founded their first colony.
No one likes to see an equal become a superior. And other Latin communities may well have been jealous of the growing power of Rome. But these communities needed Rome as their leader in struggles against common enemies. Recognition of this fact gave Rome a measure of legal recognition as the dominant city of the area. Rome herself did not want and could not afford to have any other important and independent community within the Latin territory. This may have been her reason for moving to conquer and destroy Alba Longa, the old leading city of the Latins and their politi-

---

* Plutarch: *Lives.* Romulus

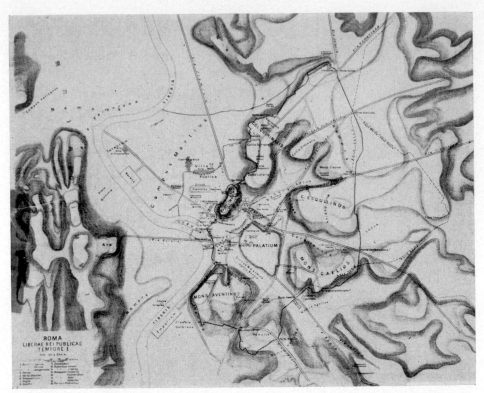

30. REPUBLICAN ROME

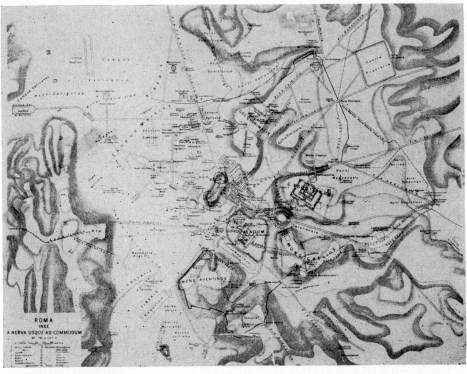

31. IMPERIAL ROME

cal and religious center. The people of Alba Longa were moved to Rome. They settled on the Caelian hill and became Roman citizens. Then Latium could be united under a Latin League. Formation of this league, like a second Synoecism, was symbolized by the city wall of Servius Tullius, built to enclose all the settlements of Rome. Latins who did not become Roman citizens had, at least, equal rights as members of the Latin League.

Rome's population increased in size and diversity as Rome's power and importance waxed. There were two main groups in the city now, each with its own aims: the Old Latin aristocracy and peasantry, conservative in character and traditional in their way of life; and the merchants and craftsmen, progressive and daring as their growing trade and industry demanded. This differentiation in thought and action intensified conflicts already inherent in Roman society.

Each group was differentiated within itself in accordance with differences in the amounts possessed by its members. Social as well as material distinctions came into being. This created another conflict, social in nature, which affected the further development of the city. A kind of timocracy appeared; people were classified according to their means. Rights and obligations, especially those related to military service, were determined on this basis.

The city enclosed by the Servian Wall was already of considerable size. It included all the hills around the Palatine on which the original city had been built. The city's stronghold had been transferred from its original position on the Palatine to the Tarpeian Hill. This hill, free at every side, could be better defended if the city itself should ever fall. A place of assembly (*area capitolina*) stood on the Tarpeian, but no private buildings were permitted there. Close to the new stronghold—the capitol as it was now called—a bridge was built across the river, leading into the Etrurian territory. To protect this bridge, the Janiculum, a hill on the right bank of the river, had to be taken and fortified. The space within the wall included the marshy valleys between the hills. To make this valuable space useful, the marshes were drained. The place of assembly could then be transferred from the capitol hill "to the flat space where the ground fell from the stronghold towards the city (*comitium*), and which stretched thence between the Palatine and the Carinae in the direction of the Vellia."

Momsen,[*] who thus describes the new location of the place of assembly, also gives important descriptions of the surroundings: "At that side of the comitium which adjoined the stronghold, and upon the wall which arose above the comitium in the fashion of a balcony, the members of the Senate and guests of the city had a place of honour assigned to them on occasion of festivals and assemblies of the people; and not far from this there soon

---

* Momsen, Theodor: *History of Rome*

came to be built a special senate house, which derived from its builder the name Curia Hostilia. The platform for the judgement-seat *(tribunal)*, and the stage from which the burgesses were addressed (later *rostra*) were created on the comitium itself. Its prolongation in the direction of the Velia became the new market *(forum Romanorum)*. On the west side of the forum, beneath the Palatine, rose the community house, which included the official dwelling of the king *(regia)* and the common hearth of the city, the rotunda forming the temple of Vesta. At no great distance, on the south side of the forum, there was erected a second round building— the storeroom of the community or temple of the Penates, which still stands at the present day as the porch of the church Santi Cosmae Damians. Along the two longer sides of the Forum, butcher shops and other traders' stalls were arranged. In the valley between the Palatine and Aventine a space was staked off for races; this became the circus. The cattle market was laid out immediately adjoining the river and this soon became one of the most densely peopled quarters of Rome. Temples and sanctuaries arose on all the summits, above all the federal sanctuary of Diana on the Aventine and on the summit of the stronghold the far-seen temple of Father Diovis, who had given to his people all this glory, and who now, when the Romans were triumphing over the surrounding nations, triumphed along with them over the subject gods of the vanquished."

For her first four hundred years, Rome depended for water supply on local wells. As the city increased in size and population, this natural water supply became insufficient. Water had to be brought into the city from outside. Appius Claudius built the first of the many aqueducts on which Rome's water supply came to depend.

After long wars and increasing struggles, especially with the Etruscans and Samnites, Rome united Italy and secured its possession with colonies, fortresses, and a system of roads connecting these outposts with each other and with the capital, Rome. National unity gradually developed out of political union. Only once was Rome taken by an enemy. The Celts conquered the city and destroyed it; only the stronghold was able to resist them. This great defeat almost ended Rome's history. Some suggested that the city be abandoned and her people and government transferred to Veji, an Etruscan city previously taken by the Romans. The patricians successfully opposed this move, and Rome was hastily rebuilt, with no regard for order and harmony. The narrow crooked streets which resulted from this rebuilding remained until Rome was destroyed by fire during Nero's reign. The city that arose from those ashes had more regularity and more harmony.

Until its transmarine conquests, Rome, like all of Italy, depended on its own resources. It was both an agricultural and a mercantile city, but the landed interests dominated the moneyed. Most of the people held property and tilled the soil. Gains made by the sword were secured by the plough. Agriculture was the main support of all communities. There were no great fortunes. A Carthaginian embassy visting Rome observed "that a single set of silverplate sufficed for the whole senate, and had reappeared in every house to which the envoys had been invited." This sneering remark, Momsen* notes, is a "significant token of the difference in economic conditions" between Carthage, rich and money-dominated, and Rome still looking to the earth for her well being. Then Rome came face to face with Carthage, defeated her after long and devastating wars, and fell heir to the Carthaginian wealth.

After the second Punic War, economic conditions in Rome began to change rapidly. The great advantages Rome had gained brought with them forces destructive to Rome society. One might say that, with Rome's success, her decline began—camouflaged as "progress."

The people hit hardest by the wars and their aftermath were the small farmers. There were more of them and they had been the backbone of the army. When wars were short and on a small scale, this military service did not too much disrupt the farmer's life. But as wars extended in space and time, the burdens the farmers carried became intolerable. They needed money to effect a recovery. But, if they went into debt, they might, under the unjust and rigid laws of the times, lose both property and freedom. They might even be sold as slaves. What a fate for men whose industry had laid the foundation for the empire, whose bravery as soldiers had brought prosperity to their country!

The very military achievements of the farmers worked toward their ruin. They helped make Sicily the granary of Rome, and its vast fields, worked by slaves after the Carthaginian system, produced such quantities of grain at so low a price that the Roman farmer could not compete. If he tried to convert his farm for a more profitable kind of agriculture, he found it hard to get the loans to tide him over transition lines. As more and more individual farmers were forced out of agriculture, their farms were bought up and combined into large estates, managed by stewards and worked by slaves after the same Carthaginian system adopted in Sicily. Where one hundred and fifty families had once made their livings, there might be left now only one family of free men and about fifty slaves. The settlement structure of the whole country was completely changed. As small farms gave way to large estates, a new class was created, the Roman proletariat,

---

* Momsen: *op. cit.*

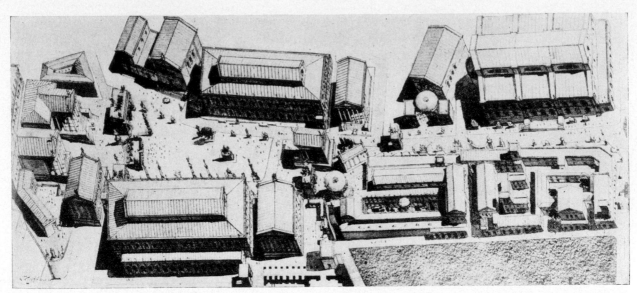

32. ROME, FORUM ROMANUM *Reconstructed*

citizens without property who could serve the state only as they had children to become the paid soldiers of future armies. Eventually, the proletarians degenerated into a city mob, tired of everything except the excitement of the Colosseum—*panem et circenses*. They were fed and amused by the money Rome took from her provinces. Originally constructive population elements became destructive.

"The nation was visibly diminishing, and the community of free burgesses was resolving itself into a body composed of masters and slaves; and although it was, in the first instance, the two long wars with Carthage which decimated both the burgesses and the alies, the Roman capitalist, beyond doubt, contributed quite as much as Hamilcar and Hannibal to the decline in vigour and number of the Italian people."*

On the whole, Italian society began to decline and disintegrate as the number of slaves increased. Money, becoming more and more abundant, also exerted a disintegrating influence. It led to speculation and to the exploitation of conquered provinces. Unscrupulous persons became very rich. The growing mass of the expropriated became discontented and helpless. The whole population was out of balance and Rome became a fertile field for demagogues. Civil wars followed each other until Caesarism emerged and emperors tried to solve the unsettled social problems by means of despotism.

Rome grew in size and population with each political and military success. After the second Punic War, in all probability, the city wall was demolished and the main obstacle to the city's expansion thus removed. On the

* Momsen: *op, cit.*

68

33. ROME, FORUM ROMANUM *At the End of the Middle Ages*

Campus Martius, the plain between the hills and the river, a new quarter arose, well built and orderly. The Rome of the Republic contained few public buildings, and most of these were located at the Forum Romanum, the political center of the city. In time, the wooden booths of the merchants were replaced by stone buildings. Basilicas and halls gave the Forum an appearance appropriate to its political dignity.

The emperors, with their passion for monumental buildings, however, changed Rome's structure. They regarded buildings as political tools and used them to impress their glory upon the people and to establish for themselves eternal fame. First, they adorned the Forum Romanum with impressive edifices, meanwhile abolishing its political function and reducing to nil the power of the people and of the Senate. Caesar planned, and Augustus built, a new Senate house to replace the comitium once the assembly of the Roman people. The political center of Rome, however, was shifted back to the Palatine Hill where Augustus built an imperial palace. The change in Rome's political structure was reflected in its architecture. The informality of the buildings on the Forum Romanum had been an expression of equality. These buildings varied in size, according to their functions, but not one tended to dominate the others. The Forum of Caesar's day was only a homogeneous temple site. The temple of Augustus dominated his forum, expressing dramatically the new spirit of government which elevated one person far above all others, subordinating aristocracy and people alike to the domination of one.

The Forum of Trajan, by Apollodorus of Damascus, expressed this imperial spirit impressively. The large square, dominated by its basilica and adjoining libraries, far surpassed all preceding efforts in scope and splendor. The columns between the libraries marked the line of the ridge which had once connected the Capitol Hill with the Quirinal, but which had been cut away to make room for Trajan's buildings and to connect these buildings and the forums south of the ridge with those of the Campus Martius and those beyond the Tiber. Between the buildings and building groups, parks and gardens with fountains united nature with the works of man.

Imperial Rome became a world city, became, indeed, the acknowledged center of the world. Underneath its glory and luxury festered all the human miseries inevitable in so vast an accumulation of people. From all over the Empire, men migrated to Rome. The influx changed the composition of the city's population to the same degree that the emperors had changed its physical structure. Some called Rome a union of all peoples; others regarded her as a city without citizens, populated by the scum of all the world.

A vast housing shortage was one result of the transformation of republican Rome into imperial Rome. This is a characteristic development in all metropolises, but in Rome the problem was intensified as available land was appropriated for vast imperial buildings. It was further aggravated because the city lacked transportation facilities to make possible expansion beyond the periphery of the already vast city area.

The atrium house, typical of old Rome, with its small rooms on the sides of the Atrium, had already been replaced by the more comfortable peristyle house, more or less elaborated according to the requirements of its owners. The imperial palace was little more than a large scale peristyle house. Only the rich adopted the new kind of dwelling. For the poor, the atrium house was replaced by the apartment. This development was brought about by lack of living space in those areas where such space was most needed. The aristocracy settled on the Caelian and Aventine Hills and had room to breathe. The lesser people, crowded into the old city area were jammed together in ever-increasing congestion. Apartment houses rose to six or eight floors to provide "relief" from overcrowding. The size of individual apartments decreased. Streets were narrowed to make space for yet more building. Land speculation aggravated the situation; rents became unbearably high.

Aristides, writing in praise of Rome, said that it carried city piled on city. If it were possible to spread them all on the ground, he estimated, the whole width of Italy would be covered by one vast continuous city extending to the Adriatic Sea. Juvenal, with more insight, remarked that in

Sora, Fabrateria, or Frusino, a house and garden could be bought for the amount of money paid for a year's rent in a dark apartment in Rome. Under Augustus, Rome's population may have reached the million mark; during the second century it was probably a million and a half.

To secure her conquests, Rome had to colonize. The conquering soldier was followed by the peaceful settler, first in Italy, then around the Mediterranean, and finally as far north as Gaul, Germany, and Britain. Roman imperialism brought peace to the world and maintained that peace for almost two hundred years. Rome tried to use her colonization to knit together spiritually her vast empire. The remotest parts of that empire felt the touch of Greek-Roman civilization. London, Paris, and Cologne were once Roman camps; they became flourishing cities. Timgad in North Africa, Palmyra in Syria, and other settlements here and there were not so fortunate; they fell into decay when the empire disintegrated. The ruins of those cities, however, still reveal the character of Roman cities.

Peace brought Rome security and wealth. It stimulated enterprise and building. Cities of a regular pattern soon began to rise everywhere. They were adorned with temples and forums, triumphal arches and colonaded streets, libraries, basilicas, and amphitheaters. Safe roads facilitated communication within the empire. Aristides wrote: "Were there ever so many cities? What ruler of the past could reach another city in his realm every day? Pass through two or three cities on the same day? Indeed all previous rulers were but kings of a desert, with strongholds; but, you, Rome, you alone rule cities."*

Libanios'** eulogy of his native city, Antioch, indicates the high level civilization reached in Roman cities, especially those in the Orient. "The water supply of our city is unsurpassed," Libanios wrote. "Others may equal us in some respects, but they are all inferior to the abundance and excellency of our water. In the public baths, and in some private baths, each stream is the size of a river, and the rest are not much smaller. He who has the means to build a new bath need not fear that it will be dry when completed. Every part of the city sees to the elegance of its public baths. . . . The abundance of the flowing water can be measured by the number of dwellings; for there are as many flowing waters as there are dwellings. . . . Therefore, we do not quarrel at the public wells as to who comes first to draw water; an evil true of so many reputable cities, where large crowds wrangle around the wells over broken jugs. As everybody has water within the house, we have fountains as an adornment of our city. . . . The sunlight is rivalled by other lights, lights which surpass

---

* Quoted by Friedlander, Ludwig: *Sittengeschichte Roms.*
** Ibid.

those of the illuminations at Egyptian festivals. In our city, nights differ from days only by the variance in illumination; busy hands notice no difference, and continue to forge and whoever wishes sings and dances, so that here Hephaestus and Aphrodite share the night."

During the third century, conditions in the Roman empire began to change rapidly. Peace was giving place to strife. The unregulated succession of the emperors caused ever-increasing struggle and civil war. Meanwhile, from without, the barbarians hammered against every frontier.

The long wars with their devastation, the huge state machine with its countless officials, the great army required to protect the empire—all these increased taxes to an unbearable height.

The number of those who received increased disproportionately to the number of those who produced. Productivity was crippled, responsibility weakened. The result was psychological and physical disintegration which touched life in city and country and which, in the end, undermined Rome herself.

For more than five centuries Rome never saw an enemy at her gates. But danger was coming nearer now. Aurelian saw it and, to protect the city against possible barbarian invasion, built a new city wall which enclosed a much larger area than the wall of Servius Tullius, long ago demolished. Protected by this Aurelian wall, Rome was able to survive the break down of the empire.

It was a city, however, of dwindling importance. Diocletian's restoration of the empire began the decline. He and the rulers who followed him lived at Nicomedia and Milano, Sirmium and Trier, closer to the zone of danger. Rome continued to be the imperial capital, but she was no longer the center of government; that center shifted, naturally, to the headquarters of the rulers. When Constantine founded Constantinople, made it his capital, and adopted Christianity as a state religion, Rome's real eclipse began.

Eventually the empire was divided. Rome succumbed to the assaults of the barbarians and lost her power completely. Two forces accomplished this destruction: Christianity from within and the barbarians from without. Each destructive force had within it elements of new life. Christianity, after destroying Paganism, created Christian Rome which, though shorn of temporal power, developed into a spiritual world center as powerful in Christendom as ancient Rome had been in her Empire. The barbarians, vigorous and vital, paved the way for the rebirth of a new spirit which, after dark ages, flowered in medieval civilization and culture.

For Rome the city this period of transition was, at first, wholly destructive. The great buildings of antiquity became quarries from which stones were obtained for new construction; this process continued until the seventeenth century. Internal strife tore at the physical as well as spiritual fabric of the city: strife between the nobility and the people, between factions of the nobility, between city and pope, between emperor and pope, between pope and counter-pope, emperor and counter-emperor. Conflict flared into violence at many papal elections, at practically every coronation of an emperor. Antique buildings became strongholds of the warring parties. The devastation of Rome, which the barbarians had been unable to achieve, now became reality. The city became a mass of ruins through which wound narrow streets and crooked alleys. Fields, vineyards, and vegetable gardens appeared among the ruins. Cows and goats grazed on the Forum Romanum. When, at the beginning of the fourteenth century, the Popes fled to Avignon, there to remain until 1377, Rome sank to the lowest point in all her history. Her population was reduced to about twenty thousand, not much more than one per cent of what it had been in the city's prime.

Out of the toil of centuries, Rome created an empire. Constantinople was a creation of this empire. Founded at a time when the empire was already beginning to crumble, it expressed Constantine's determination to build a New Rome, centrally placed within the empire, which should take the place and the function of the weakened ancient city.
Ten years after its founding, Constantinople was a good-sized city, with

34. CONSTANTINOPLE

35. CONSTANTINOPLE *View from Galata across the Golden Horn*

monumental buildings. It had grown fast at the expense of other cities, which had been despoiled of their art treasures and architectural elements for the glory of the new capital, and which had been robbed of their people that the city of Constantine should be populated. The development of a new city by the forced settling of inhabitants of other cities was traditional oriental practice, and the Diadochs had populated their newly founded cities with people from cities they conquered or destroyed. Constantinople's magnificent location made of this synthetic mass a living reality. Placed at the geographic center of the empire, it had advantages over Rome. It was the link between Europe and Asia, strategically placed near the Euphrates and the Danube from which Parthians and Germans launched their powerful inroads in the empire. It was the center of trade routes between east and west. The Sea of Marmara is here joined to the Aegean by the Dardanelles and to the Black Sea by the Bosporus. The Black Sea and the Aegean Sea were, with the Mediterranean, the main waters of the eastern part of the empire.

The site chosen for the city itself is also magnificent. Guarded by nature against attack, it was also easily accessible for commercial intercourse. The triangular peninsula on which Constantinople was built faces the sea of Marmara to the south and east. Its north side borders an inlet, the Golden Horn, forming a large natural harbor. Only the west side, connected with the mainland, had to be fortified. A chain of hills runs along this peninsula at its north side, near the Golden Horn. At the south, the land rolls in gentle waves toward the Sea of Marmara.

This excellent location had been, of course, already occupied by earlier settlements. A Phoenician settlement and later the Greek city of Byzantium had been built at the obtuse point of the peninsula. By choosing Byzantium for his new capital, Constantine proved himself an able and

far-seeing statesman. Constantinople remained the capital of the eastern empire for more than a thousand years.

Byzantium, however, had not been Constantine's first choice. He had considered Sardia (Sofia) and a number of other cities, and had finally settled on Troy because of its traditional importance as the ancient sacred home of the Romans. According to the oracle, Troy was destined to become again the seat of Rome's rulers. For centuries, sacrifices had been offered at the tombs of the Homeric heroes. In designating Troy as his capital, Constantine would have had wide support in the pagan world if not in Rome. But the gods opposed the choice, and Constantine, though no longer considered the son of a god, was obedient to heavenly admonition. The gate of the new capital had already been erected on the site of Troy—one hundred years later their remains could still be seen from the sea—when the admonition came. God himself appeared in the emperor's dream and advised him to choose another site. To be advised by God rather than commanded by the gods was a new experience for Constantine. We may assume that similar advice led to the adoption of Christianity as a state religion, and that this decision was taken because the emperor saw in Christianity a political means, a source of strength to his empire, to himself as emperor, and to the dynasty he wanted to found. History was to prove the farsighted statesmanship of this decision.

The god-guided choice then fell upon Byzantium, a site not linked to a host of pagan traditions. When Constantine, spear in hand, paced the boundaries on which the city was to be erected, his companions felt that he strode too far. One of them dared to ask, "How much farther, Sire?" Constantine replied, "Until he who walks before me stands still,"* as though he saw a super-human being, perhaps God himself, leading him.

* Gibbon, Edward: *The Decline and Fall of the Roman Empire*

Constantine transferred from the abandoned capital of Rome all that represented Rome's importance in the eyes of the world. Burckhardt says:* "Constantinople's virtual likeness with Rome was shown in the establishment of identical institutions, public offices and the privileges connected with them. Above all there had to be a Senate, even though its purpose was obscure, unless the court required figurants for its processions. A small number of Roman senators were induced to settle in Constantinople by having special concessions conferred upon them, such as palaces, villas, and landed estates. The emperor erected also a magnificent Senate house, but neither the pictures of the Muses, nor the statues of Zeus of Dodona and Pallas of Lindos at the entrances of the edifice, could alter the inanity of it."

Constantinople, as a founded city, could not grow organically as Rome had grown. The structure of the older city had expressed all the changes in its long progress from small Latin village to great imperial capital. Constantinople was built all at once. And only once in its long history was the city area increased. This took place one hundred years after Constantinople's founding and the city was then enlarged to occupy the whole peninsula.

Constantinople began where Rome ended—with despotism. To this the emperors added Christianity as the state religion, bureaucracy as the machinery of government. Together, despotism, Christianity, and bureaucracy formed so strong a unity that Constantinople was able to survive the fall of Rome by more than a thousand years.

In Constantinople, as in Rome, the poor were fed at the expense of the provinces. Egypt, for example, had to provide an annual tribute of grain. There was also a circus. There were factional and political struggles here also which often menaced the city. But Constantinople differed from Rome in that she had replaced economic passivity with vigorous activity in industry and trade.

Antioch in Syria and Alexandria in Egypt, centers where Hellenistic culture was blended with orientalism, challenged Constantinople's cultural leadership, but Constantinople eventually surpassed them both. The city became a religious center for the newly developing Christian world. The church of S. Sophia, built by Justinian to replace Constantine's timber-roofed basilica, symbolized in architecture this spiritual dominance.

The architectural character of Constantinople is determined by the topography of its site. The city was irregular on its hilly north side, more regularly laid out on the south. But nowhere were axiality and symmetry dominating factors. The arrangement of the squares, with their imperial

---

* Burckhardt, Jacob: *Die Zeit Konstantine des Grossen*

and public buildings, is free, more like Greek cities than Roman. The north side, in spite of its hills, was the more densely settled area. The south side was more open, its houses interspersed with gardens which, increasing in area toward the city wall, gave the city the look of the countryside. Around the busy harbor to the north, the Golden Horn, were the necessary harbor installations, warehouses, stores, factories, workshops, and also the dwellings of craftsmen and traders. This concentration accounts for the greater density of this part of the city. The hills were recognized always as natural sites for significant buildings. The Greeks had once built their temples there. Now they became sites for Christian churches. Later the Moslem would crown them with mosques. Those mosques, all architectural variations of S. Sophia, dominate the city with domes and semi-domes, which contrast effectively with the horizontality of the houses on the hills as these follow the elevation and are like terraces attached to it.

Constantinople's favorable location and growing splendor attracted the envious eyes of the not-so-far-off barbarians, especially when the empire weakened under their hammering. Yet the city, often in danger, was spared the fate of Rome. The city was never surrendered to the barbarians. Her downfall came at the hands of fellow Christians when the Crusaders, sweeping out of the west, stormed the city, captured it, and became its rulers for a time. The real doom of Constantinople was sealed only when the Turks overthrew the city and made it the capital of the Turkish empire.

The greatest achievement of Roman civilization was the creation of cities. They arose everywhere in the vast empire, serving as administrative and market centers, as outposts of Roman civilization, and as forces drawing into unity a widely scattered Roman world.

The new provincial cities were inhabited by Roman landlords and army veterans, who directed the predominantly agricultural economy. The landlords were responsible for taxes, measured by the amount of land they owned. They were, in effect, parasites upon a people living on the land. They oppressed the native population, reduced its members to serfdom. And yet, these cities propagated seeds of freedom, glimpsed the ideal of the self-governing community.

Colonization was possible only in an expanding empire, and Rome was long forced to continue an expansionist policy for her own protection. The time came, however, when expansion reached a limit, when it was checked by the barbarians who, feeling themselves the need for new land, made aggressive war against the empire. It had been a Roman custom to settle such land-seeking people in areas devastated by war. In this way

36. ARLES *Amphitheater*

37. ARLES *Amphitheater with Town*

78

they could recover lost land and, at the same time, appease the land-hungry. This plan no longer worked when the barbarians became conquerors in their own right. Then, the expense of defending the empire mounted rapidly, while the revenues to pay this expense declined. The whole system of colonization began to crumble. Eventually the empire itself was defeated and its civilization barbarized. Some of the conquering barbarians recognized the importance of the empire as an organization and saw the possibility of using it to their own advantage. In general, however, Rome's civilizing touch did not make a deep impression on her conquerors.

Many Roman cities were destroyed during the barbarian invasions. Many, however, survived. Especially in Latin countries, with their age-old Roman tradition, city life continued. The rural population, carrying their movable belongings, sought refuge from the havoc of war behind the city walls. Sometimes people driven from their homes found protection within a large public building. The amphitheater of Arles was so used. The crumbling palace of Diocletian became a place of refuge for people from Salone when their city was destroyed. The refugees built themselves houses inside the palace; eventually their settlement became the nucleus of the present-day city of Spalato. The Venetes, living at the shore of the northern end of the Adriatic, escaped destruction by fleeing to the islands of the lagoons; their settlements were later united and Venice came into being.

Did the barbarians deliberately destroy the cities they conquered? Certainly they destroyed many in the process of attack. Certainly they saw many burned to the ground by their defenders. They may have deliberately destroyed some cities because they considered them symbols of oppression. But they cannot be held wholly responsible for the disappearance of once flourishing settlements. Roman cities depended for existence on the empire which proctected them. When that empire fell, they were deserted. Their inhabitants were killed in the wars or fled to escape conquering armies. The deserted cities, useless to the barbarians, fell into decay. When the barbarians only wanted the land for their livelihood, this process may have well suited their purposes. Those tribes which conquered in order to rule over a subdued population may very well have saved the cities and made them the fortified centers of their petty kingdoms. Those barbarian kingdoms were short lived. They were always targets for one conquest after another. No stable rule was possible. The barbarians eventually became Christians, and Christianity became the spiritual idea shaping the western world, though it was, for centuries, obscured and almost blotted out in a darkness difficult to penetrate. Oriental tradition and Christianity flourished together in the eastern empire, until Moham-

38. SPALATO *Diocletian Palace, Reconstruction*

39. SPALATO *Diocletian Palace with Town*

med proclaimed the new faith of Islam. Dynamic, forceful, active, this new religion attacked Europe East and West and held it in pincer jaws. Constantinople, protected by its walls, held out against the onslaught. In the West, the Moslems were defeated at Tours and never again able to cross the Pyranees. Christianity was saved to continue its spiritual mission and its civilizing task.

In this struggle, however, the Moslems became masters of most of the Mediterranean Sea. Age-old communication and trade relations between East and West were disrupted. The cities of the West faced new problems. We do not know how the inland cities were affected, but we do know the tremendous changes the rise of Islam brought about in two maritime cities: Marseilles and Venice. One suffered great loss; the other great gain.

Marseilles, for centuries a link between the East and Gaul, may have been founded by the Phoenicians and settled by Greeks from Phocis. With a natural harbor, easily defended, it was the important port of Gaul. Under the Romans it became the trade center of southern Gaul. After the Mediterranean became a Moslem sea, Marseilles could no longer perform the functions of a trade city. Her trade routes were cut off. The city declined, and did not regain its old importance until the close of the Middle Ages.

What Marseilles lost, Venice may have gained. The city had been founded by people of the northern Adriatic coast who fled from the swords of the Huns to find a safe refuge on the islands of the lagoons. Life was hard on those islands; the people were pitifully poor. But they had one essential of human life in abundance—salt. They extracted salt from the sea and exchanged it for other necessities of life. To carry on this business, they had to be accustomed to both sea and land; they learned the art of sailing and became able navigators. As their islands could be approached only by secret channels, they were well protected. Their ships increased in size. They built up trade with all the harbors of the Gulf of Venice. Thanks to their enterprise and their impregnable position, they flourished. When the Moslems came, Venice was able to make a trade agreement with these people who shared her interest in commerce. The East was, to a certain extent, reopened to the West via Venice.

Unceasing wars devastated Europe, leaving destruction and anarchy in their wake. Weak and unprotected free peasants had to give up their freedom and their possessions to the lords of the large estates. This created the condition out of which medieval feudalism emerged.

The Carolingian empire brought some degree of order out of this chaos. This was the first political expression of the spiritual unity of Christen-

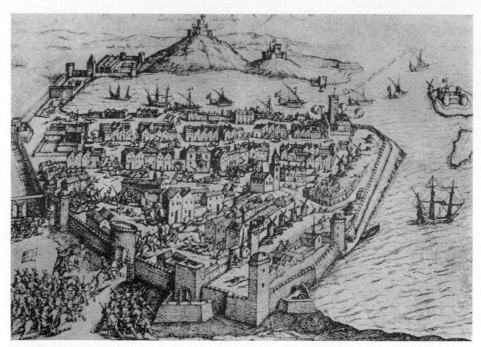

40. MARSEILLES

41. VENICE

dom, but it was too short-lived to be really successful. Charlemagne divided his empire into counties, each headed by a count. Equal in rank with the counts were the bishops. Both shared the administrative functions. Like the emperor himself, the counts traveled from estate to estate to perform administrative and judicial duties.

The Carolingian empire was quite different from the Roman in its settlement structure. In the Roman empire, based on both cities and estates, the cities had two main functions: they were administrative as well as trade centers; they were inhabited, therefore, by the landed proprietors and the merchants. In the Carolingian empire, cities no longer had those

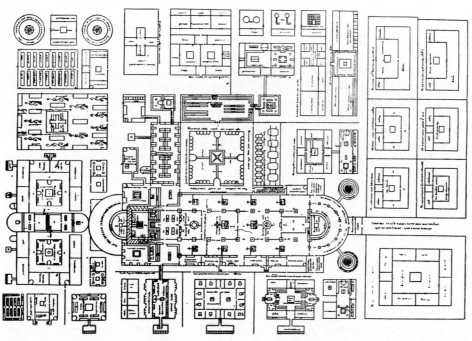

42. S. GALL *Plan of a Monastery*

functions, except those which became the seats of the bishops. The whole economy was based on landed property and was agricultural in character. The seats of the counts, as well as those of the emperor himself, were located, not in the cities, but on the estates on which, through the prevailing self-sufficient economy, their livelihood depended. There were only regional markets. Trade with other countries was small and unimportant.

Not very much has survived of this period. The plan of S. Gall, a valuable document, gives some information about the monastery, Since a monastery was itself part of a large estate, this information helps us to understand the nature of these estates also. The plan is abstract, but the general idea which guided the lay out of the monastery is clear.

Such a monastery was like a small town, except for its population. It contained, besides the ecclesiastical buildings, most of the essentials of a town. The people who tilled the monastery fields lived in villages in the midst of these fields. We may assume that the seats of the greater or lesser landlords may have had a similar layout. The domestic buildings could have been the same, the ecclesiastical buildings replaced by a palace or a manor, according to the owner's rank and wealth. We may assume also that monasteries, palaces, and manors were fortified, and that they probably served as places of refuge for the peasants, who, in time of danger found protection there and served as defenders of their refuge. Such palaces, manors, and monasteries must have been small centers of civilization. Their spirit was not passive turning away from life which characterized the monasteries in Egypt. The monks, with unceasing energy, created conditions for civilization everywhere, worked persistently to tame the barbarians. They cleared forests, drained fens, built flourishing settlements on land once deserted wilderness. Their work cannot be overestimated. They laid the foundation of western civilization. The medieval cities were the true fruit of the monastic spirit and enterprise.

The medieval city, like the Greek city, was a free, self-governing community, a free commonwealth with its own constitution. It differed from the Greek city, however, because there were no slaves in it. For the first time in history, an economy based on free work became the source of political rights.

How did the medieval city come into being? It is not easy to answer that question. Among the facts we know, it is difficult to separate consequence from cause. Perhaps, behind all the facts, some wholly new spirit, some new conception of life was at work, different from all preceding concepts and making it possible for men to dissolve the torpidity born of unceasing troubles and to imagine new creative possibilities. The emergence of the medieval city was certainly no mere mechanical process, no inevitable evolution. Was Christianity, perhaps, the driving force? Was the Christian idea of the equality of all men before God and consequently of the brotherhood of man the central force which wrought the transformation? It may be so.

One may trace the development of the medieval city out of feudalism. As the power of the central government diminished and the local officials emancipated themselves, feudalism increased in power and became supreme. The count, once a representative of the emperor, became, in effect, the prince of his own domain. Ownership of land was the source of obligations as well as rights. Absolute tenure was modified into a conditional one, and a system of dependencies grew up. A grant of land made the recipient a vassal to the lord, as the lord himself was vassal to the emperor. Such grants of land varied in size, some being very small, others very large. The obligations attached to the grant, usually military in character, were graduated accordingly. The emperor or king was the supreme land owner. Work on the land was performed by serfs and bondsmen. These, however, though dependent, were not dispossessed; each had his place in the feudal system. Everyone had his regulated share, his security in life, his livelihood. But personal freedom had become impossible. A man without a lord was a man without a livelihood. The chief occupation was agriculture. On the self-supporting estates was produced everything their inhabitants needed. Craftsmen in their workshops produced articles to meet the needs of the people living around them. On these estates what was produced was consumed. Only in exceptional cases were surplus or special products made which could be sold or exchanged at a fair, the yearly or semi-yearly market.

Whatever may have been its faults, the order established by feudalism had undeniable benefits. Under it, population increased considerably, and by its increase created new problems whose solution brought about changes in the settlement structure. New land had to be and could be cleared, drained and cultivated to provide new living space. New villages had to be established, and they, in turn, increased the revenue of the feudal lords. Some individuals, especially craftsmen, could now be spared from the routine of every-day work and permitted to specialize and perfect their crafts. The increased income of the landlords may have made it possible for them to foster and encourage this refinement of the crafts. The lords, growing richer, were able to build larger and more comfortable manor houses. The great landlords built castles. The old manor house had usually been closely connected with its villages; the new castles were separated from them and towered over them from the hills. Such hill sites facilitated the fortification of the castles; they also symbolized the power and importance of their lordly owners. What happened at the manorial estate took place also at the monasteries.

The growth of population resulted also in something more important than manors and castles. It led to the creation of cities, the greatest accomplishment of the age of feudalism. The steps toward this development may have been these. The craftsman, freed from agricultural work, could now produce more goods than the community needed. There was a surplus which could be exchanged with goods from other estates at the fairs. This development was advantageous for both lords and craftsmen. The latter could, in time, buy their release from compulsory service,

43. BERNE *Castle below the City*

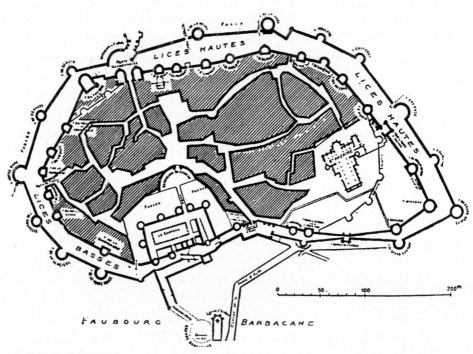

44. CARCASSONNE

45. ROTHENBURG

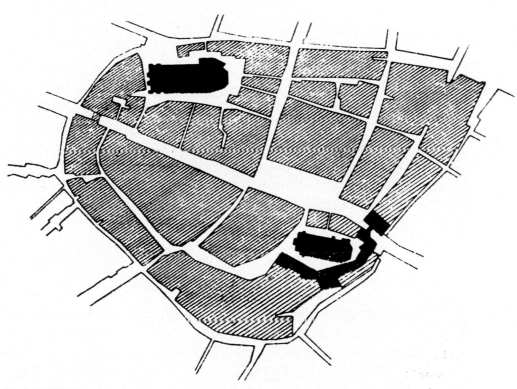

46. MUNICH

become independent, and settle with groups of their peers. Some settled in cities which still existed. In regions where there were no cities, rural settlements of craftsmen under the protection of castle or monastery became the nuclei of medieval cities. Princes and counts, bishops and abbots were quick to see advantages for themselves in these new cities. They encouraged their establishment everywhere. Bern and Nuremberg grew up under the protection of castles. At Carcassonne, the castle itself was incorporated into the city. At Rothenburg, the castle stands outside the city on a hill. S. Gall developed in connection with a cloister; Essen, in connection with the seat of a bishop. Luebeck grew up between two older settlements, one developed under the protection of a castle, the other related to the seat of a bishop. Luebeck itself became a trading center and, eventually, the head of the Hansa. Freiburg, Villingen, and Munich were all founded as market centers to serve their regions.

Cities founded by lords and princes increased the revenues of their founders. Those cities also had great historical significance. In creating them, feudalism set in motion the forces of its own destruction. But is death not the condition of life? Does not destruction often pave the way for construction?

The creative energy of the people who built those new cities was beyond measure. The crafts became differentiated; production diversified. A new kind of population arose guided by a spirit of independence. Every active individual wanted to become a member of one of these growing communities. Reintroduction of trade with foreign countries became possible when the invading Norsemen were appeased and settled in northern France and the Moslems, their strength spent, could no longer maintain their hold and rule over the Mediterranean Sea. This trade revival rejuvenated old cities and stimulated the growth of those newly formed. Venice, which had come to trade agreements with the Moslems, was already flourishing. Marseilles rose again. Pisa, Genoa, and other harbor cities on the Mediterranean became competitors as the trade with the Near East developed. Christians and Moslems were enemies, but trade was more important than religion. In the north, a similar development took place. Harbor cities like London, Bruges, Bremen, and Hamburg expanded their trade as actively as the harbor cities of the Mediterranean. Inland markets developed also where trades of north and south met for exchange. The traffic crossed the Alps along the old natural traffic routes of rivers and their tributaries. Raw material, manufactured goods, and luxuries were the items of this exchange. This commercial intercourse had a civilizing influence; gradually it lifted the less advanced communities to equality with others in the spreading civilization of the Middle Ages.

Did the medieval city arise from the market? Unquestionably some cities

47. S. GALL

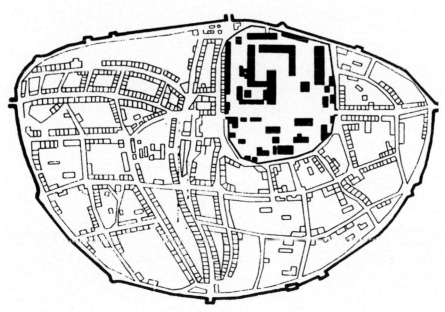

48. ESSEN

had such an origin. For instance, at Tiel on the river Waal there developed a market under the protection of a castle, which became the nucleus of a city. But this was the exception rather than the rule. The market and the city developed together.

Two distinct types of market are characteristic of the period: the fair or yearly or semi-yearly market of which Tiel was an example; and the weekly market. Each type grew out of a particular settlement structure and particular economic conditions.

The fair, whether annual or semi-annual, was the typical market for dispersed small settlements in an economy dominated by agriculture, where everything needed is produced and consumed within the house or estate. At these markets only special or surplus goods were sold or exchanged for surplus products from other estates. A few luxuries from abroad were also offered from time to time. Because the fair relied on accumulated surpluses, it could be held only at long intervals, once a year, once in six months.

The weekly market was typical of a more concentrated settlement, in which there was some division of labor and some diversified economy. It pre-supposed the city and the city economy based on differentiation of agricultural and industrial production. In the weekly market rural and urban products were exchanged; raw materials and foodstuffs from the country for the manufactured goods of the city. Such exchange needed to take place frequently. The weekly market met this need.

To make exchange between rural and urban producers effective and to integrate country with city, the cities had to be so located and spaced that the farm people living around them could travel to the city and home again in one day's time. This required the development of a new settlement structure. A well-proportioned pattern of villages, towns, and cities came into being. The size of each settlement was determined by its function, the resources available, and the travel distance between it and its neighbors. A balance was established between production and consumption, between urban and rural communities, in spite of the great differences between urban and rural life, economically and politically.

The settlements, the country, and their relation to each other were ordered organically. Geography, topography, climate and soil conditions, resources available were all factors influencing the settlement structure. And these factors, together with economic forces, tended to keep most cities small. Cities were much like villages at first, but they soon began to show the characteristics of urban development, industrial, political, and architectural. Cities had to protect themselves with fortifications. They had to have a city hall, a place of assembly where citizens could exercise their political rights. There had to be a church also, eventually perhaps

49. PISA *Cathedral Square*

a cathedral, a place of worship dominating the city both spiritually and architecturally.

Little information has come down to us regarding the number of people who lived in these cities. The typical population may have been between one and five thousand. The following figures from the fifteenth century show how widely the cities differed from each other in size and in importance. The population of Noerdlingen was 5,000; of Frankfort, 8,700; of Zurich, 10,500; of Strassburg, 20,000; of Luebeck, 22,300; of Cologne, 37,000; of Ghent, 50,000. Florence may have had 100,000 residents, Paris nearly 200,000.

What brought about such a differentiation? In most cases the development of a city was limited to that required for the fulfillment of its function as market for its rural area. Noerdlingen only once in its long history extended its city area. Why then did other cities attain such impressive growth? The answer must be particular for each city. A favorable trade location, the possession and development of special natural resources, the acquisition of special skills, the introduction of new political concepts—each of these factors contributed to the advancement of the city which enjoyed them. The spirit of a population might in itself provide the power for a city's rise, for the city depended always upon the spiritual force of its people as well as on its environment. And there are always to be found groups of people who can do the impossible, who can even turn necessity into advantage and make their very handicaps into assets. Siena and Grenoble owed their growth to a favorable trade location on

50. SIENA *Civic Square. Below Market Square*

an old route from Italy to France. Paris and Frankfurt, Strassburg and Cologne possessed even more favorable locations because they were built on navigable rivers crossed by important land trade routes. Zurich, at the northern end of a lake, stood at the point where a number of land routes from different directions converged and joined. London and Bremen, Pisa and Luebeck, beside rivers close to the sea, were natural places for the exchange of native goods for those from abroad. Lunenburg built her prestige on large salt exports from salt works among the greatest in northern Europe. Sheffield and Solingess, located in areas where iron ore was abundant, made cutlery in demand everywhere. Ghent, main center for the manufacture of the unrivalled Cloth of Flanders, was one of a number of cities owing their remarkable population increases to their development of specialized industry.

Power politics also, combined with new political concepts, played their part in the growth and importance of cities. Florence, gaining power through victorious wars, became the ruling center of Tuscany. Paris rose to be the dominant city and capital of the large centralized state of France. Both cities were profoundly influenced by this rise to power. They could not remain independent cities because the requirements of their new position were beyond the possibilities which independent cities could realize. As centers of states, they acquired new functions, and these new functions, in turn, influenced their development.

The fortification needed for the defense of a city limited its area. If the city increased in population but could not extend its fortification, it could solve the problem only by increase in population density. It usually happened that the smaller the city the greater was the density of its population. But if a city grew in prosperity as well as in population, it could often afford to extend its fortifications and add new parts to the original city. This could be done in various ways, according to local conditions, especially the topography of the site.

The population of medieval cities consisted of distinct and well-differentiated groups. There were the craftsmen and merchants, the patricians and clergymen. Craftsmen and merchants were organized in guilds which regulated the social and economic relations among their members, with other guilds, and with the city administration. These craftsmen were much less concerned with making money than they were with improving their skills. This spirit resulted in a high standard of craftsmenship which expressed itself in the smallest object and in the great cathedral.
The merchants, on the other hand, were very much concerned with money, in which they saw the source of power. As trade increased, money became more and more important, and the merchants, who served money, became important also. Some, growing rich, grew also in political power. The patricians were the administrators of the city. Once they had been the agents of the lord who founded the city, responsible to him for the

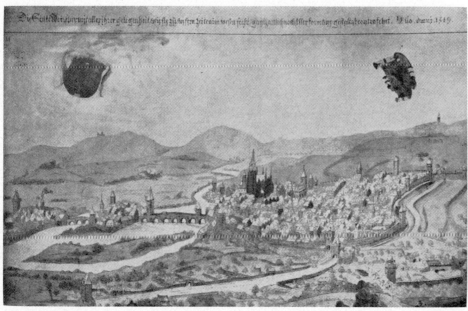

51. WETZLAR

maintenance of his rights. Their administration of the city government and its judicial functions made them very powerful.

The clergy was a class not great in number but great in influence because of their calling, their educational and charitable services. With the patricians, they constituted the city's educated class and the more conservative element of the population.

Social and economic conditions made the medieval city well adapted to the needs of life. Security and economic independence for all were possible to a degree seldom attained in history. But economic independence naturally bred desire for political independence. Conflict arose with the feudal lord, the founder and owner of the city, the guilds and the patricians fighting side by side to gain their freedom. For political and economic reasons, the city steadily tried to increase its population by immigration. By welcoming the foreigner, it could weaken the military power of the lord and strengthen its own. Gradually, cities broke away from the control of the overlord, some by open war, some by peaceful purchase of his rights. The city became an independent entity. This independence, however, marked the beginning of a struggle for power within the city itself. In some cities, the patricians emerged victorious; in others, a coalition of patricians and merchants; in still others, the guilds of the craftsmen.

The cities, through their very existence and activities, tended to undermine feudalism, but they could not wholly dissolve it. In France and in Germany the cities could free themselves from the bonds of feudalism, but they could not free the peasants from those bonds. What feudalism lost through the cities it tried to regain at the cost of the peasants. As feudalism became weaker, it became, because of its weakness, the source of new troubles. The cities were drawn into conflicts between princes and feudal lords, into wars among the princes and between the princes and the emperor. Each group wanted maximum independence; each sought only its own ends.

Feudalism, threatened by the increasing power of the city and the increasing might of the princes, tried to meet the threat by levying arbitrary custom taxes and tolls, even by resort to open highway robbery at times. The destructive effect of such disorder is illustrated in the history of the city of Wetzlar. At the end of the thirteenth century, the population of this city was about 8,000, a considerable population for that day. Wetzlar was famous for its manufacture of linen cloth; it was an important trading center on the route from Frankfurt to Antwerp. It possessed large store houses; its fairs were held twice a year. Then a wave of highway robbery rendered the trade route to Antwerp so perilous that the traders began to

avoid it as much as they could. Wetzlar's trade declined and its manufacture declined also. Craftsmen and merchants moved away. Wetzlar
became impoverished. By the middle of the sixteenth century, its population had fallen to 1,350, one sixth of the number it had boasted in its
heyday.

During the Middle Ages, extensive and varied colonization took place in
southern and southwestern France and, on a much larger scale, in eastern
Germany and along the shores of the Baltic Sea.
When rivalry between the French and the English led to wars, the cities
of France proved of great strategic value. They became sally points as
well as places of safe retreat. New cities, designed with strategic purposes
in mind, were founded; they were called *bastidas,* Bastida being an old
military word for fortified city. The bastidas were established by nobles,
by cloisters, by the crown itself. The English themselves built a number
around Bordeaux to protect that city.
Built on a rectangular plan, the bastida consisted of a central square, or
sometimes two squares, one for the church, the other for the city hall. The
streets ran at right angles or parallel to each other. Their circumvallation
was usually rectangular, but sometimes was modified by topography.
Montpazier, founded by the English, and Aigues Mortes, founded by the
French, are typical bastidas.

The Hansa established trading places which eventually became the cities
on the shores of the Baltic Sea as far as the Gulf of Finland. This Teutonic

52. AIGUES MORTES

order colonized the land behind the sea coast, built strongholds at strategic spots, and settlements around these strongholds. Marienburg was the main seat of the Order. The Grand Master moved there from Venice, made it his residence and the seat of his government.

Neidenburg is a typical settlement of the Teutonic order. Its stronghold, built on a low hill, dominates the city. The city is geometric in plan and protected by walls.

Colonization had a different pattern and a different aim in the sparsely settled provinces of eastern Germany. Here the colonies drew on the surplus population of the west. The land, owned by lords, secular and ecclesiastic, were held under royal grants which permitted the owners to found villages and cities. Such cities were a source of income for the landlords, and they also secured the possession of the land to an increasing population.

Before a city was built, a locator was commissioned. He was a kind of contractor whose job it was to select the city's site, plan its layout, and provide for its building and fortification. He also had to find its population. Such cities were usually agricultural in character. Their inhabitants were farming townsmen, who paid a yearly duty and received a lot within the city on which to build their houses and a piece of arable land outside the city for their farm. Cities of this kind, founded east of the Elbe, can be counted by the hundreds, villages by the thousands. Most of them never grew beyond their fortifications and are today still living communities.

53. GRANSEE

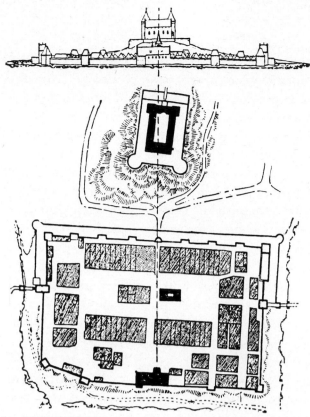

54. NEIDENBURG

The plan of these cities was of geometric pattern. Usually there were two squares, one for the church, the other for the city hall and the market. Gransee is typical. Its plan reveals the general character of these cities and their relation to the agricultural surroundings.

The medieval city ultimately expanded its economic sphere of influence and, with it, its area of sustenance. The merchants tried to buy and sell everywhere, regardless of the restriction of the city which wanted to control their trade. The city economy then became unbalanced. The restrictions became more and more meaningless. Slowly at first, but with increasing rapidity, new forms of production were introduced which required and had to serve a larger economic field.

Parallel with this development was the effort of the princes to enlarge their realms. Some, victorious in struggles with other princes, with nobles, and with cities, increased their domains and founded territorial states. Cities, as well as feudal lords, lost their independence, became subordinated to and integrated into larger political and economic wholes.

The economy of the territorial state was the economy of the mercantile system. Its policy was to secure a favorable balance of trade, to develop agriculture and manufactures, and to monopolize foreign trade.

This new political and economic development made cities a coordinated part of the state, subject to a more comprehensive economy. The close homogeneity between city and country ended. Production was now for unknown customers in far away markets. Merchants grew more and more powerful. Proletarian elements moved into the cities—ejected peasants, impoverished craftsmen, discharged soldiers. Their coming made possible new and more economical forms of production. Factories, financed by rich merchants, arose, in which the division of labor became an important factor in success. Free work diminished. In ever increasing numbers, craftsmen lost their independence; they too became proletarians.

As industries developed, workshops and factories had to be built and new residential areas established for in-migrant workers. The princes encouraged these new city developments as well as the new methods of production. They were well aware that they might thus increase their own revenues. Eventually they established factories themselves. The new city elements changed the self-contained medieval city in many ways. Where once everything had been related to the whole and had fitted into its proper place in an ordered scheme, growth without order brought evil consequences. The princes, with their swelling incomes, could build for themselves new and larger palaces, to display their power and to house the increasing bureaucracy. Usually, they chose to build away from existing cities and, in most cases, to stimulate the growth of new settle-

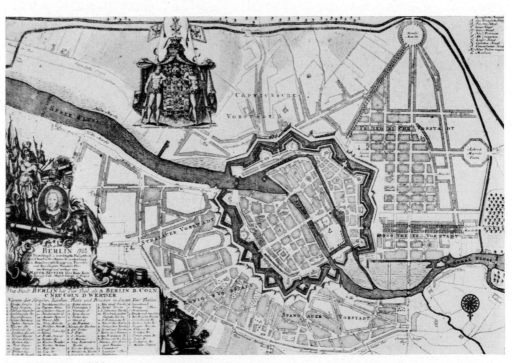

55. BERLIN, 1733

ments around new palaces. Versailles is typical. It became the prototype of many imitations which were, however, dwarfed in scale.

Everything in the state became subject to control. The political system of the territorial state became more and more autocratic. Absolute monarchy arose, then the national state. In France this development reached its maximum; in England it was checked by Parliament which changed absolutism into constitutional monarchy. The national state brought a new concept of political economy and provided the framework for the industrial revolution. The concept of a free and unrestricted economy arose first in England and there reached perfection.

The change from the free medieval city to the city of the territorial state is well illustrated by the development of Berlin. During the Middle Ages, Berlin was a free, independent, flourishing city. It acquired the land which surrounded it, and in so doing freed the peasants from their lords. It stood at the head of one of the city federations which cities founded to protect their trade. It was also a member of the Hansa. Berlin's advantage was feudalism's disadvantage, and it was inevitable, therefore, that the two systems should clash. To break the power of feudalism, to end its robberies, and to bring peace to the country, the Emperor appointed the Hohenzollern to restore order. That was like setting a wolf to mind the sheep! The Hohenzollern promptly sided with the feudal lords against the Emperor and the cities. Berlin, like other cities, lost its independence; but it gained importance and began to grow when the Hohenzollern, the founders of a new state, chose the city as their residence.

Berlin and its twin city Coelln, separated from each other by the river Spree, originated from two very old settlements at the river crossing of an old road where the river could be forded. Ill. . . . shows how the city grew by the addition of new settlements. In the center are both the original cities and a new part, all united by a fortification. Outside are other new settlements. There were at this time five different cities, kept separated from each other to prevent their united action. It is of interest to note that the now much larger city was no longer fortified and never would be again. It could, therefore, develop without restrictions until it grew into today's metropolis.

London and Paris developed along quite different patterns from that of Berlin. Both were very old cities founded in Roman times. They stood at the center of civilization, whereas Berlin stood at its periphery. When Berlin began to outgrow its medieval boundaries, London and Paris were already large cities, having governmental and economic functions unknown in Berlin. Both were capitals of growing kingdoms. They

56. LONDON *From South Warke*

differed from each other, however, in magnitude, and expressed this difference in their pattern.

Located on the Thames which flows through a wide flat valley into a navigable estuary, London was destined to become a great trading center. The river opened southeast England to her, and, through its estuary, made accessible the countries of northwestern Europe. London early became England's most important port, dominating both internal and overseas trade.

Probably London was originally a small settlement at a river ford. In Roman times, this settlement had no political importance, but it was even then a trading place and a center of maritime commerce. Roads from all directions led to London; it was one of the focal points of the Roman road system. The city declined with the decline of Rome, but soon, because of its favorable location, began to gain new strength. By the early Middle Ages, it had regained its position as trade center, holding this position in spite of frequent raids and invasions.

The boundaries of Medieval London did not vary much from those of the Roman city. East of the city was the Tower, the fortress of the king. Toward the west, the small town of Westminster was still separated from London by open country.

England, in that day, exported only raw materials in exchange for manufactured goods, her most important export being wool. Gradually conditions changed, as craftsmanship developed in the city. The guilds and the merchants were industrious and daring. They made it possible for England to reverse her trade; to make cloth for export, for example, instead of having to import it. This change, making England an exporter of manufactured goods, an importer of raw materials and food, laid the foundations for the country's future economic greatness.

100

These economic changes had their effect on the city of London. Before the Great Fire, London had acquired many of the characteristics of a city of our age. At its center was the seat of finance and commerce. Around this center and also south of the river were the quarters and dwellings of the tradesmen. Toward the east, along the river, were wharves, warehouses, and workshops for ship-building. Toward the west and around Westminster, were the seat of the government, the palace of the king, and also the houses of the aristocracy, the middle class, and the professionals who had offices in the city. There was no fortification. The city was spreading in all directions, incorporating the parishes around it. England had begun by that time to establish the colonies which were the foundation of her empire, an empire of merchants.

When the Romans advanced into and conquered Gaul, the Parisii, one of the Gallic tribes, were living in the region which we now call Isle de France. The Seine is the main river of this region. Lutetia, a settlement on a Seine island, was the most important center for the Parisii, who found protection against aggression in this island Parisii. Lutetia became Paris. It may have had some importance in Roman times because of its central location in its region, but we know very little of that part of its history. There is some evidence that a Roman wall protected Paris in the dangerous times which followed Rome's fall.

After the collapse and dissolution of the Roman Empire, Paris and all of France were invaded again, this time by the on-rushing barbarians. Kingdoms arose and vanished, amid continuous fighting. The Carolingian followed the Merovingian. Then, at the end of the tenth century, Hugh Capet became king of France and established a lasting dynasty. Paris became the capital of his kingdom. It was the age of feudalism, and the king, although he was acknowledged as such, was supreme only in his own domain. Centuries of bloody conflict were necessary to bring under his authority all the proud princes and great lords determined to maintain their power and independence even against the crown. Only when these lords and princes had been beaten into submission was the unification of France possible.

A plan of Paris, showing the walls built from the twelfth to the nineteenth century, indicates the city's steady growth. During the Middle Ages, it was already a large and important city, internationally famous for its university which drew to Paris scholars from all parts of the medieval world. Its growth was due chiefly to the fact that it became and remained the residence of the French kings, the capital of a growing centralized state. Paris increased in size and importance in step with the territorial expansion of the kingdom.

Whereas London and Berlin were never fortified after the Middle Ages, Paris always retained her fortifications. Building outside these fortifications was forbidden by law. But the law was not always obeyed. A plan of Paris by Mathien Merian shows that, in the early seventeenth century, many new settlements had sprung up outside the walls. To include such offshoots in the city proper required the building of a new wall. It was quite natural that this expensive undertaking should be postponed as long as possible. But the postponement had its effect on the city pattern. Because space within the walls was so limited, building had to be increased in height. They became out of proportion to the narrow streets. Population density increased. Like ancient Rome, Paris became a narrow

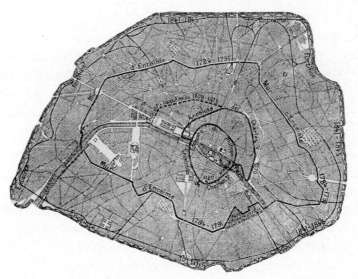

57. PARIS *Successive City Walls*

densely crowded city. Jacques Gomboust,* explaining his plan made in the middle of the seventeenth century, says: "Paris seems to be so large and its houses so high that it appears as if there were two or three cities on top of each other. It is full of people. All streets are filled with them. One could say that the whole world came together here." French civilization was revered throughout Europe. Unfortunately, admirers of France were led to copy slavishly the weaknesses as well as the strengths of their idol. Instead of following the London pattern in which single family houses prevailed, many European cities adopted Paris as their model, building narrowly and erecting the high airless apartment houses which, in some unexplainable way, seemed an expression of the admired civilization.

* Quoted by: Hegemann, Werner: *Der Staedtebau Berlin*, 1911

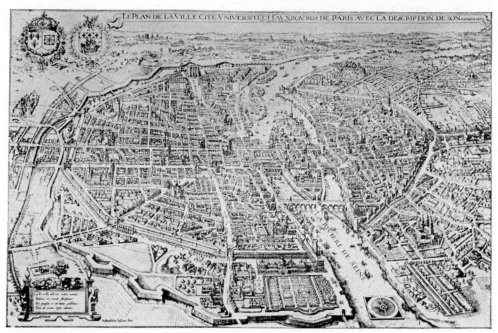

58. PARIS

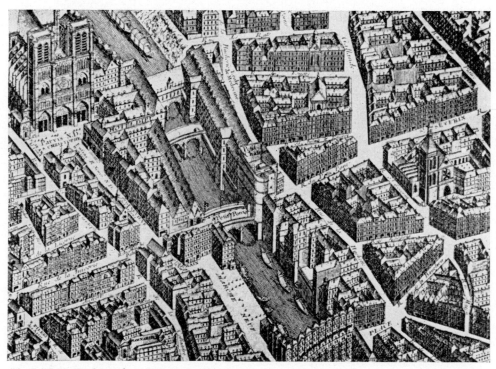

59. PARIS *Cathedral and Surroundings*

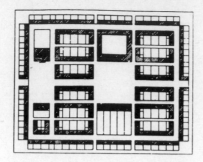

France was never greatly interested in foreign trade. She was to a great extent self-sufficient. Her geographical location, combining the advantages of northern and southern Europe without their extremes, made her economically independent. In its great fertility, adapted to rich diversified production, the country was able to meet the needs of the people. It was able to provide also all the resources needed for their industries. France's only important export was wine, so abundant and of such high quality that it was eagerly imported by all non-wine-growing countries. As skilled craftsmen and artisans in Paris and other French cities perfected their art, French fabrics and silk weavings, furniture and jewelry became as widely famous as French wine. New opportunities opened for France's export trade. But France lacked ships to transport her goods. She had to use the ships of other nations. Therefore, as Voltaire* wrote: "The English and much more the Dutch, with their ships, became the traders of France. They loaded their ships with our goods in our harbors and distributed them all over Europe." Colbert, minister of finance under Louis XIV, was one of the first public officials to recognize the importance of trade to the French state. He encouraged the building of the necessary merchant marine.

The Reformation did not affect France as much as it did the countries of northern Europe. She not only remained Catholic, but also began to persecute, as enemies of the state, the Huguenots who belonged to the Reformed or Calvinist communion. When persecution made life intolerable, over five hundred thousand of these unfortunates fled from France to the Protestant countries which were glad to receive them. To their new countries, these refugees brought highly developed skills on which new industrial development could be based. The countries where they settled could now produce at home what they had formerly imported from France. France was a heavy loser in this transaction. In London there was a whole suburb inhabited by French weavers. In Berlin a large French colony grew up. Here and in other north German cities, the skills of the newcomers helped German industry to advance. Sometimes, instead of settling in an established city, the Huguenots settled in cities built for them: New Erlangen is a typical example.

* Voltaire: *Siecle de Louis Quatorze*

Freedom of trade and the new spirit of liberalism broke the last restraints left over from feudalism. Individual economic enterprise developed freely and vigorously. All countries shared in this development, though the movement was modified, of course, by the local conditions in which it operated. Centralized national states were established all over the Western world. And, because the impulse which brought these states into being was the same everywhere, the cities which originated from the requirements of the national economy, or which were transformed by it, everywhere presented the same characteristics. To understand these characteristics, one must understand the nature of the processes which created them.

Division of labor reached its highest degree of development in the rising national economy and the world economy which finally emerged. New techniques, based on the machine and specialization, divided the processes of production to an extent hitherto undreamed-of. Meanwhile, the new production required increasing concentration of labor. Workers in great numbers had to be drawn together wherever manufacturing took place. This concentration implied the development of a labor market to meet the demands of industry. The inevitable consequence was the formation of the large settlements which we think of as contemporary.

The coming of the railroad made possible the development of even the remotest parts of the country. The railroads and the new steam-propelled ships provided a system whereby goods could be transported to and from all parts of the earth. The masses concentrated in the great cities could thus be supplied with food with comparative ease.

The world is divided into areas producing raw materials and food and those producing manufactured goods. Large industrial nations trade the products of their factories for food and raw materials. A world-wide finance economy came into being to provide credit for the development of manufacture. It created the conditions in which vast private enterprise could grow. But in this process, the obligations which once bound society together began to disappear. The workman became part of the labor process. The industrialist who directed his work was the only remaining link of communal relationship. As the development of industry moves forward, even that link is weakened. In the end, the industrialist is no longer an individual; he is replaced by the large corporation financed by banks or capital stock. Under the protection of such anonymity, there develops a freedom from responsibility and obligation unknown in other economies.

There are two forms of industrial production: prime production and manufacture. Each influences the settlement forms to which it gives rise. Prime production takes place where natural resources exist; it is relatively

61. INDUSTRIAL TOWN

62. INDUSTRIAL CITY

106

63. AIR POLLUTION

64. CITY TRAFFIC

stable. Manufacture, largely dependent on transportation facilities, must locate itself at favorable transportation centers. Both forms of production require large aggregations of workers. Prime production, because of its greater stability, is not necessarily confined to large cities. But manufacturing, subject to considerable fluctuation, depends on the labor market and must, therefore, seek the large city where that market exists. Thus two new types of city have arisen which have little in common with earlier urban settlements: the purely industrial city, located at the source of raw materials and inhabited almost exclusively by workers; and the manufacturing city, which harbors not only large aggregations of laborers, but also great numbers of office workers. Variations occur in the manufacturing city according to the importance of a given settlement in industry or in trade.

Such have been the forces which brought our cities into being. How well does this city serve the functions for which it was created? Have our cities found the pattern adequate to their purposes? This question cannot be answered in the affirmative. Our cities have grown without plan. There has never been time to think of planning. The gridiron system, adopted perhaps to facilitate the sale of land in advance of growth, has determined the layout of the streets and, making no distinction among the city's different parts, has become a guide to disorder.

Industries and mechanized transportation have made possible the creation and the rapid growth of our cities. But this growth, unplanned and undirected, has resulted in sheer chaos. Each part of the city affects other parts disadvantageously. Blight and slums appear. Traffic hazards increase. City dwellers begin to desert the city for the suburbs. The very forces which created the city seem now to be destroying their creation. Meanwhile, decentralization and suburbanization, proceeding without plan or direction, begin to create outside the city the same chaos and confusion. The slums are being carried into the countryside.

The rapid and random growth of our cities has resulted in many and serious deficiencies. Let us name only a few. Houses in the residential districts have been built without the slightest thought that the people who would live in them needed sunlight and clean air. In the worst and unhealthiest parts of the city, population density is highest and recreational areas direly lacking. Such residential slums are a danger, not only to the people who live there, but to the whole community.

Excessive use of land has simultaneously created high land valuations and reduced the value of the land. More and more merchants and business men are driven into outlying areas where lower land costs enable them to do business more profitably. As buildings rise higher and higher, automobile

65. RECREATION

66. CITY SLUM

congestion increases. This congestion "drives the pedestrian out of the business area to a place where he can shop with greater convenience and safety. We have forgotten that all shopping is done by the pedestrian."

"High buildings are believed by many to be a cause of blight. They have a depressing effect on near-by property. It is an anomaly to note that, while a few years ago, it was frequently said that high land values compelled the creation of high buildings, we now have many high buildings adjoining vacant or near vacant lots in business areas for which no stable use other than automobile parking can be found. Apparently too intensive use of land is not economic or necessary."*

No effort has been made to place industry in proper relation to residences. No thought has been given to prevailing winds. Therefore, the smoke, soot, and fumes of our industrial cities constitute an evil which threatens the health of the people who live there.

The disorder within the city area, the indiscriminate conglomeration of industrial, commercial, and residential sections, has given rise to almost insoluble traffic and parking problems. Far more conveyances than should be needed must be used—and even then traffic facilities continue inadequate. The antiquated street system, faithfully followed, has created danger for pedestrian and motorist alike, and this danger mounts as traffic increases. Parents of growing children must constantly worry because each street corner has become a death trap. It seems impossible to prevent accidents or to relieve the inconveniences and confusions of transportation.

How do cities affect the human beings who live in them? More and more people are spending their lives and doing their work in cities. Can the city-dweller live a satisfying life? Is the city a good place to bring up children? Does it promote physical and mental health? Does its slums breed delinquency and crime?

To the last of these questions, statistics indicate a sobering answer, that the incidence of crime increases as the size of the city increases and diminishes as the city's size diminishes. It would seem that there is close relationship between the slum which is the cancer of the city and crime which is the cancer of society. Within the city, crime is always more prevalent in slum areas, decreasing in the outlying, better neighborhoods. Does this mean that naturally criminals gravitate toward the slums? Or does it indicate that the slum makes the criminal? Is a criminal a human being destined, under any circumstances, to become an enemy of society? Or is it perhaps true that each man has within him seeds of evil and of

* Urban Land Institute: *Decentralization. What Is It Doing to Our Cities.* Chicago, 1940

110

67. PARIS

68. DISORDER AND CHAOS

good and that his environment may determine which seeds take root and grow? Is it reasonable to suppose that the slum boy who becomes a delinquent and later a criminal might, in the setting of a small town or the country, have grown up to be a normal law-abiding citizen? Or is crime a disease to be treated by psychiatry?

We have much to learn before we can answer such questions with certainty. Yet this much seems clear. In the slum areas of our cities, relaxed mores diminish resistance to temptations, anonymity protects, and may even attract, the criminal. Slums do breed crime.

We take vast pride in the achievement of medical science. Our great hospitals symbolize the strides we have taken in the scientific treatment of the sick. But should a healthy society require so many hospitals? Should we not give more attention to the prevention of sickness? It is a striking paradox to see masked nurses taking meticulous care of new-born babies who, within a few days, will be taken from the antiseptic hospital back to the dirty slums where their parents live.

Speaking from his experience as a practicing physician, Dr. Jonathan Foreman* writes: "In candid truth, the city is not a healthful place in which to live. Its inhabitants do not live as long or as happily as dwellers elsewhere. More of them go insane. They are sick more often. Finally, and perhaps most disastrously, they fail to reproduce themselves. The city must, as a consequence, import nearly one-half of the next generation in order to maintain its size and satisfy its civic pride. If pure surmise were one of the legitimate functions of science, it may be interesting to contemplate the fate of a metropolis in an age when new blood could no longer be piped to it from the country. . . .

"Cities have grown rapidly, without intelligent planning; indeed the rapid and disorderly growth is responsible for many of the undesirable elements in city life. It has produced poorly designed streets that are congested with unnecessary traffic and full of danger, an atmosphere that is filled with noxious gases, dust, dirt, and smoke—a blanket of smog which shuts out the health-giving sunshine. Disturbed mental poise and disordered social habits have been engendered by loss of sleep, malnutrition, and frustration. . . . Men must pay for living in cramped quarters and interdependent environments."

This human view is shared, not only by physicians and planners, but also by the Urban Land Institute, which reports: "Any observer of American cities must come to the conclusion that a larger part of the urban dwellers do not like the cities which we have built, and seek to escape from them if

---

* Foreman, Jonathan: *Biological Truth and Public Health.* In *"Cities Are Abnormal,"* edited by Elmer Peterson. Oklahoma, 1946

69. NEW YORK *Air View*

their work permits and if they can afford to do so. . . . It becomes increasingly apparent that cities are not merely machines which must be planned for services and for the highest economic utility. They are also social entities in which human beings must live, and social and sociological requirements of people are quite as important as economic considerations." Fortunately for humanity, there are forces at work which may make possible the realization of human requirements. Technical achievements tend to encourage decentralization; defense necessity may force it. At long last, it may be, human needs long neglected may come to be satisfied.

As the railroad and steam power once tended to centralize and concentrate urban settlements, so now electricity and motor vehicles are tending to decentralize them. Even before the advent of electricity, the tide had begun to turn. People, who had been moving steadily into the city, began to use the new suburban railroads to escape from the city and to found new settlements beyond its limits. As the railroads were extended, these settlements along their lines appeared farther and farther from the city center. The automobile accelerated this exodus, and widened its scope.
But this dispersion has been a random one, and has developed a chaotic suburbanization. Only with the development of electric power has genuine decentralization become possible. Electric power is a real force toward decentralization. Small settlements can now be established anywhere. New communities of relative independence can be built. Even the smallest settlements can be supplied with water, electricity, heat, and light. Power rates in them may, indeed, be lower than those in the metropolises and great cities with their vast undeveloped areas requiring extensive and expensive supply and drainage lines and complicated transportation systems.
Great possibilities lie ahead if we are wise enough to use them. This does not mean, of course, that we should strive to replace all large settlements with small ones. We should always concentrate what needs to be concentrated. We should aim, not at a maximum or a minimum size for our cities, but at an optimum size. As we learn to decentralize what can best be decentralized, we may make our communities truly serve the best good of the people who live in them.

70. ATHENS *Parthenon*

II. Pattern and Form

The pattern and form of a city are the result of an interaction of forces, both material and spiritual. Yet the city is always more than the mere sum of those factors. There is always something we can perceive but cannot define; there are irrational factors which cannot be explained rationally. Cities are like individuals. Each has its own character and physiognomy. Each possesses a pattern and form expressive of the creative forces which brought it into being.

There are, however, certain factors readily identified which, with their implications and interrelations, do much to determine the essential character of the city. Most important is the nature of the site on which the city is located, the relation of that site to the landscape of which the city is a part, the character of that landscape, its geographical and topographical features, its climatic conditions, its available resources, and its natural transportation routes.

A second major factor is always the people who make the city and live in it. Their character, their spiritual and material aims, their social and political concepts, their industrial and artistic abilities and activities will all influence the pattern and form of their city as much as the natural conditions in which it is set.

A third factor is the function the city is planned to perform. It makes a difference in the structure of a city whether it is independent and self-sustaining or part of a larger state. A functional specialization—administrative, commercial, industrial—will also set its stamp upon the city's form. These factors are interrelated always. They act together. Each depends on the others. We may consider each separately, but we should always keep in mind the fact that they are always present together, each contributing in differing degree and proportion to the totality which is the character of a city.

In the following pages, we make no attempt to investigate all the factors which influence the pattern and form of cities. We shall deal only with a few which have had, all through the ages, decisive influence: the location of the city in relation to its defense; the social-political ideas and organization of the city's people; the creative expression in architecture of the spirit of those people.

Geographers and archaeologists have discovered that even the most ancient peoples instinctively understood the importance of choosing a site for their settlements which could offer protection against primitive warfare. They knew that certain topographical features provided the best defense —islands in the sea, the lakes and the rivers; peninsulas formed by river bends or the confluence of rivers; cape formations along the shore or in the mountains; single mountains standing in the plains. These were always recognized as the best naturally protected sites, the places where even the earliest people preferred to found their settlements.

Tyre, the Phoenician city, was located on a rocky island on the coast of Syria. It was invincible because of its location. Its two well protected harbors, the Sidonian towards the north and the smaller Egyptian towards the south, made Tyre, with its industrious population, one of the oldest merchant centers of the Mediterranean.

Motya, another Phoenician city, also considered invincible, stood on an island in the midst of a bay at the west side of Sicily. As the population of this limited island increased, the inhabitants had to build their homes higher and higher until they became tower-like.

Neither Tyre nor Motya was actually invincible. Alexander the Great conquered Tyre; Dionysius of Syracuse, Motya. In both cases, however, the strength of the original site had been impaired by causeways built from the mainland to the island cities. Along those causeways, the besiegers were able to bring the towers and battering rams which finally broke down the city walls. Would the cities have remained unconquered if those causeways had never been built? It is quite possible. As late as the Thirty Years War, Stralsund, a city on an island in the Baltic Sea,

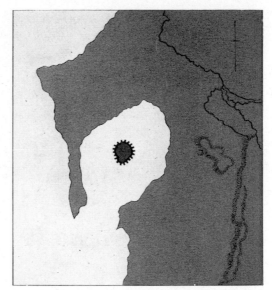

71. TYRE

72. MOTYA

successfully resisted Wallenstein's siege. Rhodes, a city founded by the Greeks on a larger island, was able to maintain its independence against the hostile kingdoms which developed on the mainland. Rhodes was built after a plan by Hippodamus. During the Middle Ages, the order of S. John built a castle there and fortified the city.

73. STRAHLSUND

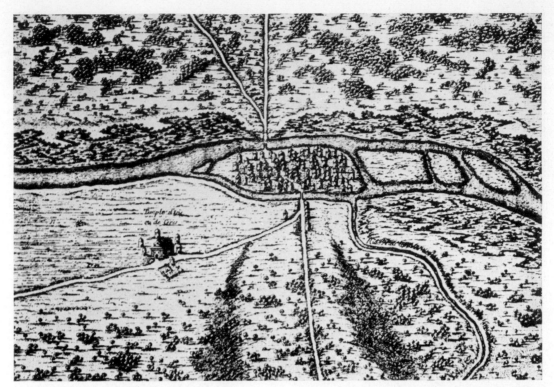

74. EARLY SETTLEMENT OF PARIS

75. DURHAM

76. NORMA

77. CARTHAGE *Reconstruction*

78. AMPHISSA

There were many such island cities in antiquity. Arne, built by the Greeks on a rocky island in Lake Copias, was one. Such sites were so highly valued for their strength that they were sometimes constructed where nature did not provide them. The lake dwellings of the Stone Age at Glastonburg and Zurich stood on man-made islands. Paris grew from its island nucleus to dominate the valleys of the Seine, Marne, and Oise. Luebeck rose on an island in the river Trave which combined safety with the advantages of an important traffic location.

Durham in England is located on a peninsula formed by an U-bend in the river Weir. Bern in Switzerland was similarly placed. Lyon in France grew up on a peninsula formed by the confluence of the Rhone and Saone. Lyon was originally a Celtic settlement. The Celts understood the defense value of a peninsula site as well as the Romans who, coming later, used the same location for a city which became the military and commercial center of the region.

Cape formations—mountain promontories or bluffs jutting into the sea or the lakes—were also favorite sites for early settlements. Such formations could be made invulnerable by special and easily arranged means of defense. Norma in Italy located on a steep mountain promontory, shows the advantage of its sheltered position. Amphissa in Greece was also placed on a promontory. Today the ruins of a medieval castle mark the site of the old Locrian city; the town below is of later origin.

79. THERA

Thera stands on a high promontory jutting out from a mountainous island into the Aegean Sea. The promontory is connected with the main mountain by a narrow isthmus, so easily defended as to make the city invincible. Thera is of Phoenician origin and was later developed by Greek settlers. Standing high and strong, with a free view over the sea, the city could ward off attacks from the pirates who then infested the Aegean. It was a long-stretched, narrow city, lying along the mountain ridge, with one main street running through its entire length and only a few crossing side streets. It had two squares.

The Dalmatian city of Corcula, like Thera, is placed on a promontory extending into the sea from a mountainous island. But its site differs from that of Thera because the peninsula formed by the promontory is a low flat hill. The main street of the city led from the gate up hill to the square in front of the cathedral and then down again, while the side streets on either side sloped gently downward.

In rocky coastal regions, promontories offer protection and form natural harbors. Cnidos, on the southwest coast of Asia Minor, made good use of this dual advantage. Here the promontory forms an island-like peninsula, connected with the mainland by a small isthmus. Toward the sea, the slope is very steep. But the gentle slope toward the eastern bay provided space for the earliest city. Between the peninsula and the coast of the mainland, two bays gave the city harbors for her sailing ships. The bay toward the east formed large harbors; part of the western bay formed a

80. CORCULA

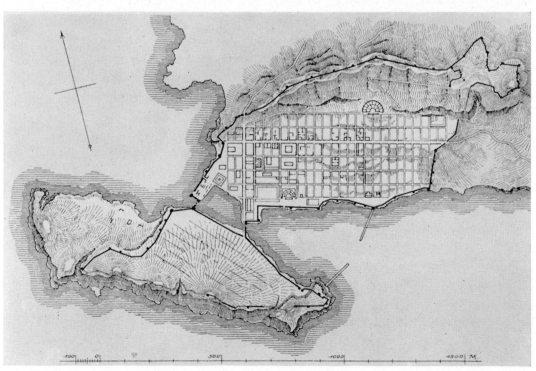

81. CNIDOS

smaller one. A canal built across the isthmus connected the harbors and increased their usefulness. As Cnidos grew, it expanded by building a new part on the hill sloping gently to the eastern bay. This extension gave the city the appearance of an amphitheater, its buildings rising in terraces along the hills.

Single elevations, rocky plateaus, isolated mountains were often chosen as safe natural sites by early Greeks and Romans. Athens rose on the Acropolis; Rome on the Palatine Hill. Both cities were close to the sea, but

82. SAN GIMIGNANO

far enough away from it to be relatively safe from the attacks of pirates. It was also on a hill, the Byrsa, that the first Phoenician settlement at Carthage was founded by men from Tyre. Soon the growing city had surpassed its parent settlement in glory and power. Athens, Rome, and Carthage quickly grew beyond the expectations of their builders. The hills which had been the sites for the original settlements became in time sacred precincts or, in the case of Rome, palace grounds.

Many hill cities survive today in Italy. Their differences in appearance are in part the result of differing topography, but are even more a reflection of differing social organization. Acerenca, on a hill isolated in a plain, gives the impression of great simplicity and suggests that political equality was the force which created it. A few ecclesiastical buildings stand in contrast to the simple houses which give the city its character. S. Gimignano, also a hill city, is dominated by a number of towers. Were they, like the towers of Motya, a result of trying to provide for an expanding population in a limited narrow space? There seems to be a quite different explanation.

As the cities of the Middle Ages freed themselves from feudalism, it was natural that the feudal lords should try to regain in the cities what they had lost on their estates. In Italy, these lords moved into the cities peacefully but with firm determination to regain power and to rule the cities once more. The houses they built are characterized by the towers which surmount them. These towers made the dwellings private fortresses, useful for both defense and attack in a city where strife was continuous. Quite naturally, these towers became a symbol of power. As the princes and tyrants put an end to the political aspirations of the aristocracy, the deposed feudal lords were more or less assimilated into urban life and began to fraternize at least with the higher and more educated classes of the cities. But their towered houses continued to stand as symbol of a reality which no longer existed. They became a fashionable decoration, widely copied though no longer serving a functional purpose. The great number of towers—700 in Lucca, 250 in Bologna, many in Siena and other cities—can be explained only by the theory that the rich merchants of those growing cities built towers for themselves in imitation of the old aristocracy in the same spirit as they imitated their tournaments.

The impress which the spirit of a people places upon the city is dramatically illustrated at Athens. Here, north of the Acropolis, stand two rectangular building groups of Roman origin: a market surrounded by colonaded halls, and the stoa of Hadrian where colonaded halls form a court with a large building, probably the library of Hadrian, on its east side. Between these Roman building groups and the Greek structures on the Acropolis there is the greatest possible contrast. The essential genius of each people, the diversity of the art impulses which guided them, is written here in stone.

A naive observer, looking at the two building groups, might easily come to the conclusion that the Romans were far superior to the Greeks. They had clear aims. They knew what they wanted to achieve and how to achieve it. They understood geometry and symmetry. They were master planners. Compared with the Roman building groups, the Acropolis seems planless. Each building there seems to be independent, unrelated to others, as though the buildings had been placed together merely by accident, with no consideration for the unity of the whole. A more thinking observer would, however, reach a quite different conclusion. He might

124

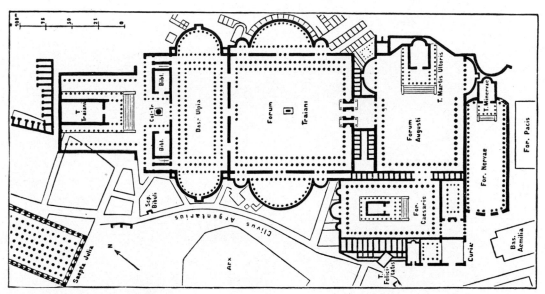

83. ROME *Forum of Trajan*

84. ROME *Forum of Trajan Reconstruction*

85. BAALBEK *Temples. Reconstruction*

86. PALMYRA *Colonaded Street*

126

note that the Roman buildings are strangely unrelated to the city. He would feel growing respect for the naturalness of the Acropolis grouping, in which the buildings are placed to harmonize with the topography. He would recognize and respect the adjustments made to religious tradition. He would, at last, come to the realization that the Greeks, with their highly developed architectural skill and artistic sensitivity, unquestionably knew as clearly as did the Romans what their aims were and how to reach those aims. He would understand that our failure to appreciate why the Greeks placed the buildings on the Acropolis in the particular way they did is only a mark of our own limitation.

Since we do not know very much about the Roman building groups at Athens, let us, for the sake of a more equal comparison, examine the Forum of Trajan, one of the imperial forums in Rome, and the largest and most elaborate among them. The Forum of Trajan expresses the Roman architectural and planning concepts as clearly as the Acropolis expresses those of Greece. Setting them side by side, we may better understand them both.

The Forum of Trajan, whose architect was Apollodoros of Damascus, lies northwest of the Forum of Augustus in the valley between the hills of the Capitol and the Quirinal. To gain the space required for the large forum and to make possible its building on one level, the lower part of the Quirinal Hill had to be removed. The Forum itself is a large square surrounded by colonaded halls. Its main entrance is from the Forum of Augustus, and it is emphasized by a triumphal arch adorned with columns. At the opposite side is the Basilica Ulpia, a large two-storied building. Toward the northeast and the southwest, the Forum is optically extended by two-storied exedras, semi-circular buildings which rise above the colonaded halls surrounding the square. Northwest of the Basilica Ulpia is the Column of Trajan, equal in height to the height of the removed hillside. It stands in the center of a small square formed by two smaller buildings, possibly libraries, and the Temple of Trajan. This temple stands in a colonaded court and was built under the reign of Hadrian. The Forum of Trajan expresses, not only the architectural concepts of the Romans, but also their fundamental planning principles. Significantly, this Forum, like other forums of Rome, has no organic relation to the city itself. One is reminded that there was no relation between the different temple courts at Baalbek in Syria. The imperial forum was superimposed upon its city, intended as an ornament and adornment for it. Imperial cities themselves became subject to this same concept. Timgad in Africa, founded by Trajan, and Palmyra in Syria, refounded by Trajan's successor Hadrian, with their colonaded streets and arched gateways, exhibit the same ornamental splendor as the imperial forums, though on a lesser scale.

Roman architecture was first influenced by Etruscan architecture, and later, as the empire spread toward the east, by Hellenistic architecture. The Romans were particularly impressed with the colonaded stoas of the Greek agoras. They adopted such ideas freely, but they always placed upon them the stamp of Rome. They smothered Greek refinement with ornamentation. They over-loaded their buildings with carved mouldings

87. ATHENS *Acropolis, Air View*

and sculptures. Their cities became subject to a rigid symmetry and axiality which resulted in ornamental compositions to which everything was subordinated. The Romans believed that, in this way, they were increasing the magnificence of their buildings and their cities, making them express the power of Rome, to impress and cow a conquered world. The Romans were law-makers and rulers. They knew how to command and how to obey. Their art and architecture speaks of discipline. "In the Roman commonwealth," writes Theodore Momsen,* "there was no

*Momsen, Theodore: *The History of Rome*

88. ATHENS *Acropolis. Reconstruction*

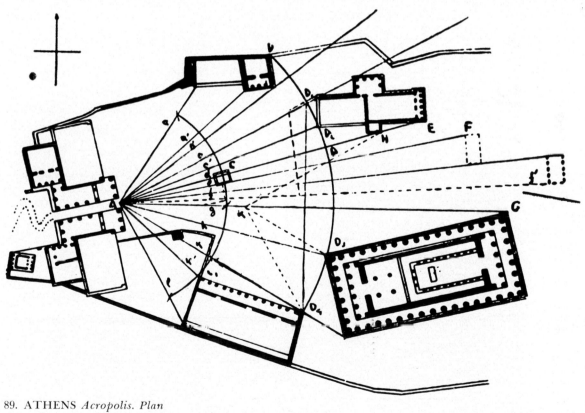

89. ATHENS *Acropolis. Plan*

129

special dependence on any one man . . . and under the rigid discipline of its moral policy, all idiosyncracies of human character were extinguished. Rome reached a greatness such as no other state of antiquity attained; but she dearly purchased her greatness at the sacrifice of the graceful variety of the easy abandon and the inward freedom of Hellenic life."

The Acropolis of Athens stands on a rocky hill, rising steeply out of the plain. Its shape is irregular, resembling a stretched hexagon. Its surface is not on one level. It rises gradually from the west towards the east. Cimon extended the surface of the Acropolis by moving the south wall. The Acropolis we know is the work of the Periclean age, when the temples and other buildings destroyed by the Persians were rebuilt in greater splendor than ever before.

The three main buildings of this period still stand. The Propylaea, gate to the Acropolis, is at the lower west side where the hill of the Acropolis joins that of the Areopagus. The Parthenon stands on the middle part of the Acropolis toward the south; the Erechtheion on the lowest level of that part toward the north. Both these buildings are nearly equidistant from the Propylaea. The huge statue of Athena Promachos, goddess of the Acropolis, stood between the Propylaea and these two temples. Farther back towards the east, two long low altars furnished contrast to the tall statue. Closer to the Propylaea were two lower buildings, placed on either side along the enclosing walls.

The order which governs the placement and arrangement of these buildings is an optical one. K. A. Doxiades* believes that he has discovered its governing principles. We should look at the Acropolis, he urges, as the Greeks looked at it, not with the romantic ideas which obscure our vision. When the Greeks entered the Acropolis through the Propylaea, they wanted to see the Acropolis as a whole, but they wanted also to see each object, building, sculpture standing free, none interfering with any others. Location as well as dimension was used to attain this optical result. All buildings are free standing; one ends where another begins. The Greeks could, indeed, as they came in by the Propylaea, see the united view with each object free of interference. That was what they wanted.

There were two groups of buildings separated by an open space between the Parthenon and the Erectheion, toward the east. Another open space, between the Erectheion and the building at its left, is optically closed by the distant hill of Lycabettus which thus becomes an integral part of the view.

So far as we know, earlier plans of the Acropolis, though they differed in the arrangement of the buildings, all applied the same optical principle.

*Doxiades, K. A.: *Raumordnung im griechischen Staedtebau,* Heidelberg, 1937

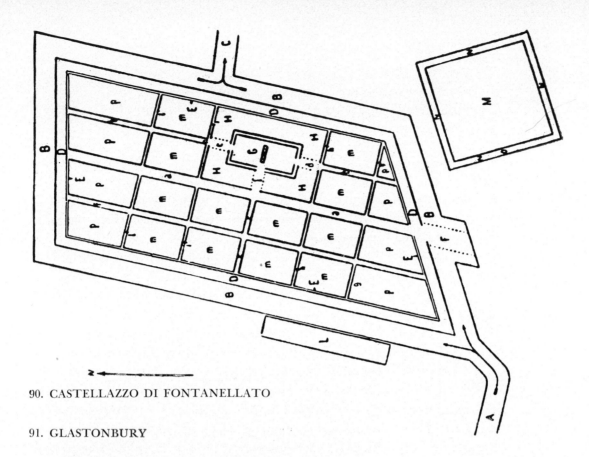

90. CASTELLAZZO DI FONTANELLATO

91. GLASTONBURY

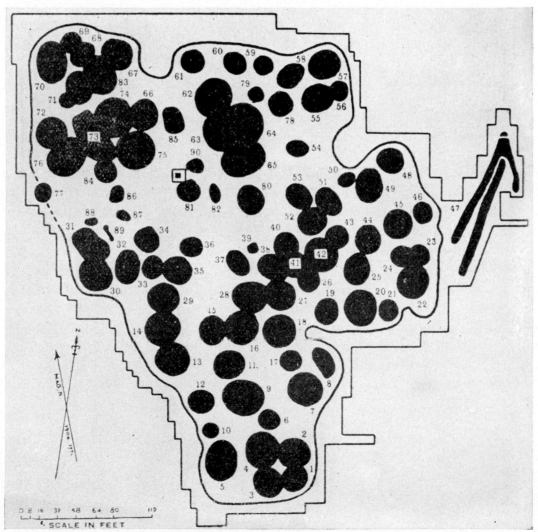

There was always the same open space toward the east. Perhaps that had something to do with the sunrise at the spring equinox and was connected with a religious concept.

The Greeks did not apply the same optical order to the building of their cities. These cities were composed of modest homes which contrasted with the monumental buildings and increased their significance. The Greek thinkers dealt more naturally with the city than we do, taking into consideration things we have utterly forgotten.

Plato and Aristotle regarded the city as primarily a social organism—the state. They were both influenced in their thinking by the Hippocratic treatise: "Airs, Waters, Places," which dealt with man and his relation to this environment, both natural and political. Hippocrates discussed the food man eats, the water he drinks, the climate he lives in, the location of his settlements and its relation to sunshine and wind. He set forth what he considered the essentials for a healthy human life. He gave great stress to the organization of the city, insisting that an eastward orientation was the most desirable. Von Gerkan,* who studied all available material, came to the conclusion that, in spite of Hippocrates, most Greek cities located on hillsides preferred slopes toward the south. The older part of Athens outside the Acropolis is described by Thucydides as "looking toward the south." Priene, founded several centuries later, had the same southern orientation.

Such an orientation allowed the winter sun to penetrate the main rooms of the houses and to supplement with its natural warmth insufficient heating facilities. At Priene, the main streets run east to west following the contour of the site, in order to secure this south orientation. On the sloping terrain terraces were formed, connected with each other by cross street which climbed more or less sharply and were provided with steps, an arrangement possible in a day when street traffic was very small.

Street orientation, however, as von Gerkan points out, varied from city to city. Each city adapted its street orientation to its own topography. Some streets ran north and south; some east and west; some at various angles in between. But the orientation of a street does not necessarily fix the orientation of a house. To get the preferred orientation then was a matter of common sense, as it is today a matter of proper planning. Where south orientation was impracticable, southeast and southwest orientations could be used. Either of these is almost as advantageous as southern orientation; combined they can be even better.

Socrates** seems to have preferred the south orientation. "A house,"

---

* Von Gerkan, Arnim: *Grichische Stadt Aulagen*. Berlin Leipzig, 1924
**Xenophon: *Memoralities of Socrates*

he said, "should be most pleasing and at the same time most useful to live in. . . . Is it not, then, pleasing to have it cool in summer and warm in winter? . . . In houses, then, that look to the south does not the sun in winter shine into the porticoes, while in the summer it passes over our heads."

Considerations like these will obviously result in an order of planning entirely different from the Roman geometric order and the Greek optical order. Here is an order which grows out of the nature of things, takes into consideration necessity and function. It is an order of naturalness, "organic" in character. There is no longer a dominating form concept to which everything must be subordinated. The organic order is autonomous; its guiding principle is that each part must develop according to its own law, that each part must also have its due place, according to its importance and function, within the whole. It means, as St. Augustine said, "the disposition of equal and unequal things, attributing to each its proper place."

Organic planning aims to find the pattern and form adequate to a city's location and function. It deals also with the forms and means of life and strives to establish a balance between things material and things spiritual. It provides the conditions in which all things can grow and unfold.

The organic order, since it takes everything into consideration, includes form values. The necessary and functional become sources of inspiration to influence the creative impulse. If all requirements are mastered, the essential nature of an object will be revealed and this revealing will prove that the useful can also be the beautiful. What Socrates* said about the house is true also for the city, and, indeed for every object, large or small, made by the hand of man. "The same houses," he said, "that were beautiful were also useful . . . for whatever is good is also beautiful in regard to the purposes for which it is well adapted."

The organic order of planning is much older than the Greeks, older, it may be, than recorded history. It also outlived the Greeks to become a characteristic of the medieval city. We know much about these cities of the Middle Ages; some have survived almost without change to our own day. Once more, in our own times, the organic order is beginning to regain influence. We have rediscovered the truth that objects made without thought for form values may be more beautiful than those whose whole purpose was beauty. The airplane, one of the representative objects of our technical age, has form values of its own of surprising quality.

The co-existence of these two concepts of order: the geometric and the

*Xenophon: *Memoralities of Socrates*

organic, can be traced back as far as the Stone Age. The prehistoric settlements of Castellazzo de Fontanellato and Glastonbury are evidence of the early existence of these contrasting types. Both are original forms and express differing concepts of life and society in their purest form.

Castellazzo was probably a settlement of the first Latins who entered Italy from the north. Its pattern expresses a well-established social order. The city was surrounded by a deep wide ditch which made the site a kind of island. Its street system was laid out geometrically; the center street was wider than the others and east of it was a square.

Glastonbury in southwest England, in contrast to Castellazzo, shows all the characteristics of an organic settlement. For protection, it was placed on an artificial island in a lake. Its huts, circular in shape, were isolated or combined in groups. In the center of the settlement there was an open space.

Castellazzo and Glastonbury represent, at a primitive level, the two universal city types: the autocratic and the free city. We find these types all through the ages. The earliest autocratic cities we know about are in the near east. In all probability these were the oldest of all urban settlements. And already they show all the characteristics common to autocratic cities. Their pattern is geometric, having dominant axes leading to important buildings. They display the power of the ruler to whom the population must bow. With their pomp and ostentation, they proclaimed the omnipotence of the ruler and symbolized the might of his rule.

The autocratic cities of the Near East greatly influenced the cities founded by Alexander and the Diadochs who followed him. These cities had little in common with the Greek city states which had been weakened by the Peloponnesian War and dissolved by the Macedonian conquest. They had quite different functions. They were parts of great empires, kingly residences and military camps, founded to express the self-glorification of monarchs building their kingdom on the oriental pattern. All had mixed populations. Some, because of their locations, had more or less important trade functions.

This self-glorification reached a climax in a suggestion which Stasicrates, a Greek architect, made to Alexander. Plutarch* tells the story: "He always promised something very bold, unusual, and magnificent in his projects. Once when they had met before (with Alexander) he had told him that, 'of all the mountains he knew, that of Athos in Thrace was the most capable of being adapted to represent the shape and lineaments of a man; that if he pleased to command him, he would make it the noblest and most durable statue in the world, which in its left hand should hold

* Plutarch: *Lives, Alexander*

134

92. MOUNT ATHOS *Its proposed transformation*

a city of ten thousand inhabitants, and out of its right hand should pour a copious river into the sea'." This noble mountain statue was to resemble Alexander. Alexander, however, refrained from ordering it built. The mere fact that it could be seriously suggested indicates the degree to which the Greek concept of freedom and independence had crumbled under the influence of the oriental concept of monarchy.

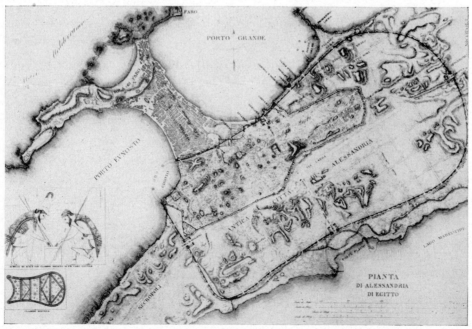

93. ALEXANDRIA

Alexander founded several Alexandrias, the most famous being in Egypt. This city, destined to importance by its location, was built after a plan by Dinocrates. It was placed on a tongue of land between Lake Mareotis and the Mediterranean Sea at the western Nile delta. The island of Pharos, connected with the city by a causeway, protected Alexandria and formed its two harbors. Alexandria became the link between the rich Nile valley and the Mediterranean world, the most important maritime and commercial city of the Hellenistic age. Its lighthouse, rising like a sky-scraper, could be seen from far away. After Alexander's death, the Ptolmies, one of the Diadoch families, made this city their capital. They enlarged it and built themselves palaces connected by a park which stretched along the eastern harbor. This park was, in all probability, the first city park ever created. Alexandria became a seat of learning, famous for its library; a great metropolis with mixed population. It remained the capital of the Ptolmies until its conquest by the Romans under Caesar and Augustus.

In the Far East, too, developing empires founded autocratic cities. The most outstanding were Peking and Kyoto, the former capitals of China and Japan. Peking was originally a tent camp. The tent of the commander stood at its center, with the tents of the generals and the army arranged in a geometric order around it. Its north-south orientation, based on a religious concept, was so completely carried out that later its layout was adopted for the imperial city. The imperial city, however, was much more than a mere army camp. It stood as symbol for the hub of the universe. At important festivals, the emperor sat on his throne facing south. Before him knelt the worshiping nobles, and throughout his kingdom his subjects, all facing north, honored him at their altars, even in the remotest huts.

Kyoto remained the capital of Japan for more than a thousand years before its place was taken by Tokyo. The shape of Kyoto is a square, divided into two parts with a wide central street. At the north end of this street is the palace ground, surrounded by a moat and a wall. The palace stands at the center of the park which completely fills this enclosed area. The city itself is divided into large squares by streets running from north to south and from east to west. Each square is divided into blocks and subdivided into lots.

Versailles, residence of the French kings, gave perfect expression to the concept of absolute monarchy, represented in its purest form by Louis XIV. The king was the glorified symbol of the monarchical system. His

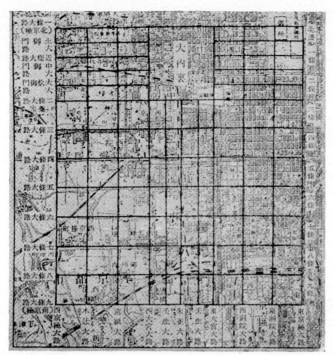

94. KIOTO

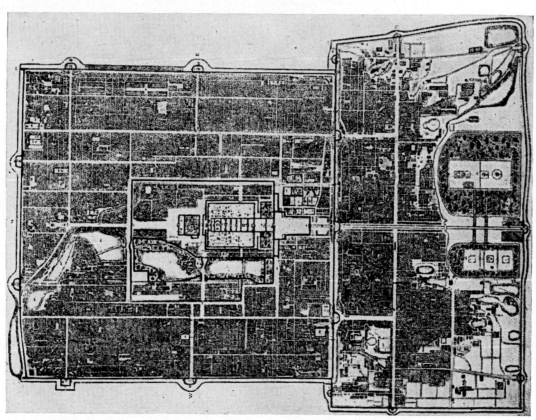

95. PEKING

palace stood at the head of the city as the king himself stood at the head of his subjects. The city was wholly subordinate to the palace. The geometrical axial street system focused upon the palace and thus emphasized its importance.

Versailles, however, was more than a place for royal aggrandisement and amusement. It had also a social-political function. Louis XIV had experienced in his youth the drive toward independence through which

96. HERACLEA

the great nobles had endangered the kingdom and the unity of France. He deliberately used the splendor and grandeur of his court, the rigid etiquette of court life, to transform rebellious nobles into obedient courtiers. With this great political achievement, Louis crowned the work of Richelieu who had originated the movement to end the independence of the great nobles, to reduce their power, and to unite France under one supreme ruler, her king.

138

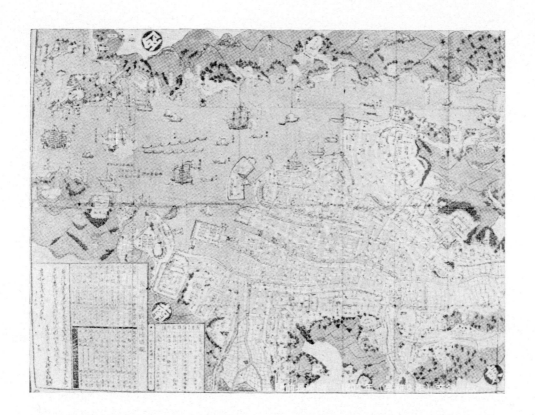

97.-98. NAGASAKI *Plan and View*

鍋冠山より見た長崎港

Quite naturally, Versailles became the prototype for capitals of territorial princes. Many princely cities show its influence. Some were sheer imitations on a dwarfed scale, like Rastatt. Others were adaptations, showing clearly the inspiration of Versailles, but showing also some originality of creation. Karlsruhe is one of these. Here, the palace of the prince is at the head of a city lying in fan-shaped formation before it. Nine radial streets are oriented toward the tower of the palace which in its prominence symbolizes the omnipotence of the prince. This tower is the center of a circle, one quarter of which is formed by the city, the palace ground; the other three-quarters by parks and adjoining forests. Interesting architectural effects have been achieved with this ornamental plan.

The pattern of free cities is of an organic order. It reflects the community spirit of cities self-ruled and based on a voluntary coalition of citizens. The founders and builders of these cities may not have drawn their plans as we would draw them; but they had a clear conception about the city they wanted, its arrangement, and the relation of its constituent parts to each other and to the whole. They tried to meet the varied needs of the community, took advantage of the topography of the site in arranging the city's defenses, carefully placed the fortification walls and the public buildings. Planning organically, they were able to make changes when change became desirable. The streets within the city and the roads which made possible communication between the city and its agricultural environment were also organically developed.

The organic order, like the geometric, is universal, appearing in widely separated countries and in widely separated times. Wherever it is found, it expresses the same basic principles, no matter how much this expression is modified and diversified by the topographical features of particular sites. Let us consider some of the cities planned in this way, cities in different ages and different parts of the earth.

Of the earliest Greek cities little remains except parts of foundations, on which once stood houses and public buildings, and ruins of city walls. Thera, which we have already mentioned, is one of the best examples, and it already suggests organic principles in its plan. Heraclea, which was built on the part of the western coast of Asia Minor called Ionia by the ancients, is another.

Ionia was a region of fertile land and natural harbors. But the coast was subject to unceasing change, as deposits of the river Meander constantly built the land farther and farther into the sea. Miletus and Heraclea, once seaports, are now miles inland. The harbors of Myus and the older Priene were already blocked with silt in ancient times.

Heraclea was located on a rocky mountain side on an inlet of the Aegean

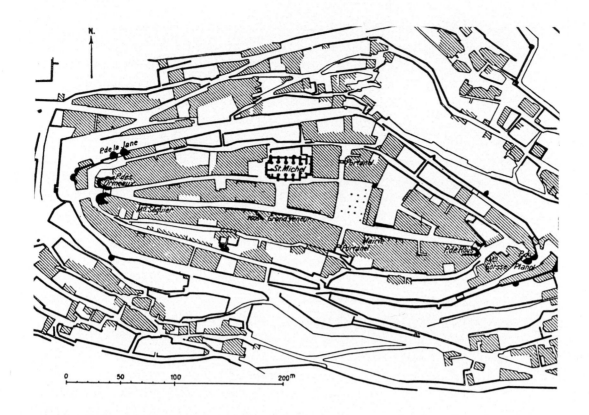

99.-100. CORDES *Plan and View*

141

Sea. This site, selected for its safety, created difficulties in the layout of the city. Until it became, at the time of the Diadochs, a naval station, Heraclea was of no great importance. Then its new function necessitated an increase in size and the city was twice extended. Ruins of various city walls make it possible to study the Hellenistic method of fortification. There were several outlying forts and an acropolis on the top of the mountain to protect the city as well as the harbor and its installations. Very little of the city remains, but the reconstruction by Krischen gives us some idea of how the city looked to its contemporaries and how it was adapted to its difficult terrain.

Nagasaki, long the only trade port between Japan and the west, is located at a bay on the western coast of the island of Kyushu. Originally it was a fisherman's settlement between two rivers. Soon it became also a harbor city. It was extended twice, and its new parts were also placed between rivers. Nagasaki's particular pattern is determined by those rivers. Until the middle of the nineteenth century, Nagasaki was the only Japanese port open to foreigners. Since these foreigners were not allowed to live in the city itself, artificial or semi-artificial islands were made for them. The Dutch traders, for example, were settled on Dejima island, connected to the mainland by a bridge. A similar island was provided for traders from China. After Japan was forced to take down the bars against foreigners, many of the people of Nagasaki became Christians under European influence. World fame touched the city at the close of World War II, when the second atomic bomb in history fell upon Nagasaki and destroyed it.

Cordes was a medieval trading city in southern France. Its oldest part stood on the top of a long-stretched hill. As the city prospered, it was twice extended. There were, consequently, three succeeding walls which, one after another, were built to enclose the growing city. Later, a suburb was added: Les Cabanas in the plain below the hill. There were few streets in the old part of the city: two main streets running from gate to gate, a third between them leading from the western gate to the church and the market square with its city hall, a few connecting cross streets. The market square was covered with a roof supported by stone piers to protect it from the weather. The first extension of the city added some new streets parallel to those already there. The second extension, built on the sloping hillsides, was separated from the older parts because of the topography of its site. The form character of the city emphasizes architecturally the natural features of its site. Houses similar in shape and form give Cordes its individuality; there are no single dominating buildings. Like the Italian hill cities, Cordes is impressive through its very simplicity.

101.-102. HERRENBERG *Plan and View*

Herrenberg was a small medieval city in southern Germany, located on the slope of a hill and bent around its spur. Its bent streets were at a uniform altitude, following the formation of the site. The few cross streets ran down hill, some of them so steeply that they had to replaced by steps. The city hall, with the market square, was nearly in the center of the main street which led to the city gates. Above it was the church and, still farther up, the castle. The city wall with its towers no longer exists. It ran parallel to the outerstreet. Herrenberg's architectural character is determined by the gabled houses and the church above them.

Noerdlingen, also in southern Germany, was originally placed upon a hill, but it outgrew that site and had to be rebuilt on the plains below. The city could grow without limits on this new site. Its shape is nearly circular. Since a circle encloses a maximum of area by a minimum of perimeter, the city wall, following this shortest possible line, could be built less expensively and defended with greater ease. When, like all growing cities, Noerdlingen needed to expand, the circular form was retained. The extension became a ring around the circular nucleus. The old wall was replaced by a circular street, and the streets within the new ring were connected with those of the old city in various ways and with the city gates of the new wall.

The cities we have thus far considered have been diversified through the influence of topography. Cities on similar locations, with similar topographical features, however, tend to follow similar patterns in their development. The Greek city of Thera, the ancient Italian city of Sutri, and the medieval city of Bazas near Bordeaux illustrate this clearly. All of them occupy good defense positions, and could be entered only by one or few gates. Their street systems and the location of their public squares reveal the same intention in the minds of their builders, in spite of the fact that centuries separate them from each other, that Bazan, in fact, is milleniums distant from Thera and Sutri. It should be remembered, of course, that the plan of a city is only its horizontal projection. Buildings erected on similar plans may be so different that they express quite different form concepts.

Organic planning does not rule out rectilinearity and rectangularity. This is well illustrated in cities planned by Hippodamus and his school. Of Peiraeus, Thuri, and Rhodos, actually planned by Hippodamus himself, very little is known. But Miletus, planned before Hippodamus's time, and Priene, planned after it, were good examples of what Greek tradition came to call "Hippodamian planning."
Miletus was a trading center, the founder of many colonies. It came

144

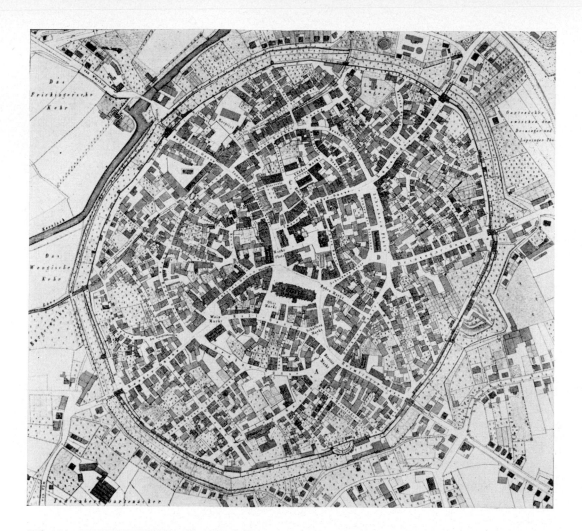

103.-104. NOERDLINGEN *Plan and View*

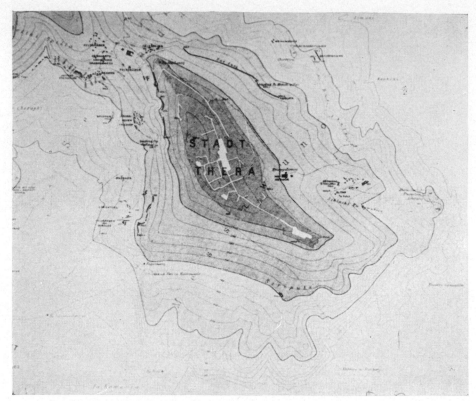

105. THERA *Plan*

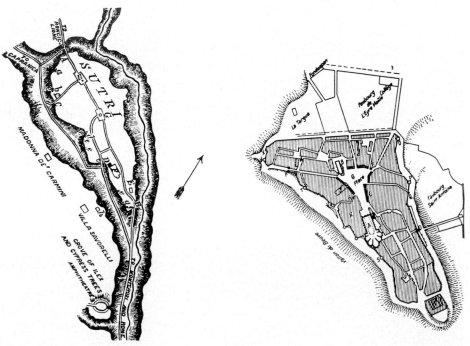

106. SUTRI

107. BAZAS

146

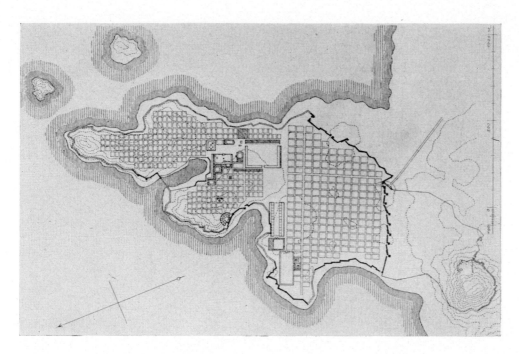

108.-109. MILETOS *Plan and View*

under the influence of Persia, and was destroyed during the revolt of the Ionian cities against Persian rule. Its conquerors sought to wipe it out as a Polis, but the few surviving citizens, strong in their faith in the eternity of the polis, restored and eventually rebuilt their community.

Miletus stands on a peninsula. At its west side two inlets form two harbors and also divide the city into three parts. The Agora and the ad-

147

joining northern and southern markets occupy the central part. West of the Agora stands the council house with colonaded court in front; east of it is the Nymphaeum, the city fountain. The markets are enclosed by colonaded halls with compartments for administrative and commercial purposes.

The Agora and the markets are determined by the rectangular street and block system, but they are not restrained by it. Their size is adequate to the purposes they served. Rectangularity does not necessarily force an axial, geometrical pattern upon the city. Miletus is developed with great freedom. The free arrangement of its colonaded halls and public buildings made possible any desired change without impairing the architectural harmony of the squares.

In addition to the geometric and the organic, there is one more universal city type: the colonial city. Colonial cities came into being for various reasons, but they were always deliberately founded and, therefore, have certain common characteristics. Their general pattern is geometric, like that of autocratic cities. But the pattern has new purposes and new uses. The colonial city was never dominated by the palace of a ruler placed at its center, as in Peking, or at its head, as in Versailles. The use of the geometric plan had one purpose: simplicity. It made possible an equal division of the city area. Wherever and whenever colonization took place, throughout all the world and in all the ages, this simple geometric pattern appears. Even colonial cities founded by people from cities built on an organic pattern followed the geometric plan.

The tent camp of the nomads antedates the colonial city and shows, in simple terms, its coordinating principles. A firmly established tent order was one of the disciplining forces in nomadic life. Every person and every thing had a place not to be changed without command or cogent reason. Encampment and decampment could, therefore, be effected with swiftness and order. The tent and all its contents could be packed and loaded in the shortest possible time. In the Abyssinian tent camp, this order is not easy to comprehend. Even in our own age, however, a military tent camp shows the same coordinating principles.

Colonial cities possessed, of course, ethnic differences as well as general similarities. Venta Silurum (Silchester), a Roman colony in England, shows the traditional colonaded forum at the crossing of the main streets. Montpazier, a medieval colonial city planned and built by the English in France, shows the two squares characteristic of the period, one for the church, the other for the city hall. This second square, symbol of the citizen's freedom is also the market place. It is surrounded by arcades. New Orleans, a French colonial city, consists of equal square blocks, but

110. NOMADIC TENT CAMP

111. MILITARY TENT CAMP

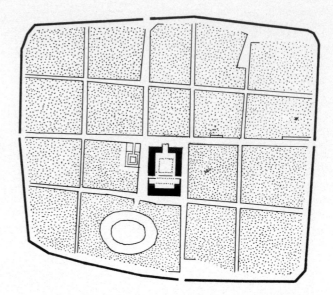

112. SILCHESTER

it has also the traditional French axis, formed by a street cutting across the middle squares, and leading, not to a palace, but to the church on the public square at the Mississippi.

Cordoba in Argentina omits the center block to provide space for the *placa,* the characteristic feature of Spanish cities.

Let us now see how the geometric and organic orders of planning affect cities in their parts and in their relation to their landscapes. Let us, for this purpose, take two cities similarly located on peninsulas formed by river bends: Verona, a geometric city, and Bern, organically planned.

Verona, founded by the Romans, shows in its pattern all the characteristics of a Roman city. Cardo and Decumanus, the main streets, lead to the forum, the Piazza Erbe, the market place of today. The amphitheater and the block and street systems are the most important survivals of Roman days. The city's geometric pattern wholly disregards the peculiarities of the site. The square blocks are spread over the peninsula and conflict everywhere with the boundaries set by the river.

At Bern, the site formation is made part of the organic plan. Three main streets run parallel with the river and are connected with each other by smaller streets. The central of the main streets gains importance by its width. Modest houses, expressive of equality rather than class distinction, contrast with the more elaborate public buildings.

The pattern of Verona clashes with its site; that of Bern is in harmony with it. What is a disadvantage to the geometric order becomes an advantage to the organic order. The flexibility and adaptablity of that order enables it to master any location. Bern's pattern is so convincing that it seems to be the only natural one.

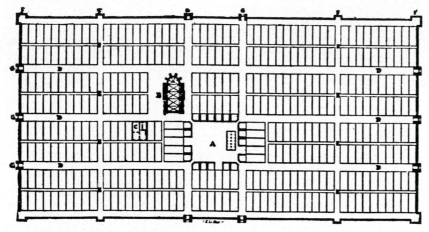

113. MONTPAZIER

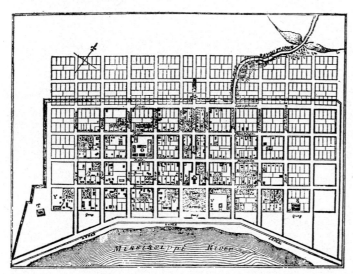

114. NEW ORLEANS

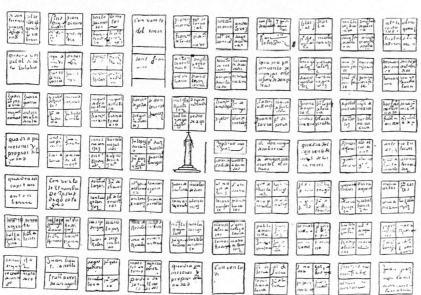

115. CORDOBA

151

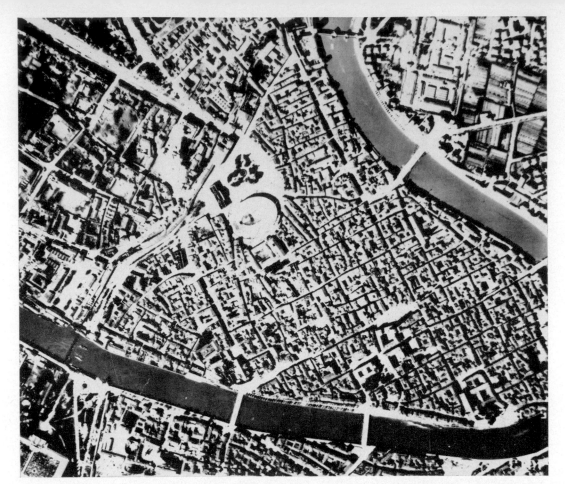

116. VERONA *Air View*

117. BERNE *Air View*

How do these two concepts of planning influence the usefulness of the city? Let us analyze the market squares of Karlsruhe and Luebeck to find the answer to that question.

The market square at Karlsruhe is part of the main axis which, like other radiating streets, leads to the palace. It is part of the extension of the city made by Weinbrenner at the beginning of the nineteenth century. The axis includes a number of squares of which the market square is the largest. Monuments and imposing buildings on these squares give emphasis to the axis. The market square is cut in half by this axis. Another important cross street cuts it again. The square, therefore, is divided into four parts, an architectural arrangement which seriously impairs its usefulness. The utility of the square diminishes to the same degree as the architectural intention dominates.

The market square of Luebeck is part of an organic city, developed according to its function. It is separated from the main street by an extension of the city hall, and from other streets by small blocks. There are no cross streets, no traffic passes through it. The market square can fulfill its purpose freely and adequately. Behind the city hall side rises the high church of S. Marien, the cathedral of the city, giving architectural significance to the square without, however, diminishing its usefulness.

Can a monument or a statue have an intrinsic value and still be in harmony with its architectural surroundings? Must such a work of art always be subordinated to the architectural composition of which it is a part? Is the placement of a statue subject to geometric or organic orders of planning? Answers to these interesting questions are suggested by two famous equestrian statues: the antique statue of Marcus Aurelius at the capitol in Rome, and Donatello's Gattamelata at Padua. Let us consider how they, as sculptural works, are affected by their placement and by their relation to architecture.

The capitol at Rome was planned by Michelangelo. We shall discuss elsewhere his architectural composition and his contribution to the then new space concept. The statue of Marcus Aurelius stands at the center of the capitol square on a low postament. Its admirable setting is like that of a jewel, but this very setting diminishes the statue's own sculptural value. It becomes the center of an architectural composition. It cannot be seen as it should be seen, because its background is always an architecture rich in its own diversity of light and shade. But should not a statue have a more natural background? Should it not stand, for instance, against a clear sky, so that its own sculptural values may be seen and enjoyed? The Piazza del Santo in Padua, famous for Donatello's Gattamelata, shows how organic planning allows each part to develop according to its

118. KARLSRUHE *Market Place. View*

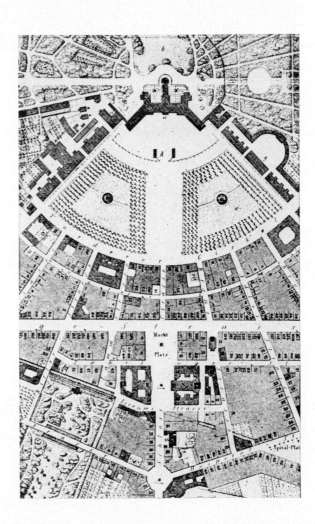

119. KARLSRUHE
*Main Axis of the City
with Market Place*

154

120. LUEBECK *Market Place. View*

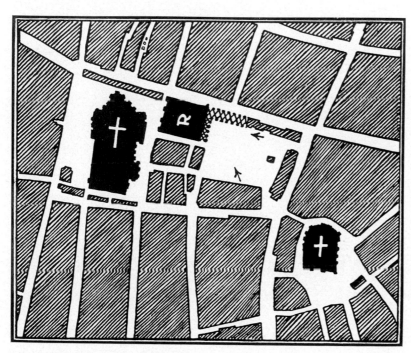

121. LUEBECK *Market Place. Plan*

122. ROME *Capitol Square*

123. PADUA *Piazza del Santo*

own laws and still remain in harmony with the whole. The placement of the Gattamelata and its relation to its surroundings is in great contrast to that of the statue of Marcus Aurelius in Rome. The "L" shaped Piazza del Santo has no special significance; neither has the seven-domed pilgrimage church of S. Antonio. The statue, on a high postament, is so placed that it can be seen both from the Piazza and from the street which enters the Piazza. It is best seen, however, from the Via Capelli. From this street, the equestrian statue appears high in the air, above the buildings of the Piazza, against the neutral background of the sky.

The relation of Donatello's magnificent sculpture to its surroundings, the church and the other buildings of the Piazza, is well nigh perfect. The degree of this perfection is shown in some small but important details. Gattamelata's staff, for instance, counteracts the falling lines of the gables of the church in such a way that the statue is brought into a form relation to the architecture of that church. Sculpture and architecture enhance each other. The Piazza increases the sculptural values of the statue; the statue gives to the Piazza significance far beyond its architectural value.

The wilderness, untouched nature, can support man only in small numbers and inadequately at best. Man must change nature to maintain his own existence. Each domesticated animal, each grain of corn, each vegetable or fruit, is a product of man's unceasing effort to tame nature. To make nature serve man is one of the chief aims of civilization. Without this taming of nature, which includes man himself, there could be neither civilization nor culture. Much of what we call nature today is of man's making, or has at least been transformed by his effort.

Man's environment, therefore, becomes subject to one of the concepts of order he has created: the geometric and the organic. Each concept has found expression in man's division and use of agricultural land, in the gardens and parks he has created.

The geometric order, with its superimposing character, must obviously conflict with nature everywhere, except perhaps on wide extensive plains. Nature, with her mountains and hills, her lakes and rivers, knows no straight lines. She is in conflict always with geometry which depends on straight lines and must ignore nature to achieve its aims. Today's mechanized agriculture, which would greatly prefer to have the landscape reduced to a hill-less, tree-less plain, is an expression of this geometric concept. Such a landscape would, it seems, be better adapted for the machine and therefore more efficient. Nature, however, has her own answer to such ideas, takes her own revenge on those who hold them. As the natural drainage pattern is disrupted, the ground water reservoirs dry up. Wind and water erosion take their destructive toll. In the end, the seemingly economical plan proves to be completely uneconomical.

124. GEOMETRIC LANDSCAPE

125. ORGANIC LANDSCAPE

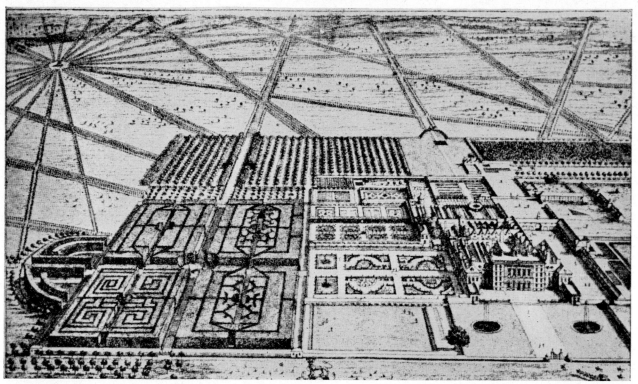

126. BADMINTON *Geometric Park*

127. BATH, PRIORY PARK *Organic Park*

The parks and gardens of princes and nobles imposed on nature the ornamentation of the geometric order. Their builders applied to nature the symmetry of their architectural concept, and, in addition, made stereometric elements of the trees and the shrubs. The parks and gardens they created were as formal as the palaces themselves. Trees were clipped into cubes, pyramids, cones, spheres. The garden became a geometric ornament with square, rectangular, wedge-shaped, round, or oval flower beds. Sometimes the grass itself was replaced by colored sand or gravel to increase the artificiality and make the abstract concept more complete. At Versailles, the creation of Louis XIV, these concepts were realized on a grand scale. The whole countryside was transformed into a work of art. Versailles was imitated all over Europe by princes and rulers. One of these many repetitions is Badminton in Gloucestershire. This estate is not a copy of Versailles, but an expression of the same spirit. Its mansion is surrounded by geometric gardens. Its park grounds are traversed by twenty avenues, converging to one point like the center of a star.

The idea of forcing geometry on nature, however, is much older than the Baroque period during which it became fashionable. It is older even than the Renaissance which admired and adapted it. The gardens of Roman villas contained clipped shrubbery. On the terrace of Pliny's villa in Tuscany, boxwood was cut and clipped into the shapes of animals. The villa of the emperor Hadrian at Tivoli had geometric gardens, with trees and hedges shaped stereometrically, and with an artificial lake. It was by no means unusual for the Romans to force nature to their own ends. We have already mentioned the removal of a hillside in Rome to provide the level surfaces required for the Forum of Trajan. We may assume that geometric gardens appeared in connection with the palaces of the Roman emperors in Constantinople, that they were known in the Near East and the Far East wherever the geometric order was adopted and builders sought to transform, not only the city, but also the whole countryside into a work of art. If the geometric order, always and everywhere, battles to force nature into its own pattern, the organic order strives, always and everywhere, to achieve harmony with nature. It must work to change nature to make her serve man better, and sometimes its efforts fail. For nature remains an eternal mystery, almost as unknown today as in the ancient past. The tendency of the organic order is, to reach agreement with nature to the greatest possible degree. It tries to adapt itself to diversities in topography, to recognize and make use of the particular features of the land, the climate, the geographical position of the areas with which it works. It treats arable land as arable land, grassland as grassland, woodland as woodland. It protects watersheds, lakes, and rivers by planting trees beside them. It provides nesting places in trees and shrubs for insect-eating birds. It uses woods and forests for the conservation of wild life.

This search for harmony guides also the arrangement and subdivision of the land. Dividing lines and roads follow natural contours. The natural drainage pattern is thus maintained and the reservoirs of underground water preserved. Crop rotation and organic fertilization maintain the fertility of the soil. The organic order recognizes the interrelation between man and the environment of which he is ecologically a part. This spirit of conservation, prevailing everywhere, touches even the parks and gardens arranged for man's pleasure. The organic planner knows that nature has a beauty of her own which, carefully developed, can achieve artistic values. The Priory Park at Bath, in Somerset, proves this. This park contrasts with the surrounding countryside in scale but not in pattern. In harmony with nature, it is also an enhancement of nature.

City architecture is architecture which deals, not with single buildings or groups of buildings, but with all the buildings which make up a city. It is concerned with the relation of the parts to each other and with the relation of each part to the city as a whole. Its objective is the creative use of the material elements of the city. Its goal is to achieve an optical order adequate to the city's physical order. City architecture has but limited means for the realization of such aims. Yet it is true that the more clearly these limitations are recognized, the more effectively can the means be used in particular tasks. The more completely the means are mastered, the more satisfying will be the results.

Means, however, are only means. Their mere application does not insure fruitful results. Artistic ability will always be a determining factor, and such ability is innate and cannot be acquired. Architectural expression will always vary also according to the concepts of its age. And the interrelation between utility and beauty requires that always a conscious goal of the city architect must be the meeting of utilitarian ends. He needs to recognize also, however, that what is planned for utility can, without sacrificing usefulness, transcend utility and enter into the higher realm of art.

It was once believed that only the geometric order of planning could effectively develop city architecture. The undeniable architectural values of organic cities were considered more or less accidental; the organic order itself was regarded as devoid of architectural potentialities. We have come to realize, however, that cities of either order may be built with or without architectural value. City architecture is not dependent on a particular order of planning. Both the organic and the geometric order may influence the architectural expression of the city. Each presents its own architectural problems and offers its own architectural possibilities in unlimited variety.

The materials of city architecture are the city's site and its topography, the city's buildings, and the open spaces within and without the city. The means of city architecture are, mainly, proportion, contrast, and perspective. We may consider and analyze these means separately, but we must always remember that they are inter-related, dependent one upon the other.

Proportion is concerned with the relation of parts to the whole and the relation of the whole to the parts. The whole city within its landscape is the concern of city architecture. The architect must consider this whole, but he must also consider the parts—the different buildings, the streets, the open spaces. Proportion may be used to make a building or a group of buildings appear solemn and grave or graceful and spirited. Deliberate contrast between small and large, high and low, can increase or decrease, at will, visual dimensions. With perspective, proportion may become a predominant spatial factor, making a small object appear large or a large object small, making distant objects seem close at hand and near objects far away.

The city, which exists in space, presents also a space problem. We cannot optically perceive unlimited space; only objects in space make us aware of it. Spatial feeling has, however, influenced city architecture of all ages. But space concepts have changed in those ages with changing material and spiritual influences. The walled-in city of the Middle Ages presented different problems and possibilities from the open city of the Baroque period. The space concept of the Middle Ages is expressed in the high narrow naves of the cathedrals, whose loftiness symbolized aspiration toward God. This spatial expression is raised to mystical heights by the dematerialized light which penetrates through the high stained-glass windows. The narrow bent streets of the medieval city reveal the same concept. Their view is always closed. If such a street leads to the tower of the cathedral, its own narrowness is enhanced by the height of the tower rising above the houses.

The space concept of the Baroque period is, in contrast, open and horizontal. In spite of the artificiality of its parks, the Baroque city was always open and in close relation with nature. Its architects tried to relate that which was far away to that which was close, as did the landscape artists in their paintings.

There are two kinds of proportion: the relative and the absolute. In relative proportion, the relation of the parts to the whole remains constant, regardless of scale. This was the proportion sought in antiquity and in the Renaissance. In a Greek column, for instance, the proportion between shaft, capital, and base remains always the same, regardless of the size of the column. In absolute proportion, the relationship between the

128. ULM *Street with Cathedral*   129. COLOGNE *Cathedral*

parts and the whole varies according to scale. This was the proportion used in the Middle Ages. A medieval column may have a long shaft or a short, but its capital and base retain the same size regardless of the length of the shaft.

The application of relative or absolute proportion many visually decrease or increase the size of a building. S. Peter's in Rome, built in the Renaissance, is subject to relative proportion. The result is an optical decrease of its dimensions, in spite of the contrast between the building and the colonades which surround the square. The windows of S. Peter's do not seem very different in size from those of the Vatican buildings close by. Actually they are much larger. The use of relative proportion diminishes this difference optically, to the disadvantage of S. Peter's.

Quite different is the effect obtained through the application of absolute proportion, especially if it is combined with contrast between large and small, high and low. Particularly impressive are the cathedrals of the Middle Ages. The contrast between the unusual scale of a cathedral and the familiar scale of the small low houses which surround it enhances the cathedral, increases its optical size beyond its actual dimensions. Absolute proportion, since it does not require that parts of buildings maintain an artificial relationship which at times creates a dwarfing effect, allows the buildings and their parts to appear in their absolute dimensions.

163

130. ROME *St. Peter's*

131. DANZIG *S. Marien*

164

132. DRESDEN *Frauenkirche*

How high the Marienkirche towers above the city of Danzig! In reality this edifice is smaller than S. Peter's in Rome. But its absolute proportions make it appear larger than reality. The houses around it seem dwarfed. The tall windows of the church are in greatest possible contrast to the small normal window of the houses. They seem oversized, gigantic. Their verticality corresponds with the verticality of the church's architecture, which also increases its height, optically, far beyond reality.

The Frauen Kirche in Dresden shows the same effect of visual increase. This building belongs to the Baroque period and, therefore, uses relative proportion. However, certain parts of the edifice, its tall windows, its slender dome rising high above the towers, depart from the proportions of the relative scale. Those elements are, in fact, subject to absolute proportion. The Frauen Kirche, combining both codes of architectural proportion, achieves an extraordinary effect.

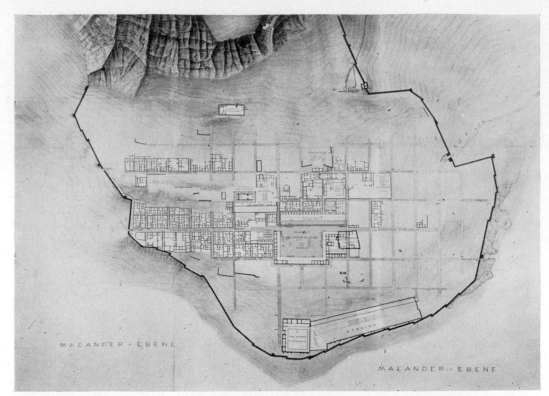

133. PRIENE *Plan*

134. PRIENE *View*

166

135. PRIENE *Agora*

Horizontality and verticality, as means of architectural expression, are closely related to the two kinds of proportion. Southern cities, generally, preferred horizontality; northern cities usually developed vertically. Priene and Luebeck impressively illustrate these differing architectural rhythms. The site of the original Priene is unknown. Perhaps its remains may have been covered with the silt of the river Meander. But the city was refounded under the influence, and possibly with the help of, Athens, and it was supported by Alexander after his victory over the Persians. This city stood on a southern slope of the Mycale mountains, a site chosen to

136. PRIENE *Theater*

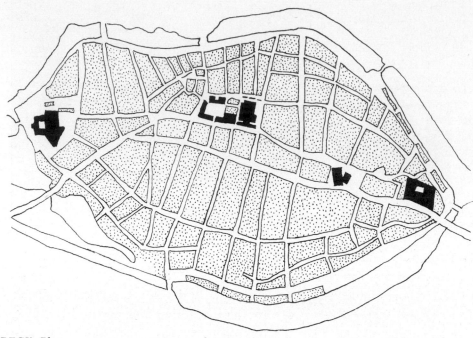

137. LUEBECK *Plan*

138. LUEBECK *Aerial View*

139. LUEBECK *View from Marli*

protect the city from the disastrous effect of the flooding of the Meander. The new site, however, had its own difficulties. Masses of rock had to be removed and retaining walls built in order to gain the even ground required for the square and the public buildings. The main streets run from east to west and are comparatively level. The cross streets, running north and south, are so steep that, at some places, they had to be replaced by steps, a solution quite possible in a city of little or no traffic.

The houses of Priene contrast sharply with its public buildings. They are modest in size and appearance; the public buildings, some of them at least, are very elaborate. The same contrast appears in the city's plan, where wide-open spaces offset the narrowness of the streets and the

140. LUEBECK *Holy Ghost Hospital*

141. VILLENEUVE—LES—AVIGNON

closeness of the houses. The architectural concept is horizontal. The horizontal masses of the public buildings, the gymnasium and the stadium below, the colonaded halls and sacred stoa at the Agora with the temple of Athena above it,—all these elements emphasize the horizontal terrace character of the city. The natural features of the site are not eliminated or neglected, but, on the contrary, are emphasized architecturally. The city is, at one and the same time, in contrast to its landscape setting and in complete harmony with it.

Luebeck, founded in the early Middle Ages, stands on a low, long island in the river Trave. This island, shaped like a low hill, is higher in its middle part, slopes gently to the rivers at either side. The plan of the city grew out of its site quite naturally and convincingly. Its architectural elevation possesses the same logic. Two main streets run north and south; others parallel them or follow contour lines. All the streets running across the island lead down to the rivers. The city hall, the market place, and the main church stand at the center of the city. The city's architecture is characterized by its verticality. The view from the east shows an impressive skyline, accented by groups of church towers and high spires. The remarkable grouping of these spires gives the city individuality. The towers increase in height from the south to the north. Churches with twin towers are impressively counterbalanced by churches with single higher spires, an effect which reaches its climax with the northernmost tower and its upward-

142. MELK

beating spire. The verticality of the towers is matched by vertical elements of other buildings: — the high gabled houses, the turreted city hall and hospital, the spire-like roofs of the Holsten gate. All these elements blend together to produce an architectural harmony of verticality.

Large buildings on hills are elements important to the city architect. An entire city may be set in contrast to one dominant edifice or building group. Medieval strongholds dominated their cities, visually as well as politically. Villeneuve les-Avignon in southern France is a good example. At Melk on the Danube a large cloister on a hilltop, in mass as large as the hill itself, contrasts with the city below. Large edifices within a city may also exert important architectural influence. At Halicarnassos, a Greek city on the coast of Asia Minor, the great tomb of King Mausolos gives the city significance. It lies at the center of the city on a long-stretched terrace, and towers above the houses built in amphitheatre formation on the lower slopes of the mountainside.

The possibilities of perspective in city architecture are well shown in the Piazza and Piazzetta of S. Mark's in Venice. The Piazza viewed from S. Mark's seems to narrow toward the rear because the palaces enclosing the space slant inward. The feeling of depth is thus increased, as the converging palaces reenforce perspective to make the square appear deeper than it actually is.

143. HALICARNASSOS *The Mausoleum*

One might expect that the opposite effect would be apparent, that, viewed from the far end of the Piazza, the square would seem shorter than reality. This is not the case. The free-standing campanile has been so placed that the shortening effect has been neutralized. Again an impression of depth is achieved. The campanile enhances this effect of depth to an extraordinary extent by interposing itself between the observer and S. Mark's, so that S. Mark's is pushed back visually. The illusion of depth is increased still further because the campanile is at some distance from S. Mark's and rises to a considerable height.

The Piazza is enclosed on all sides. The Piazzetta, which adjoins it at right angles, is open toward the Piazza and also toward the lagoon. The contrast between the two squares increases the feeling of confinement of the Piazza and emphasizes the openness of the Piazzetta. The Piazzetta seems to draw into the total spatial view, not only the island in the lagoon lying opposite, but also the remote distance.

The Renaissance replaced the mysticism of the Middle Ages with a trend toward rationalism and clarity. Man believed himself the center of the world, the scale of all measurements. The world was made for him, and for him only. Such ideas inevitably influenced the space concepts of the Renaissance. The result was a centric concept of space applied to buildings, squares, and whole cities. Cities became, or were considered, objects of art. The city was conceived as an architectural unity. Every element within the city was subordinated to this unity.

Bramantes' Tempietto of S. Pietro in Montorio, at Rome, may have been the earliest realization of this new centric space concept. The same principle appears again, on a much larger scale, in Bramantes' plan for S. Peter's and its square. In this plan, S. Peter's is placed in the center

144. VENICE *Piazza S. Mark*

145. VENICE *Piazza and Piazzetta of S. Mark. Air View*

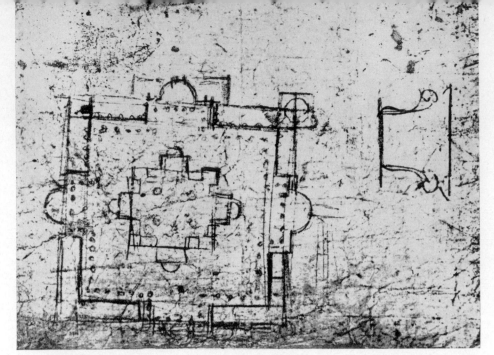

146. BRAMANTE *Plan for S. Peter's and its square*

of a large square surrounded by colonaded porticoes. At each side are exedras, similar to those of the cathedral itself. The square represents the outline of the edifice and embodies the total symmetry of S. Peter's.
Bramantes intended to give the great edifice an adequate setting. He planned that the low colonades should, by contrast, enhance the importance of the main building. S. Peter's was to be separated from the "outside", from the formless beyond which so easily might have diminished its significance.

Antonio Averulino Filarete, sculptor and architect of the Ospedale Maggiore in Milano, one of the first community hospitals, also worked on plans for an ideal Renaissance city, central and symmetrical in plan. He called his city Sforzinda after the Sforzas, the ruling family of Milano.*
In plan, the city was to be like an eight-sided star, two equal squares being superimposed with the diagonal of one square bisecting the side of the other. In the city's center, he placed a square with a tower. West of the square would be the prince's palace; east of the square, the cathedral. Sixteen streets radiated from the central tower, leading alternately to the city gates at the obtuse angle of the star-shaped city wall, or to the towers of that wall at its right angles. In the plan, those radial streets are crossed by circular streets and alternating squares and churches mark the intersections.
Filarete attained two things in this plan. He realized the centric and symmetrical ideal of the Renaissance city, and he provided the structural means for its defense. He even took into account the new possibilities created as the introduction of gunpowder changed warfare and, conse-

* Filarete, Antonio Averulino: *Trattate della architettura.* Vienna, 1896

quently, the defense needs of the city. From the tower in the city's center, in Filarete's plan, cannons could be aimed along the streets radiating to the gates, to prevent with their fire any enemy entrance into the city. The triangular bastions, which resulted from the star-shaped pattern, would make possible a flanking fire to prevent invaders from coming too close to the gates. Filarete's plan became the model for all fortified cities of Europe. The bastions were used for centuries as means of city defense.

More architectural in scope and less concerned with defense is the ideal city of Fra Giocondo, here presented in a perspective sketch. This was to be a circular city, dominated by an elaborate central edifice from which the streets, or rather the rows of houses, radiated. Another row of houses was planned to run parallel with the city wall.

The concept of the ideal city of the Renaissance found its realization in two cities: Palma Nova and Grammichele. Palma Nova was built at the end of the sixteenth century after a plan by Vicenzo Scamozzi, as a fortified place for the defense of Venice. It is a nine-sided polygon in outline, with an hexagonal square at its center. A tower is placed on this square. From the middle of each side of the hexagon, a main street leads to the gates or to the bastions. Connecting streets parallel the sides of the outer polygon, and these are intersected by other radial streets. Some of the streets cross smaller squares at some distance from the main square. The fortifications were later extended. Today, no longer useful, they are falling into decay.
  Grammichele, in Sicily was built a hundred years later than Palma Nova. It replaced the old town of Occhiola, destroyed by an earthquake. Its layout is more complex than that of Palma Nova. In addition to an hexagonal part with an hexagonal square at its center, there are also six rectangular parts, each with its central square. From the hexagonal center square, six main streets radiate, crossing the secondary squares and leading out to the unfortified edge of the city. As a geometric composition, this city is much more impressive than Palma Nova.

As the Reformation gave rise to the counter-Reformation, the rationalism of the Renaissance was replaced with the super naturalism of the Baroque. The static concept of the Renaissance changed into a dynamic one. This change is well illustrated by the successive alterations of the Cathedral and Piazza of S. Peter's in Rome.
The centric structure, based on the Greek cross, conceived by Bramante and maintained by Michelangelo, was nearing completion when the decision was made, under Pope Paul V, to substitute the Latin cross plan suggested by Raphael. Carlo Maderne added the extension in front of the central edifice, following the pattern of Il Gesu, the church of the Jesuits

147. FRA GIOCONDO *Ideal City*

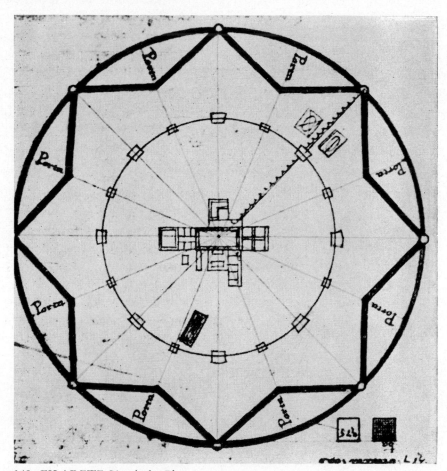

148. FILARETE *Sforzinda. Plan*

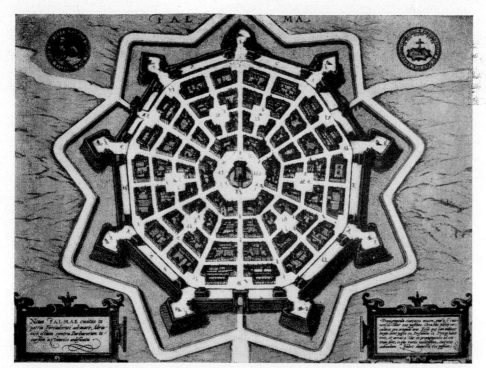

149. PALMA NOVA

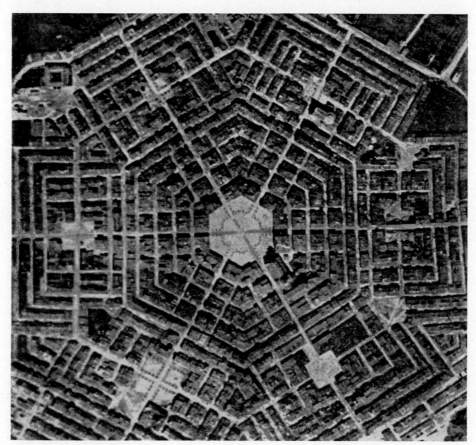

150. GRANMICHELE

151. MICHEL ANGELO *His Concept of S. Peter's and its square*

152. ROME *S. Peter's Square*

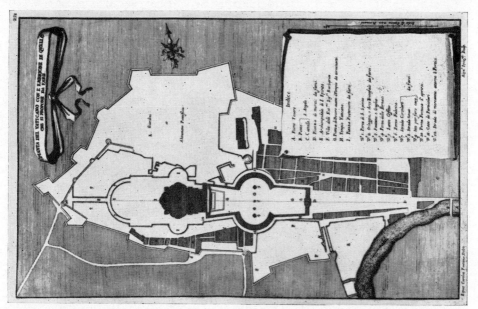

153. D. FONTANA *Proposed extension of S. Peter's Square*

in Rome. This church of Il Gesu became the model for most of the churches of that time, no doubt because it gave expression to the medieval concept of a church to which the counter-Reformation was now returning. Michelangelo's plan, like Bramante's, placed S. Peter's in the center of a square. But this idea, too, had to be changed in accordance with the dynamic concept. The Piazza no longer surrounds the edifice; it has become an entrance plaza leading to it. This new concept, it should be noted, permitted the use of terrain differences in the site which both Bramante and Michelangelo had completely neglected.

The vast impressive Piazza in front of S. Peter's is the creation of Bernini. This Piazza consists of an eliptical area with two trapezoidal extensions, one at each end of the minor axis. The eliptical area is partly enclosed by two semi-circular colonaded halls. In the center is an obelisk, with fountains on either side. The trapezoidal extension toward S. Peter's rises with the rising terrain, as do also the buildings at its north and south sides. This rising of the Piazza enhances the main front of the cathedral far beyond its architectural value.

Dominica Fontana proposed the extension of the eastern trapezoid square as far as the Castle S. Angelo at the Tiber. This would have made Michelangelo's Dome and Drum visible in their fullness. It would have revealed the whole edifice to the eye of every beholder with startling clearness.

179

154. VERSAILLES *View towards the radiating streets*

The most impressive feature of Versailles, besides its palace and its park, is the three streets which traverse the city and lead to the large square in front of the palace. They approach the palace and have it always in view. Their arrangement in relation to the square and the palace realizes both dominant tendencies of the Baroque: its dynamic movement and its trend for pomp and display.

This magnificent expression of the Baroque dynamic space concept was widely copied. The princely residence of Rastatt imitated it on a smaller scale, Christopher Wren, drawing plans for London after the Fire, reduced the three streets to two. At Karlsruhe, the number of streets was increased

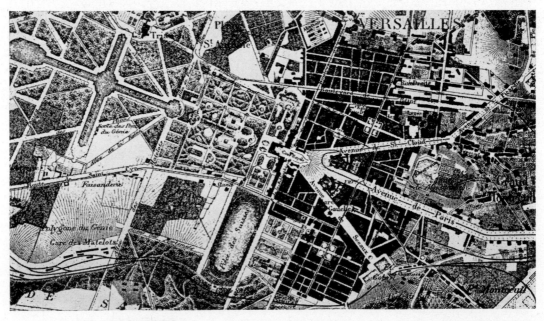

155. VERSAILLES

180

to nine, all of them oriented toward the tower of the palace; each of the nine streets had an important view, together they symbolized the omnipotence of the prince.

Versailles can lay no claim, however, to the invention of these impressive streets. They are, in a sense, only extensions of the Via Flamina which led from Rome to Rimini. A traveler from the north entered Rome at the Porta del Popolo which led to the large Piazza del Popolo. Three main streets penetrate the city from this Piazza, opening it in three directions. The obelisk at the Piazza's center marks the point from which these streets optically diverge. The impressive view is accentuated by the similar domes of two churches, each standing between two of the radiating streets.

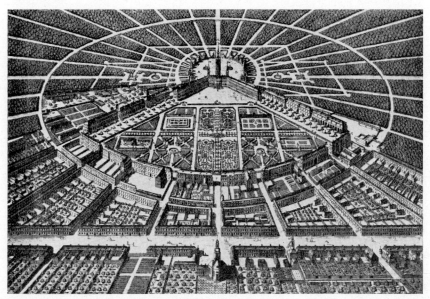

156. KARLSRUHE *Original City*

As the Piazza of S. Peter's indicates, the space concept of the Baroque does not tend to enclose an object of importance as the Renaissance did. Its object is rather to lead to the important focus; it is dynamic in character. The same tendency appears in the arrangement of squares so that, in a series of squares related to each other by an architectural composition, each, by reason of contrast, enhances the other, sometimes dramatically. Most remarkable in this respect are the squares of Nancy, built by the architect E. Here de Corny when Nancy was extended beyond its old city limits under Stanislaw Lescinski, prince of Lorraine. There are three squares. The largest, the Place Stanislas, is nearly square in shape. At its south side is the city hall and a monument in a central position. At its north side a lower building group encloses an extension of the square and leads to a triumphal arch. This arch opens to the Place de la Carriere, a long rectangle. The narrowness of this rectangle is increased by two parallel rows of trees on either side of the square whose intertwining foliage is trimmed to form cubic masses which are, in themselves, architectural elements. At the north end of the Place, another square lies at right angles. It is extended by semicircular parts enclosed by colonaded halls and dominated by the palace. Both end squares are more elaborate than the Place de la Carriere between them. The resulting contrast increases the architectural value of each square and also of the total space composition.

That a square need not be enclosed entirely, that it may be partly open, that openness itself can be a vital element in city architecture,—these ideas

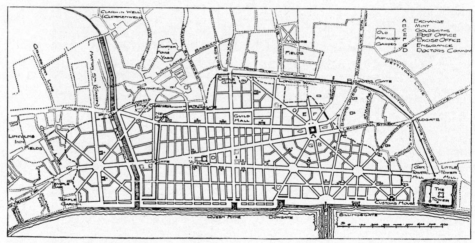

157. LONDON *Plan by Chr. Wren*

were first conceived by Michelangelo when he planned the capitol square on Rome's Capitol Hill. A wide stairway leads up to the square's platform on which three palaces stand. The Palazzo del Senatore is at the far end of the square, in the axis of the stairway and opposite to it. The other two palaces are at either side. The antique statue of Marcus Aurelius, on a low postament, stands at the square's center. An imposing flight of steps leads to the high rusticated basement of the Palazzo del Senatore. The two main floors of this palace are architecturally united by Corinthian pilasters. A tower is placed in the Palazzo's center, behind its main front. The lateral palazzos, without basements, are lower than the Palazzo del Senatore. They are two-storied and are unified by Corinthian pilasters. These two lateral palaces are not parallel to each other. Their divergence causes a widening of the square toward the Palazzo del Senatore and a narrowing

158. ROME *Plan of the City, Northern part with Piazza del Popolo*

159. ROME *Piazza del Popolo. View towards the three Radiating streets*

183

160. NANCY *Place Stanislas*

161. NANCY *Place Royale*

toward its opposite end, which remains open. The Palazzo del Senatore thus becomes free-standing, so that the square opens also at its wider end. The areas beyond the square are brought into relation to the square itself; open and enclosed spaces merge. According to rules of perspective, the Palazzo del Senatore should appear closer. Actually, in spite of its greater height and the tower which emphasizes that height, the Palazzo, because of the openness of the square, appears farther away than it really is. The more horizontal formation of the two lateral palaces increases this effect. The spatial confinement of the capitol square is simultaneously sustained and suspended. A new possibility for city architecture had thus been discovered which was to lead eventually to great freedom in planning and to make open space a recognized and important architectural factor.

The Capitol Square in Rome is a city square. The Place de la Concorde in Paris is something more. It is related to nature and surrounded by it. Originally, the Place was outside the city limits, its two large buildings by Gabriel used to house ambassadors and royal guests. These two buildings are at the square's north side and are free standing. At the south side, the square is bordered by the Seine; at its east, by the Jardin des Tuileries; and at its west, by the Champs Elysees. Behind the buildings and far away rises Montmartre, merged optically with the parks on either side of the square. The Place de la Concorde is, however, still dominated by architecture. The symmetrical arrangement of its buildings is emphasized today by the central obelisk, the two fountains, and the Madeleine, seen between the buildings and far behind them.
In great contrast to the arrangement of the Place de la Concorde is that of the Place of the Admiralty in St. Petersburg (Leningrad). Here the large buildings are freely arranged with no dominating axis. In connection with the wide square itself, this arrangement achieves unrestricted openness heretofore unknown.

This tendency toward openness is characteristic of Baroque cities. The discovery that the city may be open and connected with its landscape and even merged with it was an important one. The traditional concept had been that the city must be a closely built area, densely populated, and wholly separated from nature. Now that concept could be abandoned. Changes in the structure of the state and in the methods of warfare aided this development. The great states beginning to emerge had to be defended at their border lines. Only places of strategic importance needed to be fortified. Most cities could develop without the limitations of defense requirements. Older cities could expand beyond their walls; new cities could be built with no thought of fortifications. Kings and princes saw these new possibilities quickly and took advantage of them. Versailles and Karlsruhe

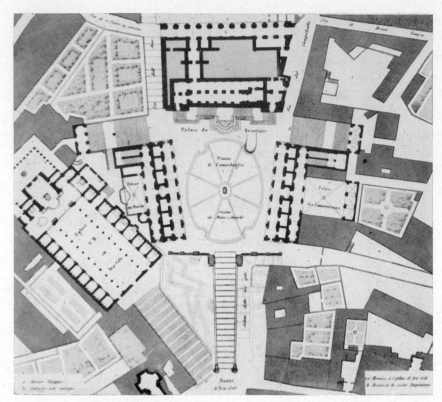

162. ROME *Capitol Square*

163. PARIS *Place del la Concorde*

demonstrated that the new princely city could be closely related to, and even interpenetrated by, the landscape around it.

During the Baroque period, the princely palace and other large buildings, changed in character, becoming, like the cities of the time, more open and more freely developed. The Renaissance palaces, all located within cities, had been influenced by the space limitations of those cities. Usually they occupied a city block, or part of a block, and were built around an inner court. The Pallazzo Farnese in Rome is typical. The Baroque palaces were built in the open, outside the old walled-in cities, often in connection with entirely new cities or new city developments. There was no longer a space limitation to hamper them. They could be opened up, and they could spread out.

At Versailles, the central part of the palace, as well as the two large buildings opposite it between the three radiating streets, is open and built around a U-shaped court. The long wings added later on either side of the palace, however, still contain enclosed courts.

At Karlsruhe, the palace has no courts at all. Three wings project from its central part: one vertical to it toward the north, ending in the palace tower toward which all streets are oriented; the other two extending at an angle southeast and southwest, each parallel to one of the outermost radiating streets of the fan-shaped city.

The movement to free the city from restriction and domination reached

164. BATH *View from Hedgemead Park*

165. KARLSRUHE *View of the City from the Palace*

its logical climax at Bath in southern England. Something new was born here which made use of the spatial concept of the Baroque, but did so without making landscape and buildings subject to any super-imposed geometric pattern. This important contribution was made by the Woods, father and son. Its influence is greater today than it has ever been.

Both the Woods worked on the extension of Bath. This city had become quite prosperous during the eighteenth century because of its therapeutic springs. Those springs had, since the days of the Romans, given Bath a reputation for healthfulness. As the town grew into a fashionable health

166. ST. PETERSBURG–LENINGRAD *Place of the Admiralty*

resort, its population increased and expansion was necessary. There was no room for the city to expand on its original plain. The sloping land to the north had to be pressed into use. At first this extension was carried out in the conventional manner, the new section being laid out with streets and squares. But Bath kept growing. And it began, eventually, to solve its problem in an entirely new way. For the first time in history, homes in the open country were built, not for princes, but for ordinary people. Free-standing, large, crescent-shaped apartment houses were erected on the sloping hillside outside of Bath.

The spaciousness of those buildings was as remarkable as their relation to the open country. Freed from the formalistic, super-architectural spirit of the Baroque, which cared so little for function, those crescent-shaped buildings could develop according to their own law. They broke the traditional confinement of the city and found harmony with the topography of their site. There was harmony between the city and the landscape. Both were equal in value. Together they achieved unity between the artificial and the natural.

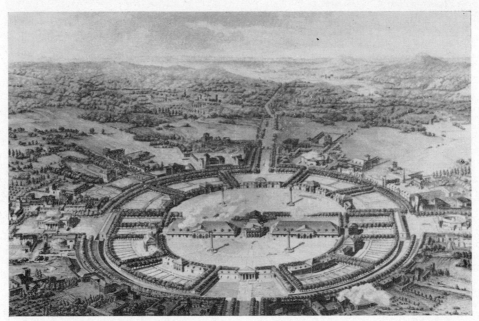

167. C. N. LEDOUX *Plan of the City of Chaux*

The city of Chaux was planned as an industrial city by Claude Nicolas Ledoux. Although only parts of it were built, it stands as the first of its kind. Chaux is located at the crossing of two roads. Its shape is eliptical, and its two parallel streets are eliptical also. Twelve short cross streets lead to the eliptical square. The outer street and the connecting streets are planted with continuous rows of trees. The square is surrounded by free-standing buildings, with gardens behind them. Here the workmen live. The factory buildings are placed along the major axis of the eliptical square. Between them are buildings for administration. Some of the connecting streets extend beyond the outside eliptical street, indicating the possible extension of the city. Chaux was planned for a new way of life. It bridges past and present, as it unifies city and country. Ledoux was not trying to make an architectural display; he was intent on satisfying needs. He was, of course, hampered by the architectural concepts of classicism to which he contributed greatly, but he tried to go beyond classicism, to plan an architecture as well as a city, to make this architecture free from the influences of the past, autonomous in its present right.

The works of the Woods and Ledoux brought to its logical conclusion the great accomplishment of the Baroque period, the relating of the city to the landscape, the penetration of the city by the country. Unfortunately, their vision was lost as our industrial age piled together the industrial cities of today, with their inhuman mass concentration and their conglomeration of quantity without quality. Instead of grasping the great heritage of free and open space, our builders adopted all the decorative elements of the city architecture of the past, as though they hoped successfully to camouflage the unbearable ugliness they had created. Growing too fast and too indiscriminately, the modern city became more and more chaotic. City building became a lucrative enterprise, whose entrepreneurs had no other aim but to satisfy the need of the day with no thought of the morrow.
We have a fatal inheritance in our cities. Their inadequacies weigh heavily upon us. Their harmful effects on our physical and social being are all too evident to us today. We can undo this harm only gradually. It may take decades to perform the tasks that must be performed. Yet surely our own age, as the ages that have gone before, will one day find the structure appropriate to its cities, the pattern and form, the architectural expression, and the relation between city and country.

168. INDUSTRIAL SETTLEMENT

III. Planing Problems

The city of our day is unlike all cities of the past. Industry and mechanized transportation have forced change, and misunderstanding of the effects of these new means has permitted cities to expand so abnormally that chaos has resulted. Traffic hazards, noise, air pollution, blight and slums have increased, and danger to human health and life has mounted. It is strange to think that the extraordinary advancement of our technology has all but destroyed the city. Technology itself, however, is not to blame. The real cause of our woe is the failure of the city to keep pace with technological development. The city built for an ancient pedestrian age has failed to adapt itself to the requirements of our motor age. This failure is underlined by countless surveys and statistics on traffic, accidents, overcrowding, slums, housing, disease, crime. But the city seems still unable to reverse its disastrous course.

Traffic and parking restrictions, smoke abatement, slum clearance, and other strongly urged reform measures are palliatives only. They can never solve the problem that faces us. This problem concerns the total city. Its solution requires the rearrangement of the city's constituent parts, and the relating of these parts to each other properly. It requires the integration of the city with its environs.

The street and block system on which our cities are built is as old as recorded history and probably even older. The function of this system has been the same all through time: it serves to group houses together in blocks and to connect them to each other and to other parts of the city by a street system. This system functioned relatively well until the coming of the motor vehicle made it out of date and dangerous. The speeding automobile requires that we replace this antiquated plan by one which eliminates, insofar as possible, the death-trap intersection.

This implies that we need to replace the archaic block or gridiron system with a new city element, a new settlement unit. The structure of such a unit should be such as to permit a general solution of all the different parts of the city and their relation to each other. It should permit free and unhindered urban growth. It should provide a framework for healthy community life.

Residential, working, and recreation areas are the main elements of any city. The problem is to develop each area according to its function, give each its proper place, and so relate it to other areas and to the whole that no area exerts an adverse influence on any other area. If these conditions are met, the result will be a well functioning unit, in which related areas are within walking distance of each other and the need for mechanical local transportation is decreased or eliminated.

The unit we propose fulfills those requirements and contains within itself all the essentials of a small community. Its size would be determined by walking distances which would nowhere exceed fifteen to twenty minutes. The number of people living within such a unit would be determined by the number of people working in offices and factories which are part of the unit. Density would vary accordingly.

Other factors also will exert a determining influence on its size. As each unit would contain all the essentials of a community, its population should be large enough to meet the social and personal requirements of the individual, large enough to offer variety in work and in life, large enough to support necessary communal, cultural, and hygienic institutions. But it should also be small enough to preserve an organic community life, so that democracy might prevail and each individual participate in community activities.

In such a settlement unit, the industrial area should be placed on one side of the transportation line. On the other side of this line would be arranged, first, buildings for commerce and administration located within a green belt, and then, beyond them, the various types of houses of the residential area. The residential area would be surrounded by a park, its natural recreation area, accessible without crossing streets. Schools and public buildings would be located in this park. Thus the settlement would become part of the landscape, and an organic relation would be established between city and country.

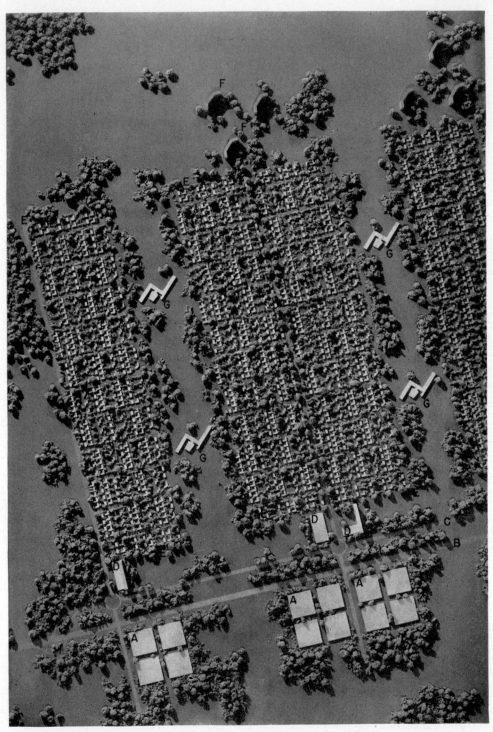

169. SETTLEMENT UNIT *A. Industry, B. Main Traffic Line,*
C. Local Highways, D. Commerce and Administration, E. Residential area,
F. Apartment buildings, G. Schools.

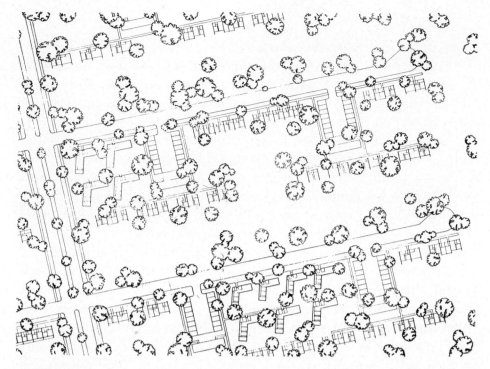

170. UNIT DETAIL

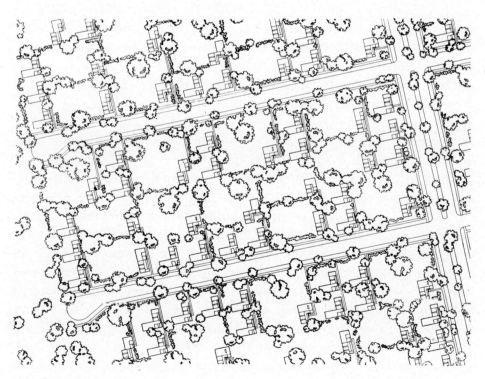

171. UNIT DETAIL

Theoretically, the shape of this unit would be a rectangle of such proportion that it would reduce to a minimum the amount of street area required. Functional organization of the street system would bring about differentiation of traffic routes. There would be residential lanes for pedestrians *only*. There would be main highways for automobiles *only*. The lanes would connect the houses with streets leading to the central streets of the unit. Those central streets would lead to the local highway and to the working area. The local highway would connect units with each other, and it would also, at convenient points, give access to the main highway. All streets within a unit would be closed-end streets; there would be no through traffic within the residential area.

The working and residential areas in each unit would be so placed that people could walk to and from their work. The question is always asked: Suppose a man chooses to live at a distance from his work? Suppose that he wants to visit friends who live outside his own unit? Obviously, such a man should be free to follow his own inclinations. Obviously also, following them would involve use of transportation facilities. But he would use such facilities under greatly improved conditions. The residents of any community within a ribbon settlement would be, so far as time is concerned, no farther away from those of other communities than the suburbanite of today is from the sprawling metropolis.

The buildings within the unit would be varied. There would be single family homes and apartment houses. To secure the proper orientation for these dwellings, the units themselves could be arranged at the proper angle; or the streets within the unit could be so arranged; or, better still, the lanes leading from the houses to the streets. Garages could be of three kinds: community, group, or individual. In the latter case, pedestrian walks which did not cross those provided for motor traffic would be needed to give safe access to the surrounding park with its schools for the children.

Such a settlement unit would meet any requirement that might arise; it would be appropriate for any settlement of any size or type or topography. It would provide maximum flexibility within itself and maximum variation in its combination with other units. No matter how many units were combined, the favorable conditions within each unit would remain unchanged. All the problems involved in the planning of settlements could be solved. A perfect solution for the problems of the motorist would be accompanied by a safe solution for the pedestrian. A framework for community life would be established. Schools could gain new significance as they became small community centers, their auditoriums available for meetings, concerts, plays; their libraries offering books for adults as well as school children; their large halls providing space for exhibitions.

172. SCHOOL

If a number of these units were combined in a row along a traffic artery, a ribbon-formed settlement would result, in which the residential areas would lie on one side of the traffic line, the industrial areas on the other. Such an arrangement would make possible free industrial development because the industries would have room to expand if they needed to do so. If this need did not arise, there might be two rows of settlements along the main traffic line.

Some industries use part-time as well as full-time workers. Part-time workers might be enabled to supplement their income by agriculture or horticulture on land made available for that purpose. Full-time workers might also have vegetable gardens, placed within the park area or, much better, connected with their own house lots. The latter arrangement would,

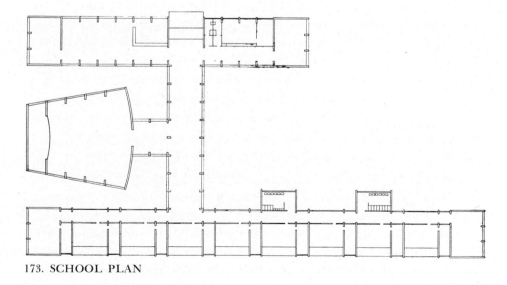

173. SCHOOL PLAN

174. ROWS OF UNITS

of course, tend to reduce density, a result often very desirable. In our study which deals with this problem, we have suggested that there be regular units of lower density, with vegetable gardens attached to the houses, and, across and along the highway, the commercial buildings and factories and also units of still another kind. These would contain houses with small farms attached. They would give the part-time worker excellent opportunity to supplement his income. The density of such units would, of course, be low.

Countless complaints have been voiced about industrial air pollution and its ill effects on health and on property values. Doctors proclaim that it is as great a crime to pour poison into a man's lungs as it is to pour poison into his coffee. And yet many industries are, by nature and necessity, air polluting. The smoke, soot, gas, smell, and noise which emanate from them are not easily controlled.

Could anything be done to eliminate such pollution? There are two answers to that question, two methods urged as the solution. One uses techno-chemical devices; the other is planning. Both natural and artificial methods, well handled, can achieve results. The artificial methods, however, are very expensive and seldom wholly adequate. The machinery required is costly to install and to maintain. The only truly efficient remedy is planning—the use of natural means to combat the evils of industrial air pollution. It may, of course, be advisable sometimes to combine with planning some use of the techno-chemical means. Certainly the possibilities and limitations of these means should be studied and fully understood.

The only completely satisfactory method of mechanical smoke abatement would be to replace coal with electricity for power and for heating. Anything short of this is too often, in spite of the large claims made by advocates of techno-chemical devices, amelioration mostly for the eyes rather than the lungs and nose! Even full electrification would not get rid of industrial nuisances other than smoke and soot. Gases and smells and noise would remain. Only planning can provide a solution which includes these in its scope.

The key to this solution is planning's goal: so to develop and relate the different parts of a settlement to each other and to the whole that each part fulfills its own function without impairing that of others. Study of prevailing wind patterns shows the manner in which residential areas may be protected from the air pollution of industrial areas.

The distribution of the air pollution caused by industry can be presented in a diagram. The accompanying diagrams show how the sector of pollution is more or less extended within a circle. A residential area placed in the sector free from air pollution will, obviously, escape its influence. Different wind conditions result in different patterns. The patterns differ in different parts of the country. Our diagrams must, therefore, be worked out for each geographical location.

The extent of the polluted area depends on the kind of industry as well as on the direction and velocity of the winds. These factors must also be taken into consideration. It is known, for instance, that the smell of

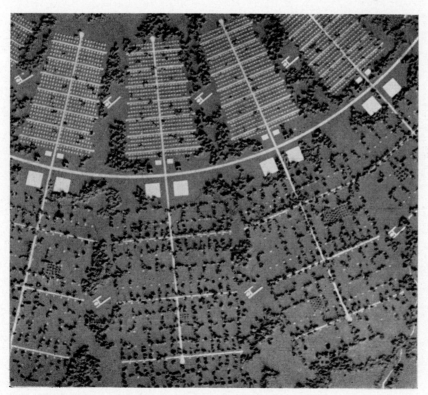

175. ROWS OF UNITS *Adjoined by Units With Small Farms*

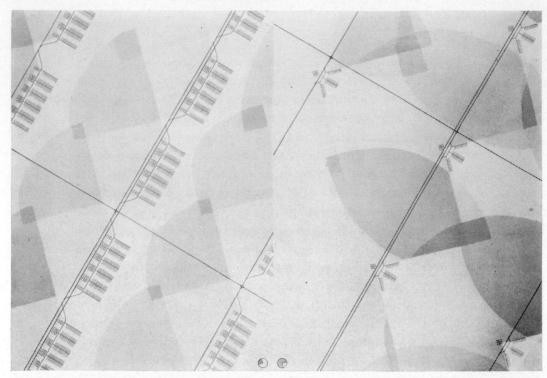

176. INFLUENCE OF WINDS ON AIR POLLUTION *and the Shape of Settlements*

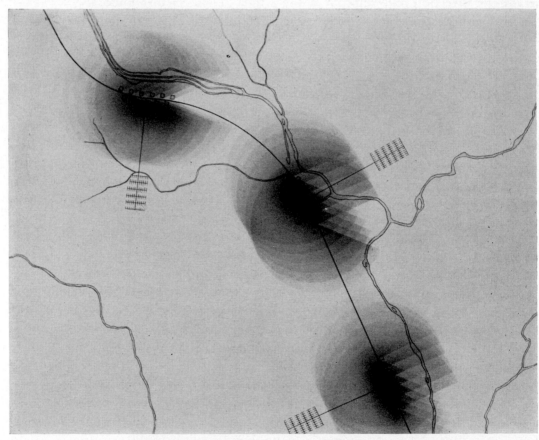

177. INTEGRATED INDUSTRIES *Wind Conditions Necessitate a Separation of the residential from the Industrial Areas.*

chocolate factories may carry for several miles; stockyards odors are perceptible for distances up to ten miles.

When prevailing winds are so distributed that the section of pollution does not exceed half a circle, a ribbon like settlement is possible. If it does, wind shadow, however, covers more than half a circle, as in our second diagram, only fanshaped settlements can be formed, separated from each other by the extension of the polluted area.

These two wind diagrams show extreme cases. Between them there can be many variations. But no matter how far the polluted area may extend, a satisfactory solution can always be found, and our settlement unit can

178. COMMERCIAL AREA

be used, although its rectangular shape may have to be modified according to wind patterns as well as geographical and topographical conditions.

Integrated industries, by their very nature, need a greater number of workers than other industries. If the pevailing winds are favorable, the residential areas for workers in such industries can be placed within walking distance of the industrial area. If, however, the prevailing winds do not permit this, we must remove the residential area beyond the area of air pollution. This would mean connecting industrial and residential areas by some mechanical means of transportation. Integrated industries need not, however, form an uninterrupted ribbon. They could, if their character permits, be placed in groups of limited area. One result of such dispersal would be greater protection against air attack.

The units themselves and the rows of units, single or double, would contain everything a small community needs. Large cities and metropolises, however, have their own more complex requirements. They must have, for example, special commercial areas to serve their own needs and those of the surrounding countryside. Such commercial areas might vary greatly in their contents. They could be placed, like the industrial settlements, on one side of the main traffic route, or on both sides of it. If they are two-sided, there might be a railroad in the center, supplemented by highways on either side, to which local highways could be joined. Commercial buildings, offices and stores would then be placed along the local highways, accessible from one side to cars and trucks, and from the other, the residential, side to pedestrians. Parking space could be provided by parking lots or by garages under the commercial buildings. People coming into the area on foot could shop at their leisure, undisturbed by traffic. The residential area adjoining this commercial center would house the people who work in that center.

The lay-out of industrial and commercial areas depends on special requirements which vary with each individual case. For a residential area, however, certain facts are constant. These have to do mainly with population density, and with the effect of sunlight and its penetration into living rooms.

Population density is both a social and a hygienic problem. It is a social problem insofar as it determines the type of building erected and the life of people who occupy those buildings. It is a hygienic problem insofar as it affects the health of people by controlling the amount of space, light, and air available in each housing unit.

The main consideration in building our cities, up to our time, has been exploitation of land. We have had little regard for the social and hygienic needs of the people who must live in those cities. The one-family house, always recognized as the ideal form of family dwelling has, therefore, been rejected in favor of constructions promising greater return on land investment. Feeble attempts to cope with the evils of too great population density have been made through zoning laws, but these laws have been wholly inadequate. They have not prevented, indeed, they could not prevent, the increase of population densities in all our large cities to such an extent that social and hygienic requirements are completely forgotten.

All cities have within them wide variations in population density. There are over-populated sections, where the density is often so high as to cause the social, moral, and physical diseases whose alleviation is one of the greatest problems of our time. There are also sparsely settled sections in the same cities, where density decreases sharply, where houses are

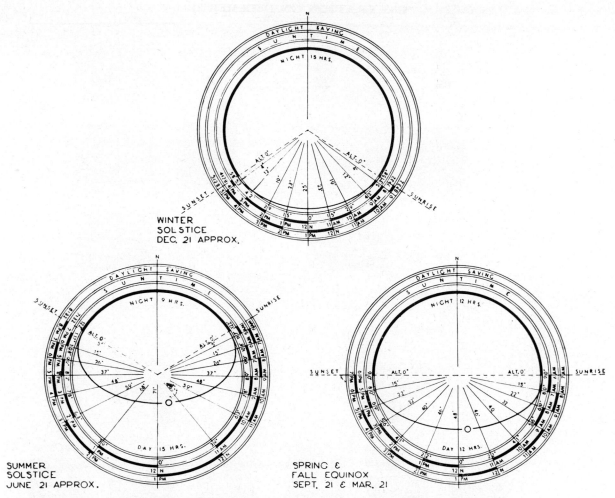

179. SUN CHARTS INDICATING THE ALTITUDE AND AZIMUTH ANGLES FOR LATITUDE 42°
Winter and summer solstice December 21 and June 21. Spring and Fall Equinox March 21 and September 21. Approximately one degree of the altitude angles must be substacted for each degree in more northerly latitudes, and added for more southerly ones.

built farther and farther apart until the city loses its urban character and gradually assumes the aspect of open country.

How great a degree of density is consonant with good city planning? In what ways does population density dictate the structures and arrangements suitable for a good settlement plan? What factors related to density must we keep in mind as we plan?

In other studies*, we have dealt thoroughly with the problems of orientation and density and their inter-action. Here we shall make only some general and supplementary observations.

---

* Raumdurchsonnung, Raumdurchsonnung und Siedlungsdichtigkeit. Moderne Bauformen, Stuttgart. 1935 & 1936. The New City, Chicago, 1944

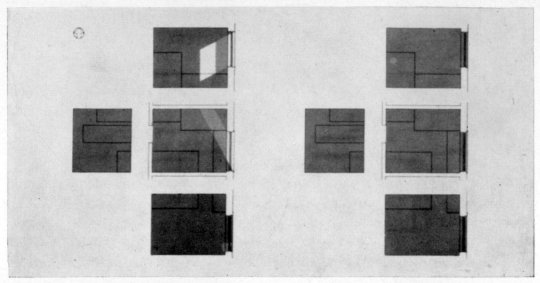

180. EAST EXPOSURE *10 A.M.—12 Noon*

181. SOUTH EXPOSURE 10 *A.M.—12 Noon*
on December 21 with South Exposure the sun in a room is at a maximum,
with East Exposure at a minimum.

Three diagrams with their respective apartment plans demonstrate the effect of orientation on density, relating orientation, hours of sun penetration, and number of stories. By an east-west orientation, four hours of sunshine may be attained with lower density than by a south or south-east orientation. For three hours it is nearly equal for all orientations. If, however, we reduce the duration of sunshine to one or two hours, the east-west orientation seems to be more advantageous than south or south-east orientation. This assumption is however erroneous. At four hours of sun penetration on December 21st, which is the criterion, the

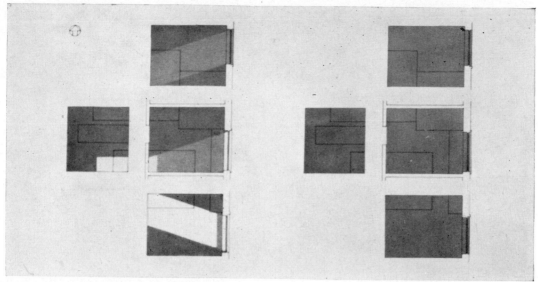

182. EAST EXPOSURE *6 A.M.—12 Noon*

183. SOUTH EXPOSURE *9 A.M.—12 Noon*
On June 21, with South Exposure the sun in a room is at a minimum, with East Exposure at a Maximum.

density would be, for the east-west orientation, less than half that for the south or southwest orientation. The amount of sun penetration into rooms oriented toward the east-west would, in spite of decreasing density, still be less than for those with south or southeast orientation, because the sun strikes the building at a flatter angle and the façade rather than the rooms gets the benefit of the sunshine.

To gain the maximum benefit of sunshine, its penetration into rooms must be determined at critical hours and at each season of the year. Sunlight is available at a low angle and for a minimum time (approx-

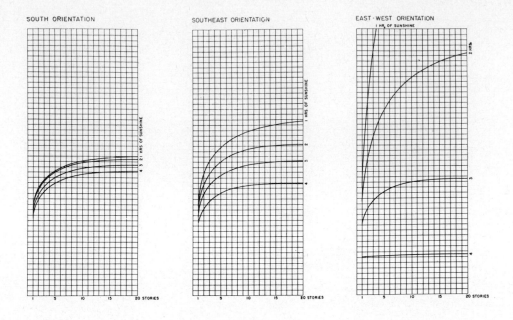

SOUTH ORIENTATION   SOUTHEAST ORIENTATION   EAST-WEST ORIENTATION

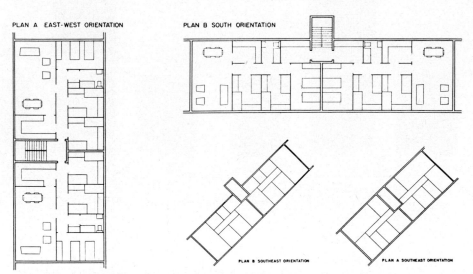

PLAN A EAST-WEST ORIENTATION   PLAN B SOUTH ORIENTATION

PLAN B SOUTHEAST ORIENTATION   PLAN A SOUTHEAST ORIENTATION

184. THREE DENSITY DIAGRAMS *their respective apartment plans Demonstrating the Effect of Orientation*

imately four hours) on December 21st. At the summer solstice it reaches its greatest duration; the sun is very low at sunrise in the northeast and at sunset in the northwest and has a very high angle at noon. All major rooms should, therefore, be oriented in a southerly direction to secure a maximum penetration of sun in the winter and a minimum penetration

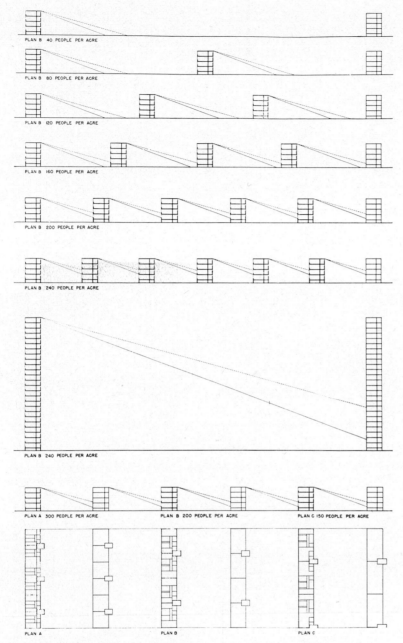

185. APARTMENT BUILDINGS *with different Plans
and their Effect on Density*

in the summer. Bedrooms might be oriented toward the south or south-east, which would be equivalent to a southern exposure. Living rooms could be oriented southeast or southwest, preferably both. This is possible in every free-standing house. Bedrooms might face east. No room, how-ever, should face west.

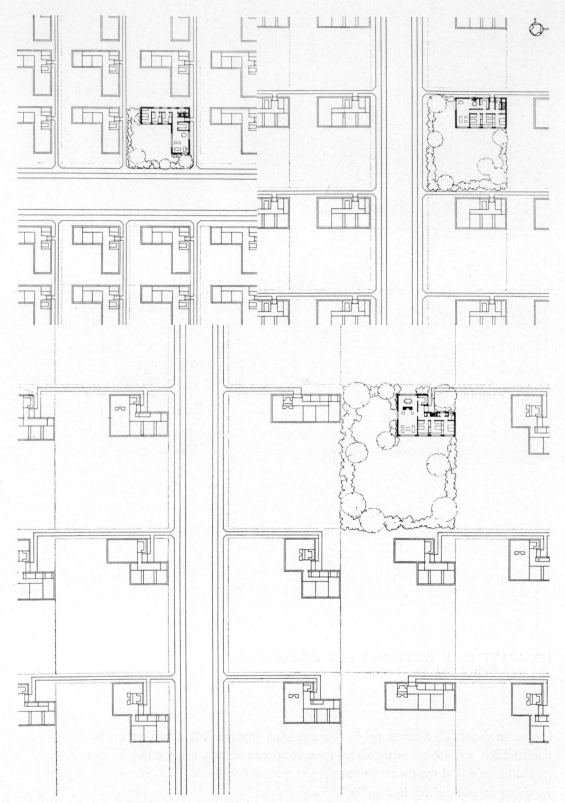

186. EFFECT OF DIFFERENT DENSITIES *on the Plans of Houses*

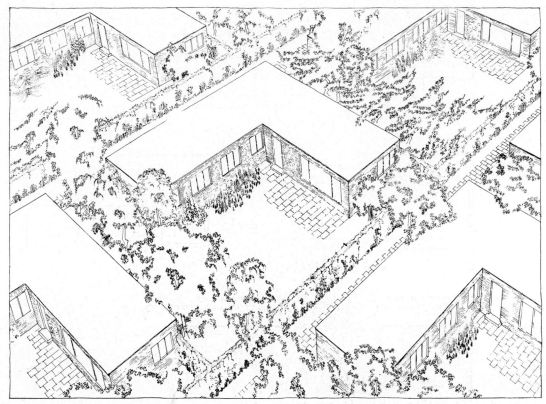

187. L-SHAPED HOUSES

To achieve satisfactory conditions in housing developments is a problem
of zoning. If we want to achieve certain social and hygienic ends in connection with population density, we must strive to influence the factors
on which density depends. Building and zoning laws are means to these
ends, but such laws, up to now, have served merely to prevent the worst
abuses of buildings. They have given no constructive aid to real solutions.

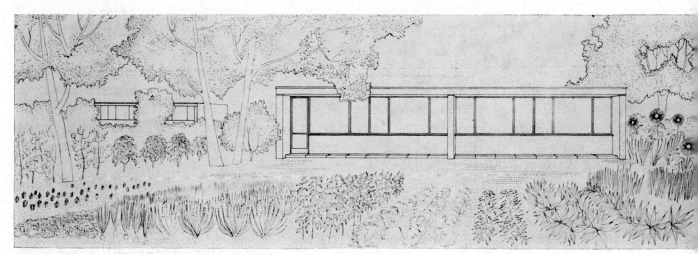

188. HOUSES WITH VEGETABLE GARDENS

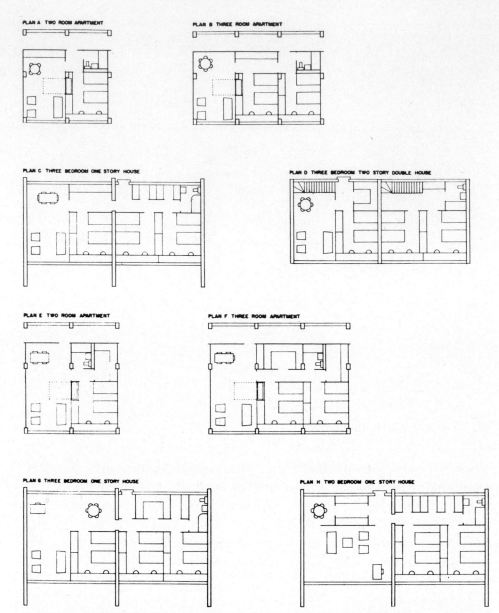

189. DIFFERENT TYPES OF APARTMENT AND HOUSE PLANS

We shall have to establish certain minimum requirements if we are to have adequate buildings. One must be that dwellings be so insolated that the precious winter sun is utilized to its fullest extent. There should be laws also limiting population density. In southern latitudes, where relatively higher densities are possible with sufficient insolation period, special laws limiting density would be required.

Far-reaching improvements can be achieved by laws based on such minimum requirements. They can encourage the erection of dwellings suited to the needs of people. No matter whether we planned a one-story building or a multi-story one, the building would have to obey the laws. But we would have, within these restrictions, very great freedom.

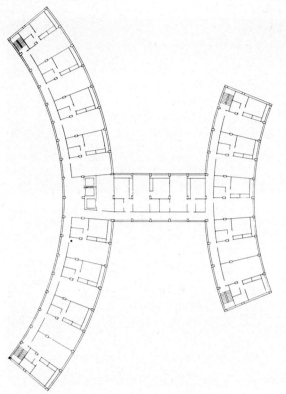

190. PLANS OF CURVED APARTMENT BUILDINGS

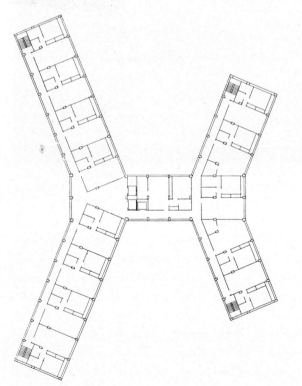

191. PLANS OF BENT APARTMENT BUILDINGS

192. STUDIES OF ARCHITECTURAL VARIATIONS
by Maintaining the same Density

Multi-story buildings do not have to be rectangular in shape. They can be greatly varied and still fulfill the requirements of the desired orientation. The curved or bent apartments illustrated here are not expressions of some fancy whim. They are rather practical results of structural considerations. If apartments located along a corridor are to receive direct sunshine and have cross ventilation, there can be only one row of apartments. The depth of the building is, therefore, restricted, and a limit is set also on the number of floors which can be safely constructed. In a curved or bent building, the possible number of floors is increased, be-

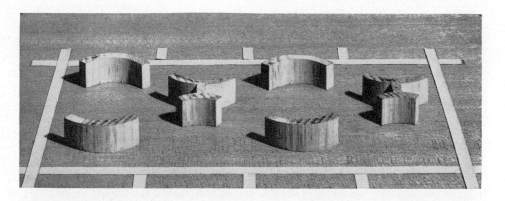

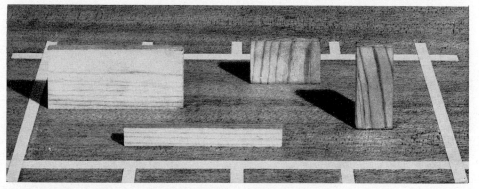

193. STUDIES OF ARCHITECTURAL VARIATIONS
by Maintaining the Density

cause the bending or curving gives the structure greater stability. Such buildings possess still another advantage. Each apartment in them has a free and unrestricted view, impossible to provide in rectangular buildings running parallel to each other.

To show how high density as well as orientation may affect a settlement's architectural character, we have taken four city blocks and developed on them six different studies. All have the same density: one hundred people on an acre. All contain the same number of apartments. It would seem

213

unavoidable that tne restrictions of orientation would result in monotony. However, as we shall see, there is, within these limitations, freedom to plan with flexibility and variety.

The first study, with its six south-oriented parallel rows of two-storied apartment houses, is without doubt very monotonous. The second, which doubles the height of the buildings and thus can double the distance between the rows is, in spite of this, monotonous also.

The third study is quite different in scope. Here all apartments have been concentrated in two multi-story buildings. The apartments are oriented toward the south, the south southwest, and the south southeast. Their concentration results in a maximum of open space, giving the plan an openness in striking contrast to the narrowness of the first two studies.

The fifth study makes this openness far more effective by contrasting it with narrowness. Here the number of apartments in the tall buildings has been decreased and the height of those buildings reduced. And there have been added rows of two-storied apartment buildings. A double contrast results: One created by the differing heights of the buildings, the other by variations in spacing. The large open space in connection with the higher buildings is now in contrast to the less open space between the rows of lower buildings.

The fourth study uses only tall buildings of varied shape, with apartment orientation toward the south, the south southeast, or the south southwest. Here again is a double contrast: a contrast between the buildings, and a contrast of space shapes.

The final study, in opposition to this formal, almost ornamental, solution, is very informal. Here buildings of varied height and length are placed with reference to the shadow areas behind the buildings. The proper insolation is everywhere secured. Such a scheme results in a very free arrangement of buildings, and opens possibilities for wide variation.

Two of these studies, the fifth and the sixth, reveal extraordinary potentialities. With their buildings of differing sizes and heights, they overcome the monotony which seemed unavoidably connected with the requirements of orientation. They create architectural contrasts and a feeling of spaciousness. The fifth study, however, does even more. When we apply its underlying principle to a larger area, we begin to glimpse the possibility of achieving a new human environment. If we reduce the density by replacing the two-storied apartment buildings with single family homes, we arrive at a solution which provides spaciousness, and provides privacy as well. Here are single homes with gardens for families with children; here are apartment houses with their free view over those gardens for single people or childless couples. This mixed type of settlement truly meets human needs. It offers man perfect freedom to choose the

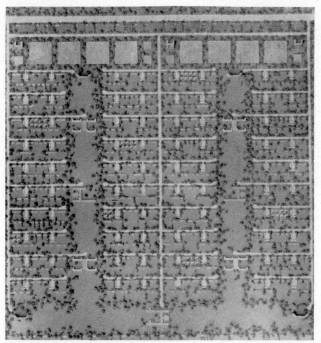

194. SMALL COMMUNITY

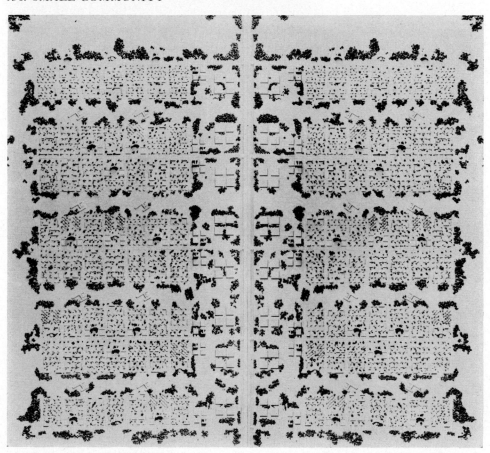

195. LARGER COMMUNITY

kind of dwelling he prefers. This may well foreshadow the community of the future.

The mixing of different kinds of building also has great architectural value. In the building groups and settlements here illustrated, the contrasting effect of buildings varying in size and height, in shape and function, in their relation to each other and to the enclosed or open space around them, presents new architectural possibilities. In spite of restrictions of orientation and density, great variability of architectural composition becomes possible.

The settlement units we propose and their various derivations can be combined into communities and into city aggregates. Each unit in itself contains the essentials of a small community. A combination of units would create a more complex community. A city aggregation, combining all the elements developed, would be a diversified city. It would have its special commercial area, and the administrative, educational, and cultural institutions which would meet its special requirements.

All communities include a working area which, as in the unit, provides space for industry and commerce and also for parking. Such communities might consist of any number of units. They would not be mere rows of units, but would be limited in size, affording opportunity, however, for the addition of new units as need arose. If the industries of such a community were not air polluting, the industrial units could be located on either side of the highway.

If, however, the industries of the community were air-polluting, they would have to be removed and placed as suggested in the wind diagram studies. To the fan-shaped communities thus formed could be added other non-air-polluting industries, with their residential units arranged in many variations.

City aggregates could be developed in endless variety. We will describe here two variants only: a somewhat formal one in which everything is more or less fixed; and one flexible enough to make possible any desired change.

The one aggregate used in ill. 239 shows the arrangement of the different areas. On one side of the main traffic line are the air-polluting industries. On its other side are, first, the commercial area, and then, beyond, a row of units with non-extendable industries, and still farther, a row of extendable industries. The areas are all connected with each other as well as with the main traffic line which connects the city aggregates. These aggregates could be at any distance from each other. They might be adjoined or surrounded by small farms, which would make possible the integration of industry and agriculture. Workshops could be provided for the people

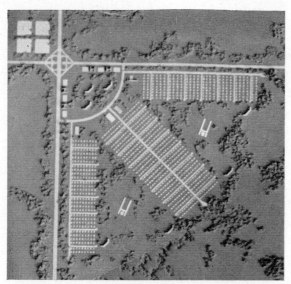

196. SMALL, FAN-SHAPED COMMUNITY

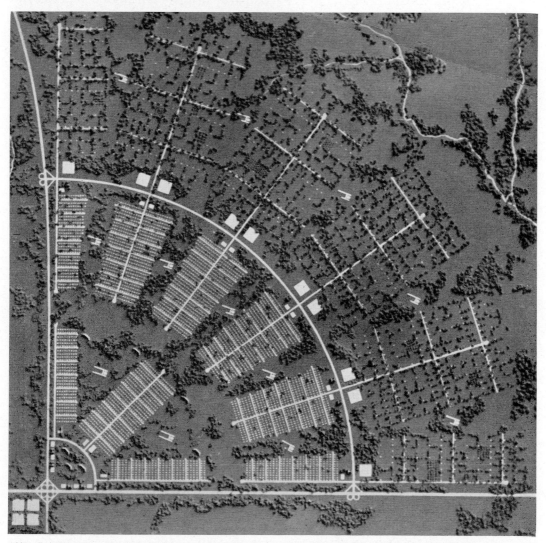

197. LARGER FAN-SHAPED COMMUNITY *with Air Polluting and Related Industries*

living on these small farms, or they could work part-time in one of the industries of the city aggregate.

The second city aggregate used in ill. 240 seems to be more flexible and, therefore, more useful. Each of its parts can easily be extended: industrial parts by the addition of new units; the commercial part by the doubling of its row. The second commercial row might become an administrative or cultural center. The various working areas are here so located that they are directly accessible from the areas of the small farms where part-time industrial workers live. Such a city aggregate would possess all that is necessary in a city. It would have the added advantage of decentralization.

Rural areas as well as industrial cities have unemployment problems. As more and more farms increase in size, become specialized and mechanized, the family-sized farm is in jeopardy because it cannot compete with the great farm operated on an industrial basis. On the large farms much of the seasonal work is done by migratory workers. New problems arise and these problems must be solved if agricultural production is to be stabilized and life continue to be good for the people who live on the farm.

As ruralization of the city would help to solve some of the city's problems, so also urbanization of the country may well be an answer to some of the country's problems.

In any region there are usually several types of farm: the large farm producing staple food; the subsistence farm supporting a single family; the small farm supplementing the livelihood of part-time industrial or migratory workers. Workshops and small factories might be connected with the small farms of the last two types; they would increase the opportunity for adequate earnings.

The decentralized city aims to supplement industrial with agricultural work. Rural planning aims to supplement agricultural with industrial work. In both cases, greater satisfaction and more stabilized living conditions for all workers would result.

The planning elements we have been discussing are only abstractions. We have kept them abstract in order to demonstrate their underlying principles, and to keep them flexible and adaptable in their various combinations in communities and city aggregates. In reality, these elements will always be subject to modification by special natural features, by topography, and by soil conditions.

Let us now consider, with the use of the accompanying illustrations, the architectural possibilities of these structural elements. These possibilities are unlimited in their variety.

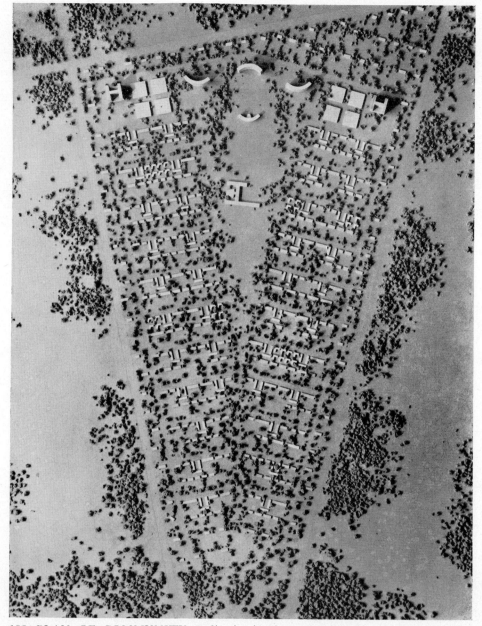

198. PLAN OF COMMUNITY *Indicating its three dimensional appearance*

The plan of a city is the horizontal projection of its three-dimensional reality. Both are aspects of the city. Both must be kept constantly in mind if we are to achieve the ends we seek.

The usual city plan, quite naturally, does not go into much detail. It deals mainly with the location of various city areas, their connection with each other and with the city as a whole by a traffic system. The planner must, however, always have some conception of how his plan will eventually appear in its three-dimensional reality. Our settlement unit and its various derivations simplify, not only the structure of the city, but also its archi-

199. PARK BETWEEN SETTLEMENT UNITS *with Community and Apartment Buildings*

tectural problems. Because these units are limited in size, they can easily be comprehended and conceived in their architectural entirety by any planner with imagination.

It is both structurally and architecturally important where what is located. Unless this fact is understood, the result can only be optical disorder. Only where everything is considered both structurally and architecturally is an optical order attainable. City architecture is, however, not to be regarded as something superimposed on the city. It should grow out of the nature

200. COMMUNITY AROUND A LAKE *View*

of things. Only then will a free development be possible, in which every part has its proper place according to function and importance, and all parts together form a coherent ordered whole.

The space concept of our age tends toward openness and breadth. The mixed type of building we have proposed provides means for the realization of this space concept. The single-family house, most desirable for a family with children, should be unpretentious, built on one level, located in a garden, and hidden by shrubs and trees. Community buildings and apartment buildings will gain importance through contrast to these homes.

201. FAN-SHAPED COMMUNITY *View*

Apartment buildings, tall, free-standing, spaced so that they do not interfere with each other but assure a free view from each apartment, could become important architectural elements.

Two illustrations show how this might be done. One shows uniform apartment buildings dispersed over the residential area. The other shows buildings similarly dispersed, but these buildings differ in size, shape, and height, and thus present a quite different architectural appearance. Those apartment buildings might be combined into groups and located in parks adjacent to or surrounding the settlement units. Because there are relatively few of them, the tall buildings, whether dispersed or grouped, will gain optical and architectural significance and will emphasize the feeling of openness and breadth. People living in the single-family houses would have their own gardens; people living in the tall apartments would be able to enjoy the view over these gardens, a view extending out over the parks to the landscape beyond with its fields, pastures, and forests, its hills, rivers, and lakes.

Buildings for other than residential use can also contribute to the open-

202. UNIFORM APARTMENT BUILDINGS *dispersed within a Residential Area*

ing up of the city. Two variations of groups of dormitories, fraternities, and apartment buildings planned for the Illinois Institute of Technology show how this can be done. These buildings, differing in size, shape, and height, are planned for a densely built area. Their arrangement demonstrates that, even under such adverse conditions, spatial aims can be realized.

The buildings for the Illinois Institute of Technology are relatively close together. In contrast, the project for the University of Berlin is less dense, more open, and more diversified. The University is located within a wooded area at the western outskirts of the city. North of the highway leading into the city, are the departments of liberal arts, humanities, and natural sciences. South of the highway, are the medical school with its hospitals and the institute of technology. The prevailing three-storied classroom buildings contrast with lower buildings planned as auditoriums, libraries, laboratories, and with the covered walks which connect the buildings of each group and form open courts. High above these buildings tower the dormitories, placed in front of the courts.

The view from the highway bridge reveals the same idea as that underlying the architectural development of our settlement units. Here only

203. DIVERSIFIED APARTMENT BUILDINGS *within a Residential Area*

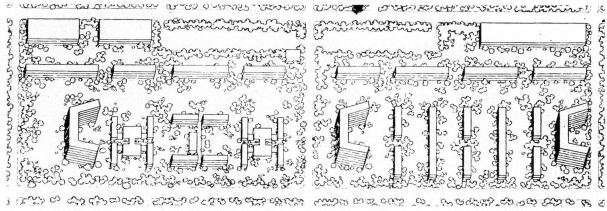

204. FRATERNITY-DORMITORY AND APARTMENT BUILDINGS
Project for Illinois Institute of Technology, Chicago

223

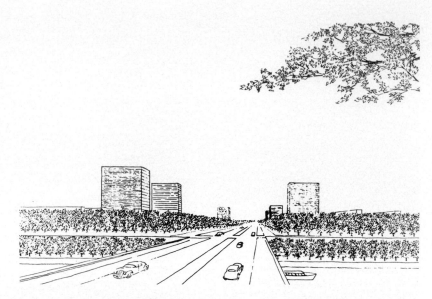

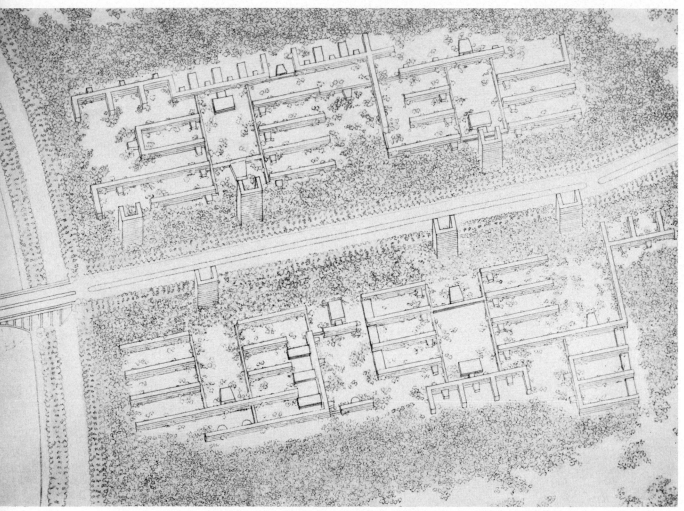

205. PROJECT OF THE UNIVERSITY OF BERLIN

206. PART OF A COMMUNITY *View*

the tall dormitories set back from the highway are visible. Like the tall apartments of our settlement unit, they accentuate the view and give it significance.

We have become more and more concerned with widening and opening the city and merging it, eventually, with the open space of the landscape. We are helped in this endeavor by certain forces tending to dissipate the confinement of the city, to liberate its buildings from the city's narrowness. If we achieve our goal, man will again be linked with nature, to the benefit of his health of body and mind, and to the benefit and health of society as well.

Our cities must be changed. How can we change them? How can we eliminate their defects and so transform them that they meet man's need for health and safety? Could we achieve this end by applying to the existing city the planning principles we have established? Could we, in this way, transform a city into a well-functioning organism? Could we, in so doing, create lasting values?

Those questions, we firmly believe, can all be answered in the affirmative. Studies already made and presented demonstrate the possibility. All that is needed is a comprehensive plan, within which every change, every new thing built, including traffic routes, could be integrated. Each step taken would be an accomplishment in itself, serving the present and pointing the way to the future. Gradually the whole city could be transformed.

To illustrate this process, we shall first apply our planning principles to parts of the city, to discover what might be achieved by such application. Then we shall apply the same principles to the replanning of whole cities. First, let us take a residential area in Chicago. Its layout is determined by the usual grid-iron system, characterized by numberless intersections. Connected with this residential area is a park, its recreation space. Because of the many street intersections, however, it is dangerous for children to go to this park, and even to their schools. This danger could be very simply eliminated by closing some streets and removing others. It would then be possible to reach park and schools without crossing a single traffic street. This could be done at relatively little expense.

If, however, we took one farther step and eliminated a number of blocks, we could extend the park and bring it into closer connection with the residential area. Schools could be located in the new park strips. Safety would everywhere prevail. Such a solution comes very close to our proposed settlement unit. But there would still be this great disadvantage. Since no working areas are related to this neighborhood, its people would have to rely still on mechanical transportation to their daily work.

All cities are today faced with traffic and parking problems which, particularly at the city's center, seem to be insoluble. Some planners have suggested that the automobile be kept entirely out of the city's center, that private drivers be required to park outside the central area and use streetcars and buses to reach that center. This is a solution which meets resistance from the individual driver. Is there another solution?

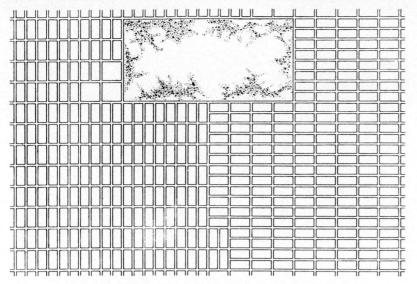

207. **CHICAGO MARQUETTE PARK** *and Two Proposals*

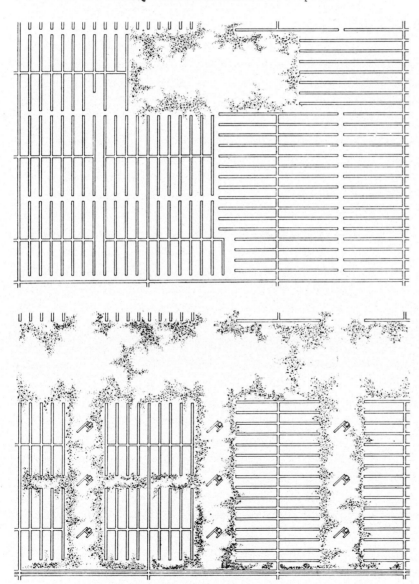

St. Paul illustrates the development of the traffic problem and the destructive effects it can have on a city. St. Paul early established itself as the trading center of a rich agricultural area, where furs and produce of the expanding west were exchanged for manufactured goods from the east. The coming of the railroad made its position more secure. But the coming of the automobile wrought a different kind of change. As traffic increase made it more and more difficult to find space to park within the commercial area, customers began to go elsewhere. Business declined. Land and building values fell. The whole health of the city's economy seemed dependent on the provision of adequate parking space. Could this problem be solved?

One theoretical solution would be to place the commercial center in such a way that it might be entered from two sides. Motorists could approach it on one side, pedestrians on the other, without interfering with each other. Motorists would come from the traffic street, enter the parking space and then go into the buildings where they worked or had business. Pedestrians would enter from the other side without having to cross the traffic street or parking space.

The simplest way to solve the traffic and parking problems of St. Paul would be to surround the commercial area by a parking space large enough to hold all the cars. This parking space would be circled by a traffic street into which all other traffic streets leading to the commercial area would feed. Thus no traffic streets would cross the commercial area.

Such a solution seems very convincing. It has, however, some serious disadvantages along with its obvious advantages. In the first place, the pedestrian entering the commercial area would have to cross the ring-like traffic street and the parking space. In the second place, the commercial area would be forever limited in its size. Any future expansion would be effectively blocked.

These disadvantages would disappear and greater safety would be provided if we placed the traffic street in the middle of the parking space. Cars could then be parked alongside the traffic street in space provided for them. The commercial area would extend along this street. The area could be reached from either side: by cars from one side, by pedestrians from the other.

The functional value of such a solution is evident. It would, at the same time, provide for present need and for future expansion. If the commercial area needed to expand, it could do so towards the northwest or towards the southwest, retaining the same favorable conditions always. Yet even this solution is not without its disadvantages. Since no special residential area is provided for the people working in the commercial center, mechanical means of transportation would still be needed for them.

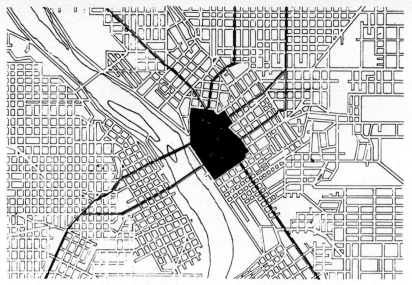

208. ST. PAUL. COMMERCIAL AREA *Two Proposals*

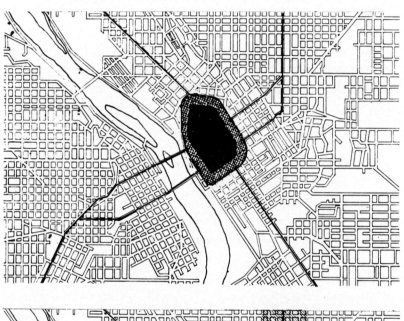

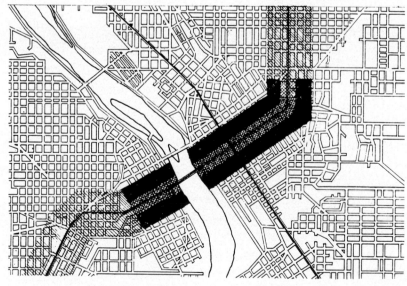

229

Zurich, a Swiss city, planned a national fair during the '30's. Some permanent buildings, as well as the usual temporary ones, were contemplated. The plan we present here, avoids the costly temporary buildings, useful only during the fair, and replaces them with permanent structures which, it was hoped, might become the cultural center of the city. These buildings are placed in a park which stretches along the lake shore. It is not a very large park, but it is increased optically, not only by the lake which opens its vistas, but also by the arrangement of the buildings, not in a wall-like row but with open spaces between them. A feeling of openness results, which is enhanced by the distance between the buildings.

This park, small as it is, is crossed by a traffic street which cuts it into pieces and which introduces an element of serious danger. In the plan which we suggest this traffic street would be removed and placed behind the new buildings. As those buildings attract traffic to themselves, it is logical that the whole area underneath them become a parking space. People could park their cars there and enter the buildings directly from the parking area. The present street behind these buildings would be widened and connected with other traffic streets of the city. The park would thus be free of traffic. Unfortunately, it still could be reached only by the crossing of dangerous traffic streets.

This is, of course, only a general suggestion: it would have to be worked out locally with all its implications and in full detail.

Replanning parts of the city—residential, working, recreational—may achieve good results, but we can never solve the problems of the city as a whole merely by replanning parts of it. Each part of a city should fulfill its own function as perfectly as possible. But all parts must be related to each other so that mechanized transportation requirements are reduced to a minimum. Only when we have taken this into full consideration shall we have replanned a city in a truly satisfactory way.

If we can replan part of a city by closing and taking out streets and by replacing other city elements, why should we not apply the same method to the city as a whole, thus arriving at the same satisfactory solution on a larger scale?

To demonstrate how this could be done, let us consider planning possibilities for several cities: a very small town, a medium-sized city, and two large cities.

The town we have chosen is Elkhorn, Wisconsin, the county seat and market center for the adjoining agricultural area whose fairgrounds are also located here. Elkhorn is quite a nice town. It has no slums, and it has many trees. There is only one thing wrong with it: the highways which pass through the town and cross each other in its commercial area. Once

209. ZURICH, LAKE SHORE DEVELOPMENT *View and Plan*

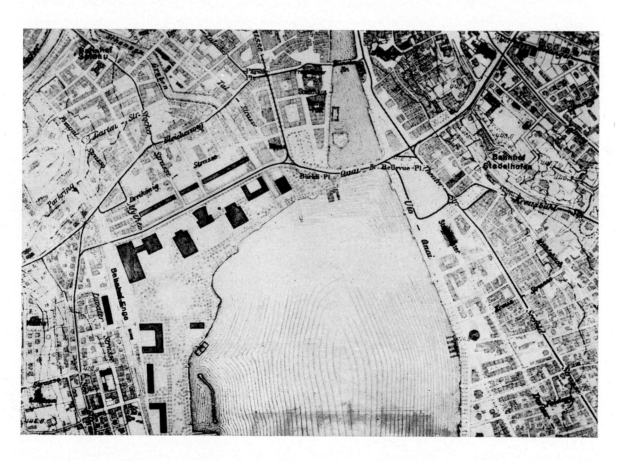

those highways were an advantage to the town; today they are a dangerous nuisance. Plans under way for the rebuilding of these roads provide an opportunity to remove them to the outskirts of the town. Secondary roads could be provided to make these highways still convenient for the people of Elkhorn.

This secondary road connecting with the highway should be so placed as to connect all other residential streets and to make all streets within the town closed-end streets. This could be easily achieved by taking out some of the residential streets and closing the rest of them. There would be no more through traffic, and yet each house in the town could be reached by car.

The industries, now dispersed within the town, could be grouped and placed across the railroad tracks where they belong according to their function.

The small outmoded commercial area needs renovation. Perhaps all these small business establishments could be placed in a single building, similar to a shopping center. Such unification would combine the advantages of the big store and the small store. Shoppers would find everything under one roof, but the small shopkeeper could still have his own business and could have his independence by cooperation. Our plan shows such a building and some other commercial and public buildings between the town and the highway. A parking space for shoppers from out of town might be provided. Such a parking area placed close to the commercial area would relieve the town of all except local traffic, and even local traffic would be reduced to a minimum because every part of the town would be within walking distance of every other part. The town would be surrounded by a park in which schools would be placed. If the community needed to expand it could do so toward the east. All these changes could be brought about gradually. Each step taken would be an improvement in itself and each step would bring a better future nearer. All that is needed is a clear concept of what the town might become, and a firm community will to make that concept reality.

Our medium-sized city is Rockford on the Rock River, the largest industrial settlement created in the development of that river valley.

Originally, the Rock valley was an agricultural area. It was settled by people who came to find land and to cultivate it. There was some home industry, but most manufactured goods were imported from the East in exchange for wheat and lumber. Saw-milling and flour-milling were Rockford's first industries. Both declined rather quickly because the small forests in the valley were soon exhausted and wheat farming gave place to dairying. The production of agricultural implements was the next step in the city's development. The river, not very well suited for transporta-

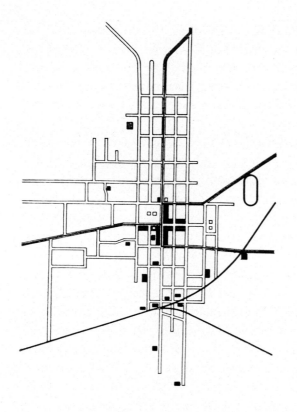

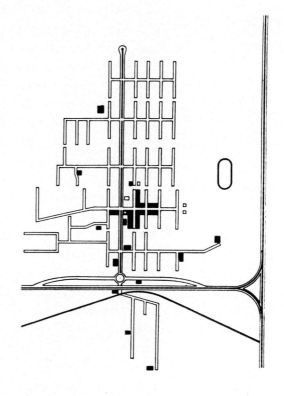

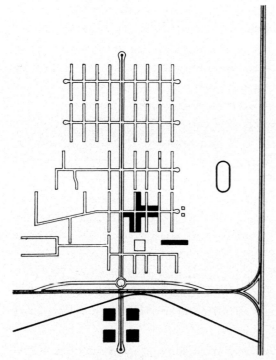

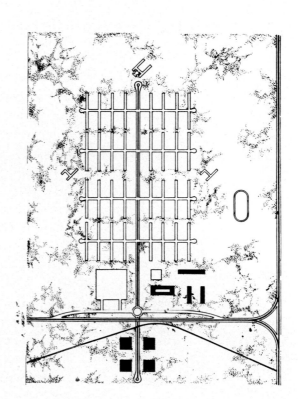

?10. ELKHORN REPLANNED *Different stages*

233

tion, became a source of power. Dams were built. The first extensive development of this water power took place at Rockford, and Rockford became an industrial town. A mill race was built, and the power of the waterwheel transformed directly to a rotating shaft connected to the machinery by power belts. This motive power ran the factories until the application of hydro-electric power.

Rockford's first industries served the local market primarily. Then, with the establishment of its furniture industry, the city began to produce for a distant market, a market becoming nation-wide. Walnut stands in the valley bottom land provided materials for this industry which made Rockford famous. But these trees were soon depleted, and the furniture factories, forced to import raw materials, saw their costs increase. The industry declined, though it did not wholly disappear.

Rockford and its valley have few resources except skilled labor. New industries were introduced to make use of this human resource. Textile and leather working industries were established; a varied and flourishing metal-working industry came into being. Materials for these industries had to be imported from the East: raw material for Rockford's few remaining furnaces; semi-fabricated materials to be manufactured into machines, tools, stoves, hardware, and automotive parts.

Rockford's older industries had been placed in the city, along the river. The newer plants sprang up at the city's outskirts, west, north, and south of the central industries. The southern industrial area, where the factories are adjacent to a railroad belt line, is the most important.

Our proposal for Rockford is that the railroads and highways which cross the city be relocated so that they by-pass it. One railroad and highway would run parallel with the river on the west side. The others would cross the river south of the city. The main station would be placed at the junction; other stations wherever they were needed.

The commercial area would remain at its present site, but it would be modified and given sufficient parking space. The residential areas also would be modified in structure, but not moved from their present position. The main industries would be left, temporarily, in their present position. But, as their buildings became obsolete, they would gradually be relocated along the traffic line running parallel with the river. The air polluting industries would be moved far enough away from the city to prevent their vapors from poisoning the city air. They should be placed along the railroad tracks leading southwest, their exact location being planned according to wind conditions. The industries dependent upon these major plants could be moved to the same area.

The old industrial areas within the city are obsolete. They and the slums should be evacuated. The people now living there should be transferred into a green area which might be extended along the river. This may seem like a bit of luxurious planning. It might, should aerial warfare become reality, prove to be the most practical feature of the whole plan. Rockford is an important industrial city and, therefore, a potential target. To minimize fire hazards during and after an air raid, the city should be open. It should have open spaces between its parts and should extend such spaces as far as possible so that they become effective fire breaks.

The four plans we present here are part of a comprehensive study. They show how the city could change itself gradually. The first plan shows the present street pattern; the second and third two stages of transition; the fourth the possible end state.

Plans two and three demonstrate the way in which the closing and elimination of streets, and eventually blocks, could create fire breaks useful also as a natural recreation area. The simplification of the street system would make it more functional. Through traffic could be completely avoided. And if residential areas were related to their working areas within walking distance, even local traffic would be reduced to a minimum.

The fourth plan shows how decentralization could be achieved with the full use of the existing city, its streets, its buildings, its utilities. Each step toward the accomplishment of such an over-all plan would be worth taking for itself. Each new construction would be placed according to this plan and would contribute to the transformation of the city.

Rockford's industries, producing for a national rather than a local market, are subject to the fluctuations of that national market. Rockford workers, therefore, are faced with periods of unemployment or part-employment. If these workers had vegetable gardens adjacent to their homes, the hardships of those slack periods would be cushioned. This suggests that the density of their residential areas should be as low as possible. Small farms might be provided for those able to handle them. We suggest that such farms be placed on the east side of the traffic line which runs parallel to the river. Workers living on these farms could find part time employment in the near-by industries.

It is in the nature of the proposed plan that all its parts can be extended and new parts added whenever necessary or desirable. Such extension would eventually involve the planning of the whole river valley and all the communities within it. The valley could become an economic unit without the sacrifice of local independence.

A metropolis seems to defy comprehensive replanning. So many factors are involved that it seems as though nothing fundamental could be achieved. But this is not really true. To demonstrate how even a large city could be replanned, let us take Chicago, the metropolis of the Middle West. The rapid growth of this city during its short history is like a symbol

FIRST STAGE

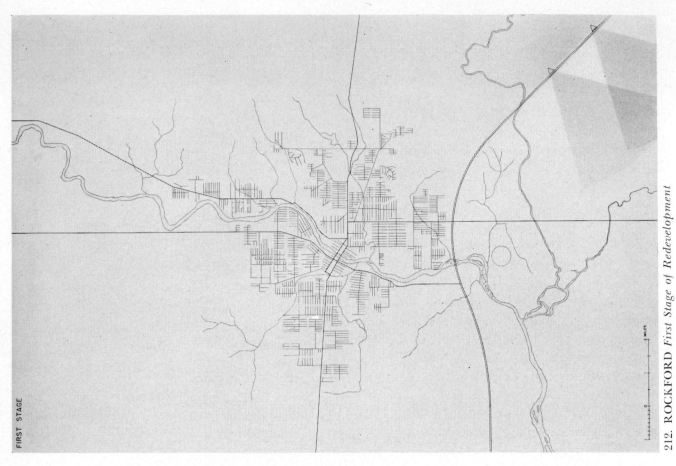

212. ROCKFORD *First Stage of Redevelopment*

½ MILES

EXISTING PLAN

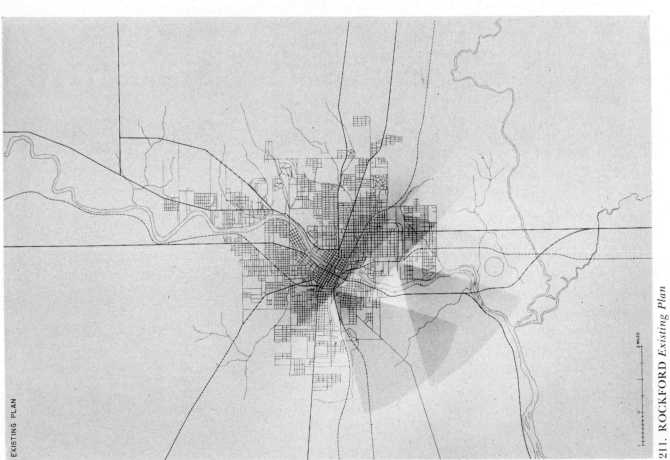

211. ROCKFORD *Existing Plan*

½ MILES

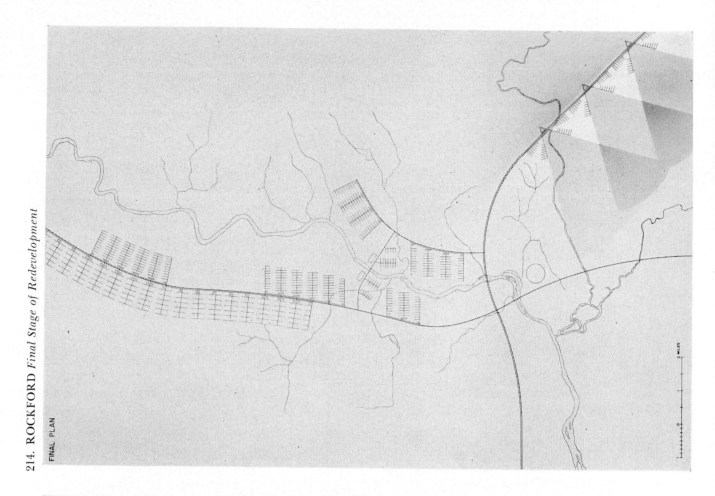

FINAL PLAN

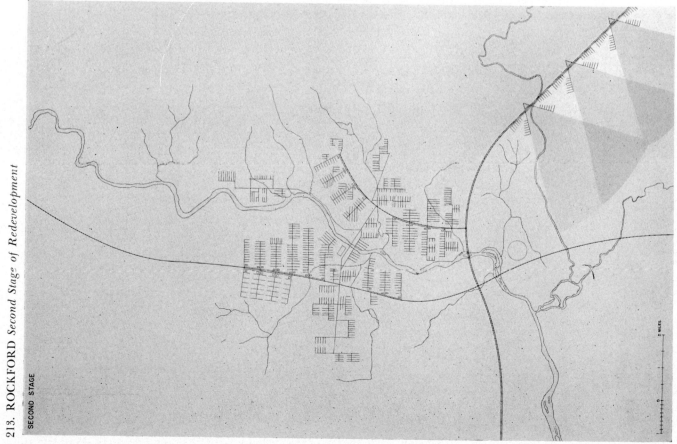

SECOND STAGE

of our industrial age. Chicago expresses fully all the advantages and all the disadvantages of that age.

Fortune favored Chicago's development. Strategically located from its very beginning, the settlement's first function was to be the trade center of its rich agricultural region, exchanging agricultural produce for the manufactured goods coming in from the East. The town was located on a continental waterway, which via the Great Lakes connects Chicago with the East and which, through a canal, the Illinois River and the Mississippi, gives access to the South. It was an ideal position for a trade city which soon began to add its own manufactures to the goods it sold. The coming of the railroad enormously increased the city's trade function.

Chicago lies between the coal of the South and the ore of the North. It was natural, therefore, that heavy industries, using the materials brought together here so easily, should come into being, and that there should also be developed extensive and diversified manufacturing.

As industry developed, Chicago's population grew by leaps and bounds. People from all over the world came to man the new mills and factories. Chicago boosters began to talk of the day when their city would contain forty-two million people within its limits. They even started to zone the city for that day. They were, fortunately, over-optimistic in their forecasts. The population of Chicago seems today to have reached and even passed its peak. It is probable that the population of the city proper is on the decline, though that of the metropolitan area is still increasing.

Let us now consider the physical structure of the city in which this phenomenal growth took place. Did Chicago ever find a pattern adequate to its greatness and suited to its varied functions? This question certainly cannot be answered in the affirmative. The city has grown so rapidly that there has never seemed to be time to consider planning problems and to develop planning principles. To plan at all has seemed impossible.

So Chicago has grown without plan. The gridiron, so useful for parceling new land for sale, has determined its street pattern and has become a guide to chaos. Streets and alleys occupy more than one quarter of Chicago's 212 square miles. What a waste of space! What a peril for people! Since the advent of the automobile, every corner has become a death trap. "The people of Chicago," wrote David H. Burnham* in the introduction to his famous plan for Chicago in 1909, "have ceased to be impressed by the rapid growth or the great size of the city. What they insist upon asking now is, How are we living? Are we in reality prosperous? Is the city a convenient place for business? Is it a good labor market in the sense that labor is sufficiently comfortable to be efficient and content? Will the com-

---

* Burnham, David H. and Bennet, Edward H.: *Plan of Chicago*. Edited by Charles Moore, Chicago, 1909.

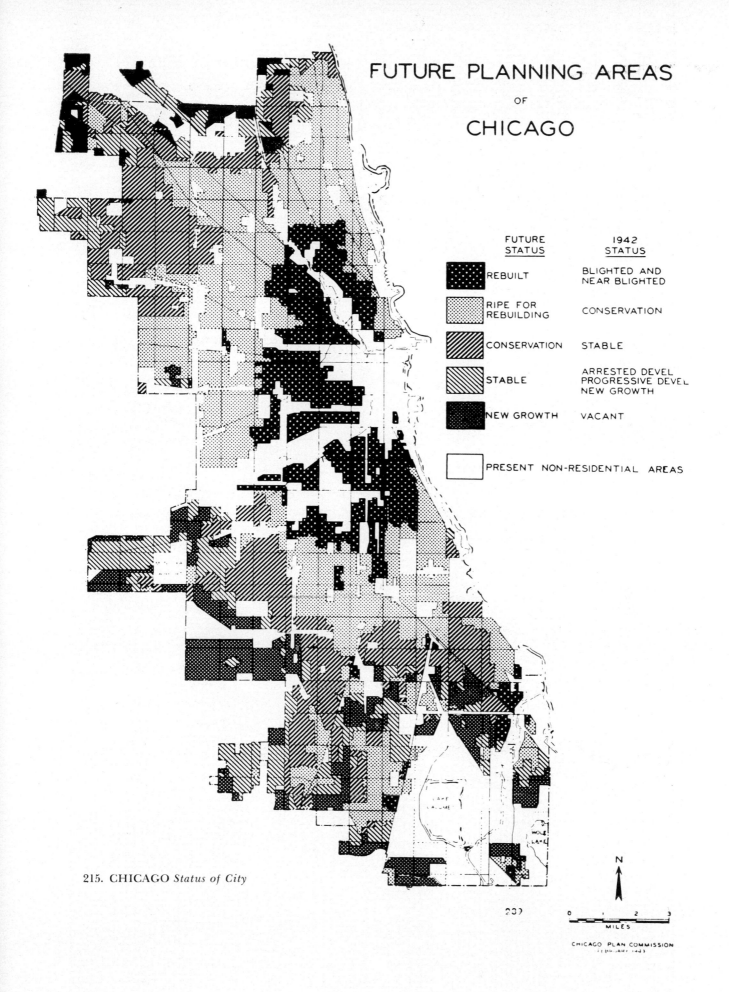

FUTURE PLANNING AREAS
OF
CHICAGO

FUTURE STATUS	1942 STATUS
REBUILT	BLIGHTED AND NEAR BLIGHTED
RIPE FOR REBUILDING	CONSERVATION
CONSERVATION	STABLE
STABLE	ARRESTED DEVEL PROGRESSIVE DEVEL NEW GROWTH
NEW GROWTH	VACANT

PRESENT NON-RESIDENTIAL AREAS

215. CHICAGO *Status of City*

N

0 1 2 3
MILES

CHICAGO PLAN COMMISSION
FEBRUARY 1943

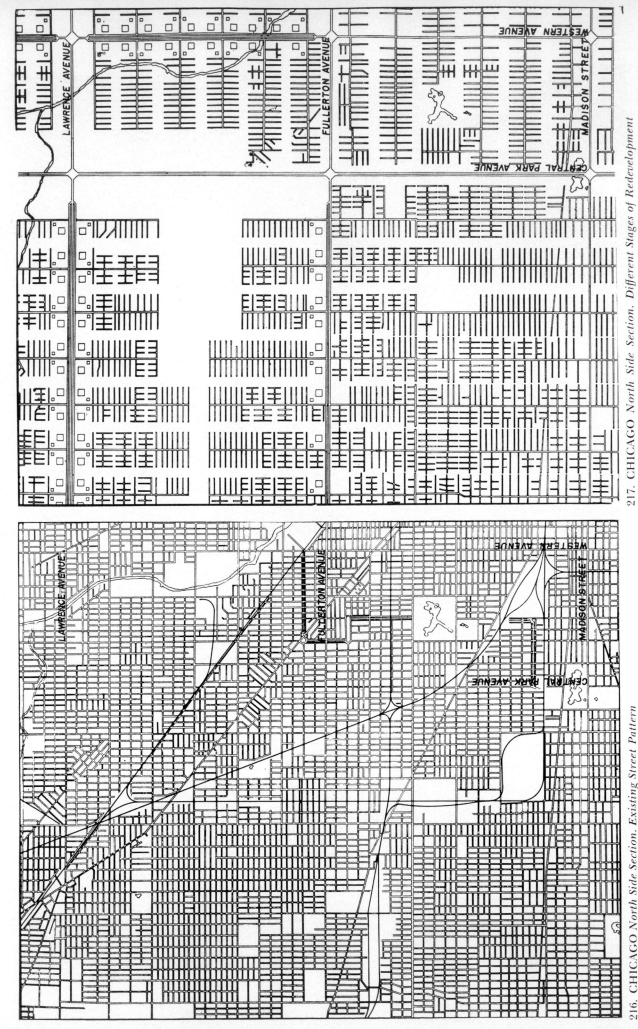

217. CHICAGO *North Side Section. Different Stages of Redevelopment*

216. CHICAGO *North Side Section. Existing Street Pattern*

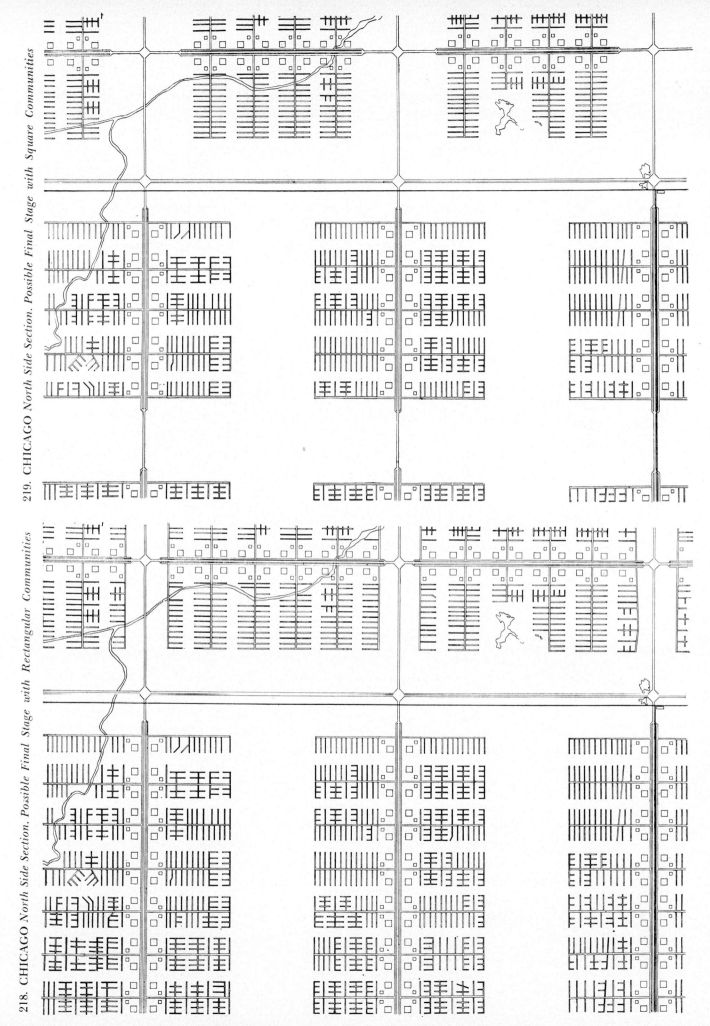

219. CHICAGO North Side Section. Possible Final Stage with Square Communities

218. CHICAGO North Side Section. Possible Final Stage with Rectangular Communities

ing generation be able to stand the nervous strain of city life? When competence has been accumulated, must we go elsewhere to enjoy the fruits of independence? If the city does not become better as it becomes bigger, shall not the defect be remedied? These are questions that cannot be brushed aside. They are the most pressing questions of our day, and everywhere men are anxiously seeking the answers."

More than forty years have passed, and these questions are still unanswered. The problem remains as Burnham saw it. Chicago is now much larger, more densely populated. Its difficulties have increased even more than its size. Slums, eating into the city like a cancer, have spread until they now contaminate the countryside. There are many reasons for the growth of these slums. The most basic is unrealistic planning—or no planning at all. Uncontrolled growth has inevitably resulted in social disorder. A map prepared by the Chicago Plan Commission strikingly shows the coincidence of factors indicative of blight and their effect upon the city. It shows the location of industries, some of the railroad lines, the commercial areas, the residential areas differentiated according to their condition, and the larger park areas. Of greatest interest is the location and the size of the slums. The areas designated as blighted or near-blighted are close to the industrial and commercial areas; they comprise nearly one-quarter of the city's residential area.

Could our planning principles be applied to a metropolis like Chicago? We believe that they could and that, by their use the city could gradually be transformed. Let us take first one part of the city and replan it, using existing streets, utilities, and buildings.

The area we have chosen for study extends from Madison Street to Lawrence Avenue and lies west of Western Avenue. It contains more than forty square miles, nearly one-fifth of the entire city area.

Our illustrations show four stages in the development of this area. The first shows the present street pattern; the second the steps in its redevelopment before the end state is reached. The other two illustrations show alternate arrangements for the final stage: one with rectangular, the other with square communities. The traffic arteries, from the residential lane to the superhighway, are so planned that they serve the city during the time of transition as well as when the desired replanning has been completed. Here, as always, an orderly progress from step to step serves both present and future.

East-west highways, separated from each other by three miles, are located at Madison Street, Fullerton Avenue, and Lawrence Avenue. The main north-south highway is at Western Avenue. At Central Park Avenue will eventually be located a superhighway into which all highways leading to the city will feed. Close to it is the main railroad line. Parallel to and

242

221. **PLAN OF CHICAGO** *Firebreaks One Mile Wide.*
New Railroads.

220. **PLAN OF CHICAGO** *Firebreaks One Quarter of a Mile Wide.*
Using existing Railroads.

on each side of the main highway are local highways. These connect with the main highway and collect all the center streets of the future units, which will be half a mile apart from each other.

The prevention of through traffic in residential areas with retention of access to each house is an important and difficult problem. It could be solved here simply by closing street ends. The lower left of Ill. 217 shows how this might be done. Only the center streets of the future units are still through traffic streets; all others are closed. The lower right of the same Illustration shows how, by the elimination of the blocks between the future units, a park might come into being, a naturally located recreation area in which schools and other public buildings could be placed. This park and the buildings in it would be accessible without crossing a traffic street. Children could go to school safely.

The same illustration at the upper left shows a further important step toward the desired pattern. The center streets of the future units are no longer through traffic streets; they have been closed and traffic within the future units has thereby been greatly reduced. Industrial and local commercial establishments are now located at their logical position along the highways. The park between two rows of units begins to emerge and to assume its future shape.

The upper right part of our detail shows the final stage. The units are now in their desired shape. Every part—working, residence, and recreation—is within walking distance of the others. Local transportation is no longer needed, and thus traffic is greatly reduced. The parks between the rows of units are now united with the parks between the units, forming firebreaks and providing the recreational area necessary for the activities of people in a large city.

The communities, rectangular or square, will be the end stage of the replanning. They will eventually be relatively independent of the city. Each square community will contain between 50,000 and 70,000 people, which is equal to the average density of Chicago. The density should be as low as possible. The working areas of these communities will provide space for offices, stores, and factories, so that workers may have opportunity for varied employment and for a diversified life. There will be adequate parking space. Local traffic will be reduced to a minimum. The communities will not be all alike; they will vary in structure as they vary in function. Each community will present its unique problems; and these problems will have to be individually and locally solved.

Since the communities are relatively independent and limited in area. people who live in them have opportunity to realize common interests and to create a community life, which the big city now discourages. But these same people can also enjoy the advantages of the big city because the com-

244

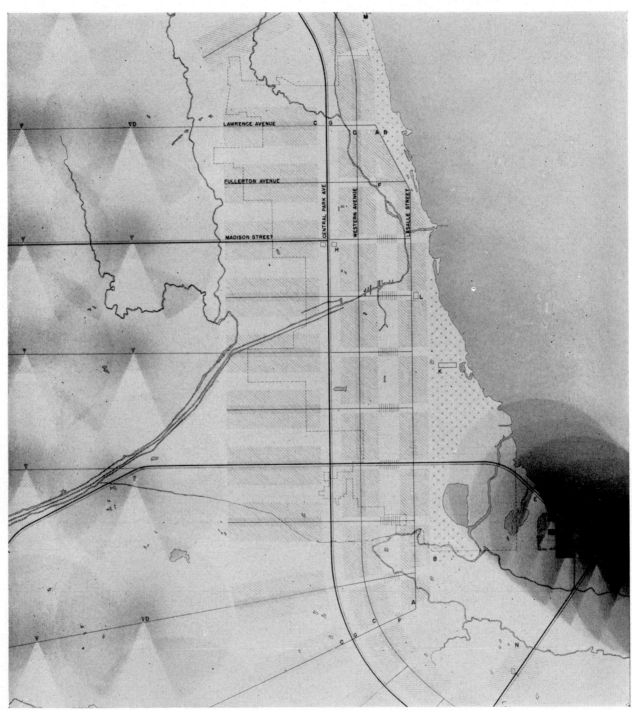

222. PLAN OF CHICAGO *with rectangular Communities*

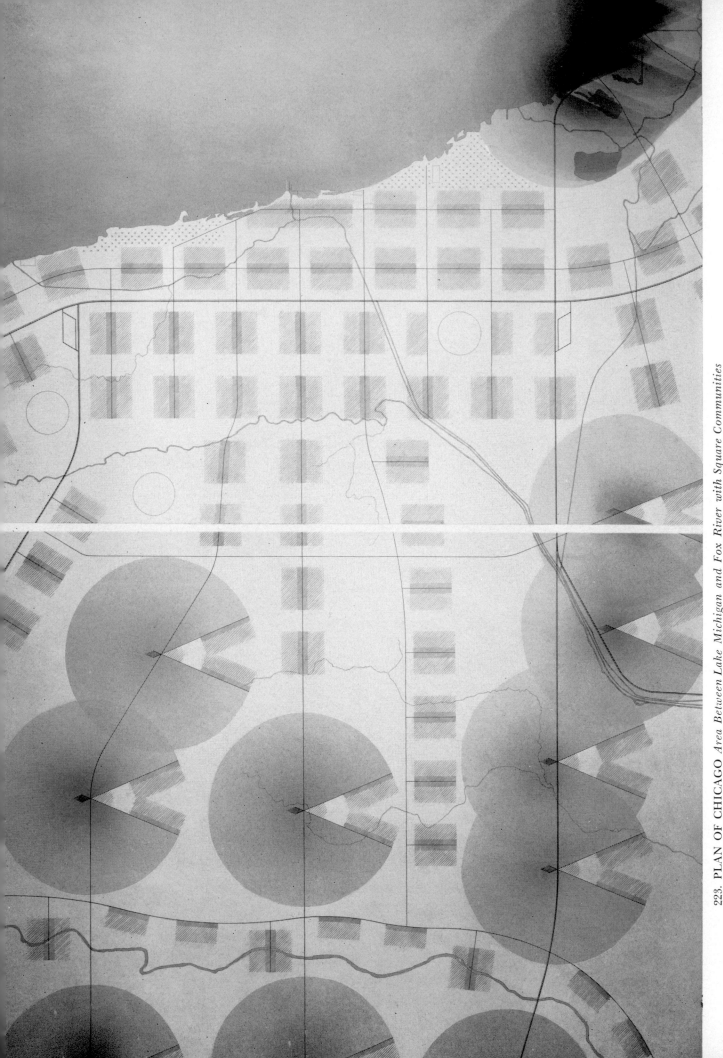

223. PLAN OF CHICAGO *Area Between Lake Michigan and Fox River with Square Communities*

munities are connected with each other by an integrated transportation system.

Firebreaks separate the communities from each other. There is no general agreement as yet regarding the desirable width of such a barrier. We do know, however, that the firebreak needs to be as wide as possible, if it is to give the city maximum protection against fire hazards connected with aerial bombardment. In two studies (Ill. 220,221), we show how the width of such firebreaks would affect the city. One shows firebreaks a quarter of a mile wide; the other firebreaks a mile wide. In our plan for Washington, D.C., we have carried the idea farther, placed the communities four or five miles apart.

The plans for Chicago here shown show a possible end stage. The older one (Ill. 222), with rectangular communities, deals with Chicago only. The newer one (Ill. 223), with square communities, covers a larger area, extending from Lake Michigan to the Fox River Valley. Both plans are extensions or repetitions of the parts we have worked out in detail. They include, in addition, city areas with special functions which must be incorporated in a total city plan. These special-function areas are mainly of three types: the commercial area, the area for air-polluting factories, the area for heavy industry.

The commercial area has been left in its present position, but extended north and south in accordance with its natural trend. This area needs to be remodeled. Is there any way to make it adequate to its function and to its traffic and parking requirements? Today there are too many streets and dangerous street crossings, no adequate parking facilities. The buildings are too close together; each deprives its neighbors of light and air. Parts of the area are blighted; some parts arc slums.

We suggest that these conditions could be transformed if the present block system were replaced by considerably larger blocks and a more adequate street system. Every building should provide its own parking space, and might do so if it used for parking its street-level floor and its basement. The buildings we suggest for the commercial area are basically of two types. One type requires large uninterrupted space. Stores, department stores, and banks fall into this classification. By the very nature of their requirements, such establishments must depend largely upon artificial light. The other type of building is suitable for office buildings, large and small. They can be open to light and air, using artificial lighting only in winter.

The solution presented in our diagram would fulfill all the requirements of such a commercial area. There would be large blocks, fewer but more efficient streets, adequate parking space. Combination of the two building types would achieve openness.

At the lower left, at -A-, our diagram shows the normal block and street system. In -B-, eight of those blocks have been combined into one large block. Instead of eight streets and fifteen street crossings, there are now four streets and four crossings. The streets are wider and differentiated according to function. There could be a highway traversing the commercial area, connected at convenient points with the local traffic streets. The necessary space for it has to be provided. On the larger block is placed a building four or five stories high, used for stores and banks. Its street-level floor provides parking space for visitors and customers; its basement is the parking space for employees. -B- also shows how free-standing office buildings could be placed on top of the store building. There might be one of these office buildings to correspond with each of the former blocks; or one office building on two of the former blocks. An even better arrangement might be to place a single building on space originally occupied by four half-blocks.

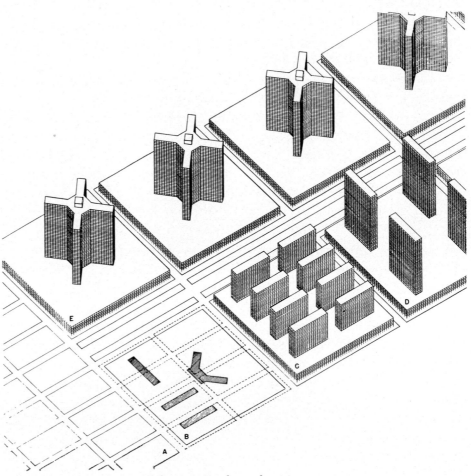

224. CHICAGO *Commercial Area Replanned*

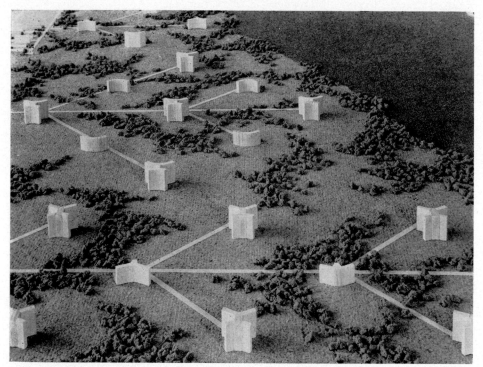

225. CHICAGO *Apartment Buildings in Park Along Lake Michigan*

Parts -C-, -D-, and -E- of our diagram show such free-standing buildings. In -C-, there are eight buildings; in -D-, four; in -E- only one. The amount of office space available would be the same in all these arrangements. The number of floors has been increased as the number of buildings has been decreased to achieve this equality. Many variations are possible besides the ones shown here. The office buildings could be mixed in type, but the combination of two different building types into one would always follow similar plans. At the ground floor would be parking space, inside streets, shopping arcades with show windows and small shops. These arcades would lead to the elevator core. A roof garden with cafeteria and restaurants might be placed on top of the store building. Such combination of building types, with appropriate differentiation, would achieve both compactness and openness, in use as well as appearance.

We have already pointed out that the main parts of the new building types, the offices, are so planned that they could be started on one, two, or four half-blocks. This means that the change could be begun on a relatively small area and gradually extended until the whole area is transformed. The function of the commercial area would at no time be disturbed. Rebuilding could begin in the obsolete parts of the area, already ripe for rebuilding. It would certainly take time to rebuild the whole area. Yet we should remember that rebuilding is always going on. It is only

228. CHICAGO South Side Section. Second Stage in Redevelopment

229. CHICAGO South Side Section. Possible Final Stage in Redevelopment

226. CHICAGO South side Section. Existing Street Pattern

227. CHICAGO South Side Section. First Stage in Redevelopment

231. CHICAGO *South Side Section.*
Detail, Possible Final Stage of Redevelopment.

230. CHICAGO *South Side Section.*
Detail, Different Stages of Redevelopment.

232. RE-PLANNED CHICAGO *View from Lake Michigan*

necessary to require that such rebuilding be executed within a plan for the whole area. The transformation of the commercial area and the achievement of a pattern adequate to its function would follow naturally.

The residential section of Chicago's commercial area is, as in all communities, directly related to it. We propose that, since space is lacking toward the east, existing parks be extended north and south, and that apartment buildings be erected in these parks, far enough apart so that the park character is retained. People living in these park apartments would, of course, have to use mechanical transportation.

To protect the city from air pollution, we propose that manufacturing industries which, by their very nature, pollute the air be located outside of the city, east and west of the Fox River and along the Illinois River. Industries related to these factories could be placed here also. The residential areas for these plants would be situated in a triangle free from air pollution because of the wind pattern.

The heavy industries in South Chicago and Gary would be left in their present positions. They should, however, be broken up and interspersed with firebreaks for their protection. The residential areas for people working in these mills would be so placed as to be free of air pollution. They would have to be connected with the industrial plants by mechanical means of transportation.

All parts of the city are connected, in our plan, by a highway system. There is a major north-south line for long distance motor traffic, with which all east-west lines connect. The major railroad line is so located that it can serve the entire city without interfering with any particular area. This major line connects all railroads leading into the city. Its central station is in the vicinity of Madison Street and Central Park Avenue. There are other stations at the junction points of other lines. Major switching yards and freight yards and warehouses are provided. Ill. 220 shows how, eventually, existing railroads could be combined, the Pennsylvania and the Northwestern forming one through route with which all other roads would be connected. This is not a good solution however, for this railroad would have to traverse residential areas, a condition not to be tolerated. Existing airports have been enlarged and integrated into the city's transportation system.

A more detailed study, made at the request of the South Side Planning Board, shows that part of the south side of Chicago which extends from 31st Street to 55th Street and from Wentworth Avenue to Lake Michigan. This area forms one-half of a community such as we have previously discussed. The same methods as those used in the studies of the north side have been applied. For part of this community, details have been worked out to show how the changes could be effected systematically and in stages, so that slum areas might be replaced by new housing developments. Diversified housing, commercial and industrial areas along the highway, tall apartment buildings along the Lake, and schools in the parks are all properly related.

If Chicago were reconstructed after our suggestions, disorder would be replaced by order. No new slums could grow. No wild suburbanization

233. PART OF WASHINGTON *Opened up by Fire Breaks*

would take place. Traffic hazards would disappear. Parking problems would have at least found solution. Such change could be gradually accomplished, preserving as much as possible of the existing city. The resulting stabilization would prevent deterioration and make real conservation possible. Chicago would become a city healthy and good to live in. It might, indeed, with its parks and gardens, achieve at last its one-time goal. and become what it has supposed itself to be: *Urbs in Horto*—a City in a Garden!

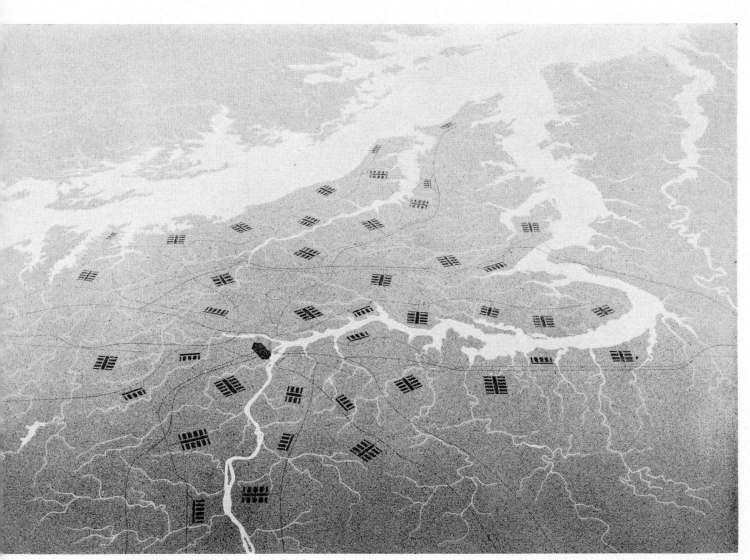

234. WASHINGTON *Decentralized*

In our plan for Chicago, we have made firebreaks one mile wide and suggested that they might be even wider. While, as we have noted, experts do not agree on the proper width of firebreaks, it seems obvious that they should be as wide as possible. The smaller individual settlements are in themselves and the wider the spaces between them, the greater will be the protection afforded the people who live there. A low population density is also an important consideration.

If Chicago as an industrial city needs to provide this kind of protection, Washington, the capital of the nation, needs it even more. A national capital located on the periphery of a country is not in the most advantageous position. St. Petersburg (Leningrad), for more than two hundred years the capital of Russia, was abandoned as the capital in favor of Moscow because that ancient capital seemed in a less vulnerable position. For the same reason, China's government was once removed from Peking to a more centrally located place. Washington, because of its peripheral location, is in special need of the protection which decentralization can give.

For this decentralization, we have suggested the use of the same method employed in our plan for Chicago. The city could and should be opened up by means of firebreaks. Its decentralization could be carried farther and the distance between its communities increased. A sketch map shows how effectively this could be done. The Washington of that sketch has been reduced to the size and condition of one hundred years ago. The city has become primarily a national monument, in which the Capitol and the White House regain their original prominence. All governmental departments have been moved and arranged to form new communities with their residential areas and the necessary community and commercial buildings. Those communities vary in size according to their functions. They are located along the Potomac and the ocean inlets. Distances between them would be four or five miles. They are all connected with each other and with Washington by the existing railroad and highway system.

The first phase of our industrial age has been characterized by concentration and specialization of production, exploitation of resources, both natural and human, and a high degree of material progress. City and country became separated. Serving different ends, they came to be in opposition to each other. Will the second phase of our industrial age reverse these tendencies? Will that phase be marked by decentralization and diversification of production, both industrial and agricultural; by the intergration of these two kinds of production and of the city with country? Will the city become more rural, the country more urban, and both more human? Will exploitation of resources be replaced by their planful use and careful preservation?

These things could come to pass. And if they did, human beings, no longer regarded as means to an end, could again be able to seek that self-improvement which might, at last, replace the ideal of material progress with the ethical ideal of human welfare. Egotistic self-interest might become secondary, in such a world, to the altruistic concept of the welfare of others and of the community as a whole.

We cannot foresee the future. Yet we know that the realization of these human ideals will depend on the mind and will of man. And we may add, with assurance, that the very survival of civilization as we know it may depend on the degree to which man approaches this ideal.

Decentralization already exists as a trend, not to say as an established fact. It is gaining more and more momentum, especially now that the trend is reinforced by the new concept of defence and security. Defence necessity forced the concentration of cities of the past; defence necessity may force the dispersal of the present city. Incredible as it may seem, we may be on the way to realizing our human aims in an effort to save ourselves from military destruction! It is strange, but true, that the very developments which would solve some of our greatest social problems—decentralization, diversification of production, the creation of self-sustaining regions—are also the developments required by defence necessity in this Atomic Age.

How will decentralization affect our cities? It is already affecting them to a far larger degree than we are willing to admit. Since it has been thus far largely undirected, there is real danger that its chief effect may be to

bring into the countryside the chaotic conditions and the blight characteristic of our cities. We can see this uncontrolled process going on around
all our cities.

If it is to be effective and to create lasting values, decentralization must be
planned. The planning elements, communities and city aggregates we
have developed may prove helpful means to achieve such planning. We
are now able, as we have never been before, to concentrate what needs to
be concentrated: for example, the great industries for which concentration
is essential. We are also able to decentralize and to disperse what should
be decentralized. We should avoid the assumption that smallness, *per se,*
is better than bigness, minimum size than maximum size. Our intention
should rather be to find the optimum size, according to its need, for each
settlement.

Integration of industry and agriculture will influence the city as much as
decentralization. If the unlimited city is superseded by the limited city,
city and country will come into closer relationship. Then the space
needed to grow food for the city's population can be directly related to the
city. The distance between any two cities will be determined, in that
event, not only by topographical and geographical features, but also by
the extent of agricultural area needed to feed their people. This would
inevitably tend to disperse the cities. It would make it possible for cities
to develop their own close connection with agriculture. If they come to
be surrounded or directly connected with small farms for part-time industrial workers, this, too, would lead to further dispersion.

Integration between industry and agriculture is an important tool for
decentralization. Such an integration should be twofold in its function.
In the larger agricultural areas, farms of varying size should be concerned
with providing the food needed by the inhabitants of the region. In areas
where industry is dominant, small farms for part-time workers, vegetable
gardens for men employed in industry, would supplement and stabilize
wages and also add richness to life. Subsistence farmers could work on
the larger farms at peak seasons, or they could find employment in the
processing of agricultural products. Such division and integration of work
should be more satisfactory for both the industrial worker and the small
farmer. A higher living standard would be possible for each. A more
general well-being and a more balanced economy would be attained.
Living conditions would be more adequate to the real needs of man.
There would be sunshine in every house and clean air everywhere. There
would be no slum-infested cities. Life would become vigorous and healthful once more. Personal security and independence would be fostered,
to the benefit of the individual and of the society of which he is a part.

Decentralization and the integration of agriculture and industry are, by their very nature, problems of regional planning. The planning problems of the city become part of a more comprehensive planning for the region of which the city is a part. Two factors determine a plan for a region: the physical structure of that region, and the use to which man intends to put its potentialities and resources.

To comprehend a region's physical structure and its potentialities for development, a thorough-going survey is required. Such a survey must deal with natural factors such as geography and topography, climate, soils, vegetation, growing seasons, water, mineral and other resources. But it must deal also with man-made things: with the distribution of people and their occupations; with the existing settlements and transportation routes; with production, agricultural and industrial.

Analysis of those factors will determine the use of the region, so far as its industrial development is concerned. Study of soil and climate conditions will be the basis for a land use map, showing how the various parts of the area could be put to the best possible use; which parts should be arable land, which grassland or forest. Whether the land and its resources will actually be so used depends, however, on the human factor. Man has freedom to choose and to act. He may exploit the resources and exhaust them. He may exploit the land and destroy its productiveness. Or he may, on the other hand, use the resources wisely, in conformity with the laws of nature. He may learn to think of his region as a living entity, capable of supporting and maintaining life. He may come to understand that, striving to make the region useful in the present, he should strive also to preserve its usefulness for generations to come. Whatever man does influences his region and influences also the life which he and his descendants can create there.

What exactly is a region? How can it be determined and defined? These questions are fully discussed in "The New Regional Pattern." Here we shall merely summarize this discussion.*

A region may be defined as an organic entity, in which the whole is related to the parts and the parts to the whole. It is something which can exist and can support life. A region is an interrelated section of a country, a natural unit, self-contained by reason of a balanced production based on a diversified agriculture and an industry devoted to the processing of the raw materials which the region provides.

A balanced regional economy can, obviously, be established only through diversification of employment and production. In some regions, natural conditions prevent this. There are, for example, regions which must

---

* Hilberseimer, L: *The New Regional Pattern.* Chicago, 1949

depend on the exchange of their principal natural resources for food and other needed goods. Such regions are the exceptions, however. They change our regional economic concept only in degree, not in principle. Trade is indispensable. Its true function, however, is to supplement the deficiencies of one region with the abundance of another. Regional economy merely suggests that a region ought to produce and consume a large proportion of the food and goods it needs, importing nothing that it might produce itself. It should exchange its surpluses for those things it is unable to produce itself. Exchange of goods on this basis, among all regions and among all countries, would eventually bring about a new and sound world economy.

To show how decentralization on a large scale might affect the country, we have developed a sketch map of the Eastern United States. It shows the coal fields and the ore deposits, the waterways and the main railroad lines. It also indicates how manufacturing industries, now concentrated in the industrial cities between the northeast coast and Lake Michigan, could be decentralized within that area and extended toward the South. The tendency to move industries from the North to the South for economic reasons already exists. We are moving also to decentralize for defence reasons, realizing that people and industries concentrated in our industrial cities are dangerously vulnerable to air attack. Economic forces also are working toward this decentralization.

Decentralization of the kind we suggest could bring about a more even distribution of population and a better spread of industries. It could establish a close relationship between industry and agriculture, so that these two important aspects of our economy might, in their integration, stimulate each other and bring about a higher productivity. This process would eventually lead to a true regionalism, both economic and cultural, a regionalism relatively self-sustaining and self-supporting and, therefore, less vulnerable to any dangers which may lie ahead.

The industrial belts we have suggested are located along main railroad lines and waterways. Some are close to coal fields but must import their iron ore. Our main source of iron ore is now the Mesabi range in Minnesota. But this rich deposit may, it is said, be exhausted in one more generation. There would then be no comparable deposit in the United States, except the abundant low-grade ore in the Mesabi range which is expensive to process. We might then have to look to the deposits in Labrador and in Latin America. Water transportation will again become very important. The St. Lawrence Seaway, which now seems on the way to realization after years of delay, may prove of both economic and strategic importance. Like the railroads and highways along with our industrial belts

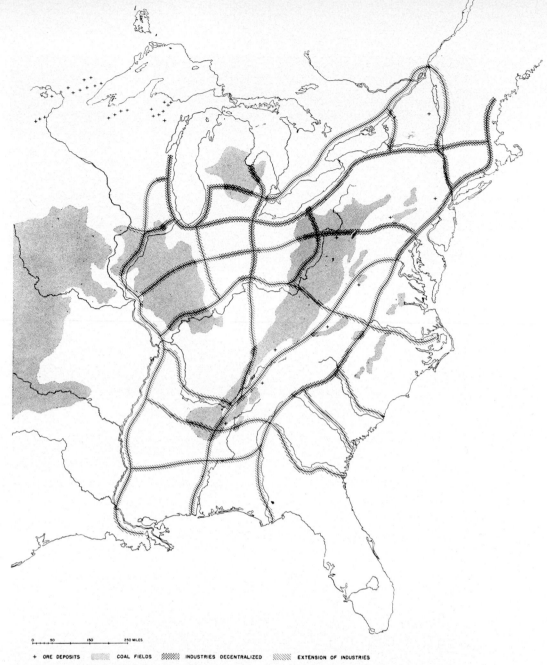

+ ORE DEPOSITS   COAL FIELDS   INDUSTRIES DECENTRALIZED   EXTENSION OF INDUSTRIES

235. EASTERN UNITED STATES *Industries Decentralized and Extended to the South*

are located also the waterways would assume new significance for our future industrial development.

The industrial belts would have to be supplemented by branch belts developed wherever necessity arises. They would, of course, be modified according to their purpose and the geographic and topographic conditions of the area.

We have developed diagramatically some studies showing different belts. Diverse as they are, they are all based on the planning elements of the communities and aggregates we have already discussed. They indicate the variety of arrangements which could be achieved.

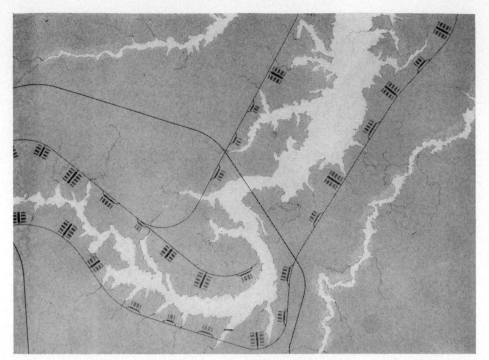

236. SETTLEMENT DEVELOPMENT ALONG AN INLET

In its simplest form, a belt might consist of communities developed, perhaps, on either side of an inlet, varying in size according to their diversified functions. Highways could be separated from them but connected with them. Since the industries of these communities are powered by electricity, there would be no problem or air pollution and the communities could be very freely placed.

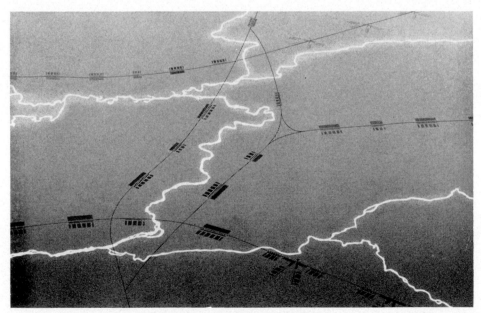

237. DECENTRALIZED CITY IN A RIVER VALLEY

However, some manufacturing industries have to be supplemented with industries which cause air pollution. Such plants would have to be separated from their communities. The study of a belt in a river valley shows communities adjoined by settlements of small farms. The air polluting industries are located toward the east, along the highways that cross the valley. Special commercial and administrative communities appear at the highway crossing.

The belt developed on hilly ground consists of a number of fan-shaped

238. INDUSTRIAL COMMUNITIES *Developed on Hilly Grounds*

communities, placed along a traffic line, in locations determined by the topography of the area. An administrative and commercial area beside a lake serves also as a cultural center for the adjoining settlements.

In another study, we have used city aggregates surrounded by small farms. The main belt formed by these aggregates stretches along the east side of two lakes and a river, connecting them. West of the main traffic line, toward the lake and the river, are the air-polluting factories and the integrated and heavy industries. The wind conditions in this area are much

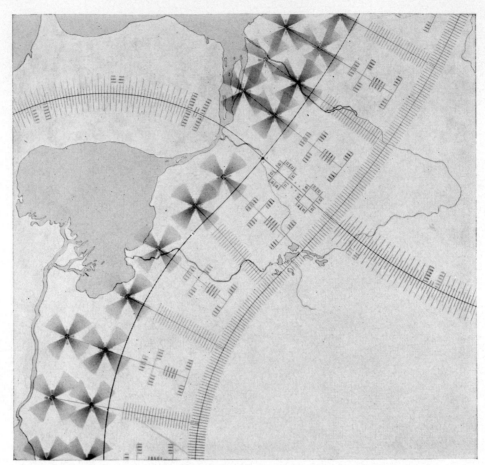

239. BELT OF CITY AGGREGATES *Surrounded by Small Farms*

more favorable than in the area mentioned before. Therefore the integrated and heavy industries can be within walking distance of their residential areas. This main belt is crossed by a minor belt, more rural in character. Commerical, administrative, and cultural centers are located where these belts intersect.

Our next study, a belt along a river, shows how freely such belts could be developed. The city aggregate use is flexible and adjustable to any purpose. Its parts can be made larger or smaller to fit any requirement. The working area of these settlement units are in direct connection with the areas on small farms, so that part-time workers living on those farms can find employment there. The open space between the aggregates, as well as between the small farms, are penetrated by a forest which stretches along the river, forming a natural recreation area for the settlements of the main belt. East of the main transportation line, are the obnoxious industries and their subsidiaries, each with its own residential area. At the south, the main belt is crossed by a minor belt. Towards the east, it consists of smaller aggregates, towards the west a belt of small farms, with some dispersed towns, is located. Factoris and workshops provide part-time work for the people who live on these farms.

The last study, a decentralized city around an inlet, uses communities, diversified in size and shape according to their function. It seems that those communities may prove to be the most useful planning elements developed. They are flexible in themselves and adaptable to any conditions. They can easily be extended if the necessity arises. They are free from any rigidness and can be spaced so as to fulfill any defence requirements. Vegetable gardens are attached to every house and small farms, for part-time workers, could be placed wherever necessary.

Each community has its own working area which provides space for factories, stores, and offices. Towards the north and the south special administrative and commercial centers are located, to which cultural centers are attached. At the east side there is a university community which pro-

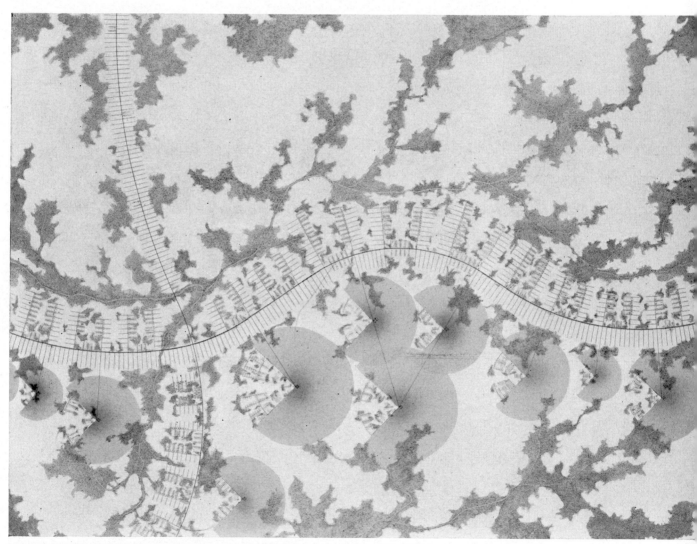

240. BELT OF CITY AGGREGATES *Along a River*

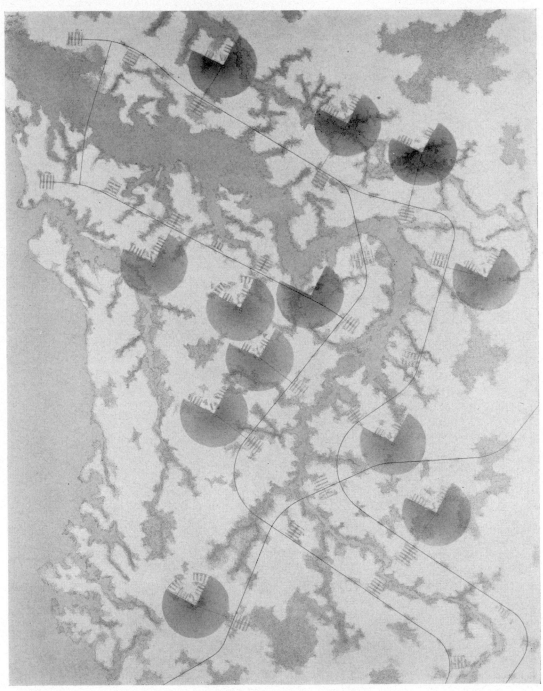

241. DECENTRALIZED CITY AROUND AN INLET

vides, besides its residential areas, also space for dormitories and fraternities.

These studies aim at a ruralization of the city. They may achieve also an urbanization of the country. If the active forces now concentrated in large cities could be more evenly distributed, activity would be spread through all the country. City and country, coming closer to each other, would influence each other to their mutual benefit, materially and spiritually. Healthy conditions would be everywhere restored. What is pleasant in city life could be combined with the pleasantness of country life. The disadvantages of each way of life would disappear. The woods and forests along the river and around the lakes, penetrating into the settlements, would become better recreation spots than costly city parks. With the adjoining fields and meadows, they would form a productive landscape.

To keep the cultivated landscape in a state of active production requires that certain natural requirements, such as water and soil, be constantly maintained. These elements, with the sun, are the sources of life. We could learn to live without steel, never without food. Man has no power over the activity of the sun, but he has learned to manipulate water and soil, to make them serve him and to support his life. He has also the power, however, to disrupt the interaction of water and earth and, in so doing, to create a desert in once fruitful land.

Like the natural landscape, the cultivated landscape depends on the maintenance of the hydrologic cycle, the result of alternating precipitation and evaporation. To maintain this cycle, ridges, hills, and mountains should always be covered with woods and forest, slopes with grassland, so that rain water is stored and does not so quickly run off that it causes erosion. Naturally concentrated and dispersed woods and forests not only protect watersheds, but they also preserve wild life and furnish timber for the needs of the region. The timber, of course, should be harvested with care. Cut trees should always be replaced by the planting of new ones. If this is carefully done, a continuous supply of timber can be assured for present needs and for those of coming generations. Woods and forests act also as windbreaks and thus prevent wind erosion. Trees and shrubs beside a river or lake protect its banks and shores.

Soil is not a mere mechanical mixture. It is the result of the interaction of animate and inanimate forces. Not only is it full of life; it is, in truth, the source of life. The interaction of the soil material, its physical and chemical constituents, the sub-soil conditions, water and sunlight: these are the factors which make plant growth possible. On plants, animals depend for their food. Man depends on both animals and plants for his own existence.

Soils differ according to their constituents, and according to their degree of maturity. They are also affected by the vegetation they support, and influenced by climatic conditions, by the amount of rainfall, by their elevation. Some soils are better adapted for growing trees and grass; others for various kinds of crop. In general, we can divide land into three classifications: forestland, grassland, and arable land.

There is always a certain relation and interdependence among these three kinds of land, although it cannot be expressed in any formula. We know that the relation will vary and be influenced by the character of the soil, by the climate, and by the geography and topography of a given landscape. Regional planning requires the study of the ecology of a region, the analysis and mapping of its physical features, geographical and topographical, the examination of its rainfall, its climate, its wind conditions, and its soil. Only through such study and charting can we discover how the land can best be used and how its usefulness can be preserved for the present and for the future.

But regional planning deals not only with the physical structure of a region, but also with the use made of it and with the sub-divisions created to serve this use. This may well become a political-economic problem, involving understanding of the means of agricultural productions, the tools and machines being applied. For example, a given area may be suitable for division into subsistence farms or large estates. Each solution is possible and practical. But a solution better than either of these would be a combination of both. If to the small farms and large estates could be added small holdings for the agricultural workers, there could be diversity of both size and production. Crops might be planted in rotation to prevent the soil exhaustion to which all one-crop farming inevitably leads.

To illustrate how a rural area could be developed, let us take Maui, one of the Hawaiian Islands, an essentially rural region. We chose an island because it shows better than an unlimited area all the advantages and disadvantages of the use of land in all its implications.

Once the Hawaiian Islands were self-sustaining. Production, both agricultural and industrial, was diversified and well balanced. Today that diversification and that balance have been destroyed. The Hawaiian Islands produce two main crops: sugarcane and pineapples. These crops dominate the highly specialized production. Since they require the use of practically all the arable land of the islands, the people living there have to import most of the food they need.

Specialization seems to work well at first. Then, as new plantations are started in new areas, competition comes into play. Desirable in itself, this competition may have disastrous effect on a specialized region. The

242. HAWAIIAN ISLAND MAUI *View*

price of the specialized product goes down; the price of foodstuffs imported remains at its former level. The inevitable result is a deficit which, eventually, can not be balanced. The system which once worked so well can become a total failure.

When the Hawaiian Islands were discovered in 1778, their population may have been around 250,000. Continual warfare among feudal chiefs, epidemics and disease brought by the white man, reduced this number to around 50,000. A hundred years after its foundation, the sugar industry, facing a shortage of native labor, was bringing to the islands workers from all over the world. By 1900, the population had risen to 154,000; it may be close to 500,000 now, twice as large as it was when the islands were discovered. Maui had 63,479 people in 1938.

Maui, like the other Hawaiian Islands, was formed by volcanic activity and, to a lesser degree, by reef-building corals. The island has two mountains: the smaller one rising to 6,000 feet; the larger one to 10,000 feet. These mountains give Maui an 8-shaped form. The wide valley between the mountains is, agriculturally, the most useful part of the island.
The prevailing winds are trade winds from the northeast. The rainfall is highest on the northeast side of the island because the moisture-laden trade winds blown against the mountains here precipitate their moisture. Rainfall on the slopes of the smaller mountain is especially heavy. Its cliffs and canyons, formed by rain and wind, cause updrafts which increase the precipitation. The perennial streams are mostly on the northeast, or trade-wind, side of the island. Other streams appear in times of heavy rain, are waterless during dry seasons.
About one-seventh of Maui's total land area is arable land under cultiva-

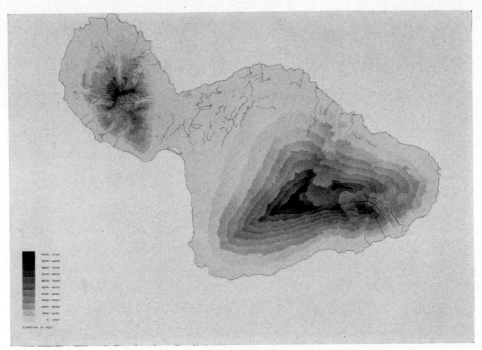

243. MAUI *Topography*

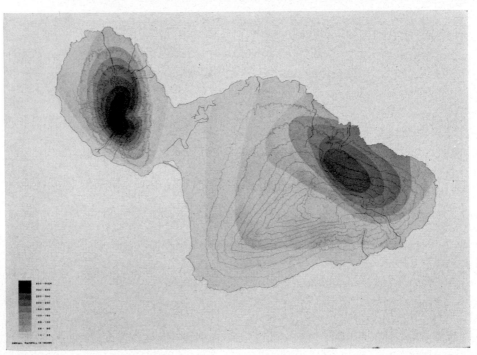

244. MAUI *Annual Rainfall*

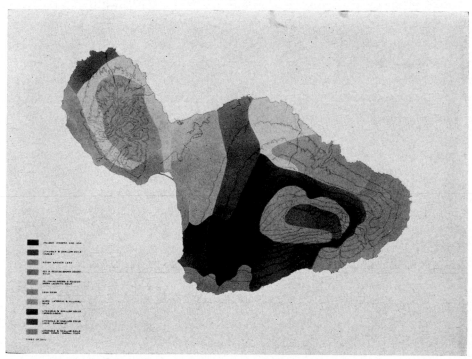

245. MAUI *Types of Soil*

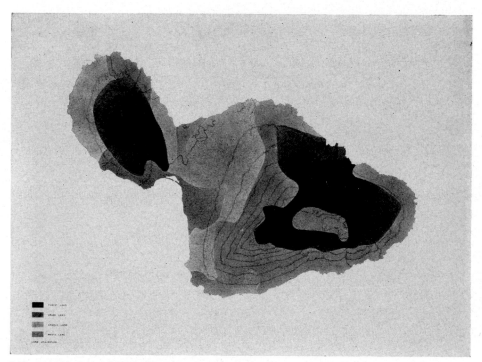

246. MAUI *Land Utilization*

tion. The rest is grassland, forest, and wasteland. Two-thirds of the cultivated land is given to sugarcane. Five-sixths of the remaining third is
planted to pineapples. Only one-twentieth of the total arable land is used
for diversified farming.

This over-specialization is already having a disadvantageous effect on the
economy of the Islands. Import exceeds export and the whole economy is
out of balance. The production of more varied foodstuffs and the introduction of some local industry would help to restore the balance and
create a stable economy.

Our proposal is that the plantation workers of Maui be settled upon land
of their own, where they can engage in diversified farming. The land
assigned for such farming should be increased to at least one-fifth of the
arable land. Each family should work a farm of about four acres. raising
on it food for its own use and, possibly, some surplus produce for those
living in the denser settlements. The position of the agricultural workers
would thus be made more secure and their lives would have more stability.
In our plan, these small farms form ribbons, running parallel with the
contour lines and along the traffic route. The great sugarcane and pine-
apple plantations lie between these ribbons, within easy reach of the
workers.

The small farms could also be placed close together, around the communities in which the agricultural workers live. Or the workers' homes
could be on their small farms. In either case, the workers would be within
walking distance of the larger estates on which they are employed.

If this island is to fulfill our concept of a self-sustaining region as one
which produces most of the goods it needs itself and exchanges its surplus
only for goods it cannot produce, still more land should be given to necessary diversified production. Since one-crop farming always exhausts the
fertility of the soil and that soil is the only natural resource Maui has,
diversification should become the general rule on the larger estates. Those
who think that land is made to be exploited and who take no thought for
the future will not welcome this suggestion. "Never mind what we leave
behind" seems still the maxim of the exploiters.

If considerations of welfare and conservation are not cogent enough to
bring about the change, however, there are other considerations which
cannot so lightly be thrust aside. The Hawaiian Islands are in a vital
strategic position, a defense post of first rank. Pearl Harbor is one of our
important naval stations. During World War II, a food shortage developed on the Islands. The well established and calculated system of
exchange broke down because no ships were available for transportation.
The military authorities, brought face to face with this crisis, began to

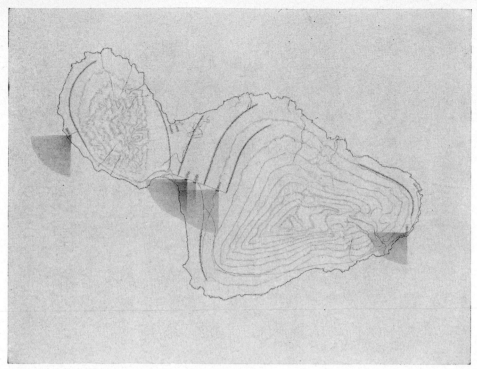

247. MAUI *Proposed Plan*

advocate the raising of subsistence crops to feed the population. This need did not disappear with the close of the War. A diversified economy for Hawaii is important to our security.

248. MAUI *Different Arrangement of Small Farms*

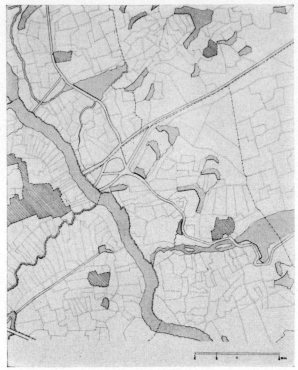

249. INDIA *Villages with Small Farms*   250. INDIA *Villages with Proposed Larger Farms*

For India, our proposal is directly opposite to that made for Hawaii. We suggest that, instead of giving small farms to workers, we take land away from the small Indian farmers. Why this seeming inconsistency?

During the period of British rule, the rights of the autonomous Indian village were suppressed. Village industries, therefore, declined, and the balance between production and consumption was disturbed. The self-sufficiency of the Indian community was lost. Meanwhile the population increased. Already small land holdings had to be sub-divided. Production became inefficient; life was impoverished.

Now that India is free, she is eager to raise production and living standards. Her Prime Minister Nehru* is convinced that "rapid industrialization is essential to relieve the pressure on the land, to combat poverty and raise the standard of living, for defence and a variety of other purposes." Nehru significantly adds: "I am equally convinced that the most careful planning and adjustment are necessary if we are to reap the full benefits of industrialization and to avoid many of its dangers." His proposals for decentralization of industry and its integration with agriculture are not unlike those made for the United States by Henry Ford.**

* Nehru, Jawaharlal: *The Discovery of India.* London, 1951
** Ford, Henry: *My Life and Work.* New York, 1922

The first step in the achievement of these aims would be, we believe, the consolidation of small land holdings into parcels adequate to the tools employed. As the agricultural tools now in use are replaced with more efficient ones, land in the villages could be further consolidated to form optimum units for efficient cultivation. Fewer people would then be needed to work the land, and diversification of production would become possible. The surplus agricultural population would furnish workers for new industries. These new industries should be of optimal size: small, medium, and large according to function and need. The smaller industrial aggregates could be placed in the villages where the surplus population now lives. Workers in these new industries could be given garden plots for their own use; by cultivating these the workers could supplement their livelihood and diversify their lives. Farmers could have such garden plots also to supplement the produce of their agricultural holdings. These farmers might find part-time employment in the village industries. Farming, especially in India, is seasonal and forces upon those who engage in it off-seasons of idleness. People released from agriculture who could not find work in the village industries could be settled in new industrial communities, placed along existing or planned highways. Dwellers in these industrial communities could also be given garden plots connected with their houses. Produce from these gardens would supplement industrial income, and their cultivation would provide relief from industrial monotony.

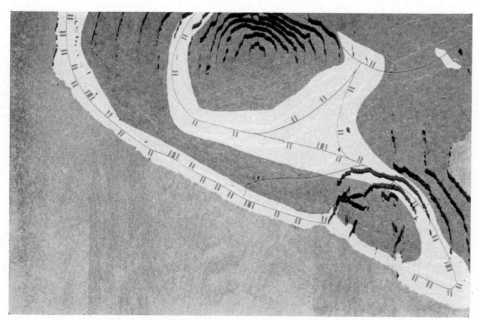

251. INDUSTRIAL VILLAGES ALONG HIGHWAYS

The planning elements and planning principles we have developed are based on research and investigation. These elements are capable of many combinations. Their flexibility makes them adaptable to any purpose, to any location, to any geographic or topographic condition.

We have, in this study, applied our principles and elements to increasingly complex problems. We have used them to replan old cities and regions and to plan new ones. We have suggested their application to bring about decentralization of industries now concentrated in the cities between our East coast and Lake Michigan and the extension of these industries into the South. Such a rearrangement would result in a more even distribution of these industries, in their closer relation to agriculture, in the integration of industry and agriculture. It would lead, eventually, to the establishment of the self-sustaining region essential today for our national defense and for the security of our people.

The diagrams we have presented make no claim to be complete solutions of the problems involved. They are rather a framework within which possible solutions may be found. They are abstractions only; and abstract cities and regions do not exist. Until they are put to use, the elements we have developed and their manifold possibilities of combination must remain in the realm of theory. Such theory provides the necessary starting point for the discovery of sound methods of work. Our purpose has been to encourage discussion about the planning problems we must face. Understanding of a problem and its implications is always prerequisite to any accomplishment. Only when we have reached this understanding can the real work of planning begin. The application of our principles will then be modified by reality. For planning is not an abstract task. It is the fulfillment of human needs, the realization of human aims.

Planning is often misunderstood. Some believe it to be a kind of strait jacket, which fixes and restricts. On the contrary, the purpose of planning is to create a framework within which the city can develop freely. Such a framework should provide for the development of each city area without restricting others. It should facilitate any desired extension, while maintaining everywhere the proper relation of the city's different parts.

If the decentralization of industry and its integration with agriculture were to become an accepted goal, then our every effort should be directed toward the attainment of this goal. Each step of such a transition should be an accomplishment in itself, as well as an advance toward the desired end. The method we have suggested for the replanning of Chicago, whose different stages we demonstrated in some detail, could be applied equally well to the replanning of a region. Each street we closed or eliminated, each block we took out, each street or highway constructed, each settlement, factory, or office building built was, in our Chicago plan, designed to serve a present need as well as to effect a final transformation. We noted that a city is always in a state of transition. The problem of the planner is to shape that transition toward a desired end. The same thing is true for a region. The only difference lies in the region's greater complexity.

Are there, in our world today, ideas, concepts, forces which support our regional concept and which may make its realization possible? There are! There is, first of all, the concept of a life better adapted to human needs, though this concept has too often been brushed aside as sentimental, too difficult and costly to be practical. There is also the evolutionary force inevitably moving our industrial age from its first stage to its second. We are aware that this transition is taking place; too often we think of it as beyond our power to shape. There is, finally, the force of defence necessity. And this we can ignore only by jeopardizing our lives and our security. Fear of possible catastrophe, stirring our will to survival, may well drive us to realize long-neglected human aims. New defense requirements may force decentralization of industry, hasten its integration with agriculture, and thus bring into being a better human environment.

Our growing dissatisfaction with life is related to the kind of work we are performing. As the process of production is perfected, the work of human beings becomes more and more repetititive, monotonous, impersonal. Workers, no longer able to act according to their will, become instruments, parts of the machines they tend. They have their place in industry only because the machine is not yet so perfect as to displace man entirely. As the machine comes closer and closer to perfection, fear of unemployment is added to the worker's frustrations. The job he does gives him no satisfaction, but he must not lose it for on it his livelihood depends. Work, once a blessing, becomes a curse. Man cannot live without it, but his very existence is threatened by it. He tries to escape this dilemma in every possible way.

Improvement of methods of production has made possible the decrease of working hours, the increase of so-called leisure time. But mechanized man no longer knows how to spend his leisure. He tries to solve the problems it creates mechanically. Canned entertainment has become as staple as canned food. Twentieth century man increasingly prefers the passive role of spectator, even in sports. His leisure-time activity, losing creativeness,

277

is too often merely an escape from self. If he can afford a car, he uses it in a frantic search for a dreamland. Back in his slum apartment on sleepless nights, thinking of his discontent with his life and his work, worrying about losing his job, brooding on the lack of satisfaction in his work and his play, such a man may, perhaps, sometimes come to himself and discover, at least dimly, the sources of his frustration. But does not frustration itself diminish man's ability to deal with frustration? "Almost any investigation of modern life," Jonathan Forman* wrote, "leads to the conclusion that white man, with his machines and his cities, is definitely on the road to insanity. While the Selective Service recognized many reasons for rejection, reliable authorities now claim that the nearer one lives to the center of a metropolitan area, the more likely he is to become insane."

If this is the end result of the progress of which we have been so proud, the situation is grave indeed. Human beings are indispensable resources of any country. No national health is possible unless the people of the nation are kept in physical and mental health and vigorous activity. If we look at the problem of human needs from this point of view, surely we can no longer push it aside, calling its solution sentimental. The de-humanizing, disintegrating effects of our mechanical age present us with a problem today on whose speedy solution may depend the survival of our country, even the survival of mankind.

A society as complex as ours could probably never get along without the labor market which brought our great cities into being. But the importance of that market may diminish. Both labor and management are encouraging a trend in this direction. It could bring important amelioration of the effects of the labor market on the city.

Many an industrialist and many a corporation will agree with Henry Ford's** statement that "the overhead expenses of living and doing business in the great cities is becoming so large as to be unbearable. It places so great a tax upon life that there is no surplus to live on. . . . All the social ailments from which we today suffer originated and center in the big cities. . . . [The idea] that an industrial country has to concentrate its industries . . . is not well founded. That is only a stage in the industrial development. Industries will decentralize. . . .The modern city has been prodigal, it is today bankrupt, and tomorrow it will cease to be." They may also agree that "the best possible conditions, as far as employees are concerned, are also the best possible conditions from the manufacturing standpoint."

---

* Forman, Jonathan: *Biological Truth and Public Health*.
  In: Cities are Abnormal. Oklahoma, 1946
** Ford, Henry. *My Life and My Work*. New York, 1922

The pension plan for which the unions are striving today will itself foster decentralization. Such a plan presupposes stabilized production and stabilized employment. This means less opportunity for the worker to shift his employment. While younger men may change jobs as frequently as they do today, the older men with families will have to settle down. But what are workers to do in those industries which cannot provide work the year around? They cannot change their jobs without losing pension rights. What kind of compensation can be provided for their security? In our opinion, only land can do this. This fact was well understood by Henry Ford when he said, "The men will have plots of ground or farms as well as their jobs in the factory. . . . Then we shall have the combination of agriculture and industrialism and the entire absence of all the evils of concentration." The same idea was expressed more than half a century ago by Peter Kropotkin.*

Patrick Geddes** has discovered an interesting parallel between prehistoric and contemporary periods. In the Stone Age, he writes, two distinct phases of development can be distinguished: the Old Stone Age and the New Stone Age; the Paleolithic and the Neolithic. Our industrial age shows a similar development. As in the ancient society, new and more refined means of production, resulting from scientific and technical achievement, are replacing older, rougher means. Geddes believes that this transition, when complete, will humanize industry and living conditions. He says: "Simply substituting -technic for -lithic, we may distinguish the earlier and ruder elements of the Industrial Age as Paleotechnic, the newer and still often incipient elements disengaging themselves from these as Neotechnic."

The Paleolithic Age was characterized by its rough stone implements, by hunting, and by war, but it was not without its vigor of artistic presentation. The Paleotechnic Age has been characterized by its mining towns, its steam engines and railroads, its concentrated and overcrowded cities—smoke filled, soot covered, slum infested and reaching out endlessly to blight the landscape. It has been characterized by degraded human lives, by instability of employment, by waste and exploitation of resources, by imperialism and wars.

The Neolithic Age brought the use of polished stone implements, cultural advances in such arts as pottery and weaving, the domestication of animals and the cultivation of grain and fruit trees—all elements of a more peaceful development. It may well be that the Neotechnic Age will be known as the age of electricity and the motor vehicle in which became possible de-

* Kropotkin, Peter: *Fields, Factories and Workshops.* London, 1898
** Geddes, Patrick and Branford, Victor: *The Coming Policy.*
  London, 1917; Geddes, Patrick: *Cities in Evolution.* London, 1915

centralization, the integration of industry and agriculture, the preservation and conservation of resources, the stabilization of production and employment. If so, the skill of man may once again be directed by life, towards life, and for life. Geddes* states in these words his vision of that future: "As there will be no need for aggression, peace may replace war. The task of peace will be a positive and constructive rebuilding, first of man's environment and then of society. . . . For social health, as for individual health, must not the essential matter be hygiene? *Il faut cultiver son jardin.* That is the hygiene of Peace."

"When all the peoples of the world become developed in the art of self-support," wrote Henry Ford,** "business will once more become service. There will be no competition, because the basis of competition will have vanished. The varied peoples will develop skills which will be in the nature of monopolies and not competitive. From the beginning, the races have exhibited distinct strains of genius. . . . The sooner we get back to a basis of natural specialities and drop this free-for-all system of grab, the sooner we shall be sure of international self-respect and international peace. Trying to take the trade of the world can promote war. It cannot promote prosperity."

Times of transition are times of creation as well as trouble. The transition from the Paleotechnic to the Neotechnic is not proving as peaceful as Patrick Geddes expected it to be. There are many unsolved human problems. Technical and human possibilities do not move forward at the same rate, and as one lags behind the other, conflict results which sometimes seems insurmountable. Times of transition are always pregnant with conflict. Sometimes everything gets out of balance and we seem to be rushing headlong down the path to war. We are so deeply concerned with the symptoms of such dislocation that we cannot or will not look at the causes from which the symptoms arise. Future historians may very well see in the two World Wars the expression of inevitable transition; they may go farther and see in them the instruments of necessary and desirable change. We all hope there will be no other war. Hopes, however, though they may influence reality, cannot actually control it. In times like these, it is wisdom to prepare for the worst, while continuing to hope for the best. What does such preparation mean in terms of planning? What means do we have to help us meet an emergency? What could we do to make ourselves invulnerable as a nation and safe as individuals?

Decentralization, combined with the integration of industry and agriculture and the creation of self-sustaining regions, is a complete answer to our problem. Providing relative security in time of war, such planning would

---

* Quoted from: Boardman, Philip: Patrick Geddes. *Maker of the Future.* Chapel Hill, 1944
** Ford Henry: *My Life and My Work.* New York, 1925

also establish the frame work for a better and more satisfactory life in time of peace. It would cushion the destruction of war. It would, at the same time, relieve people from the destructive impact of our industrial age. The life of an individual and of society would gain new health and freedom.

This is no vague Utopia. This is the most practical course we can take for our defence. It cannot be followed without large expenditure; but defence has always been costly. We go on inventing and producing expensive weapons which may become obsolete before they come off the assembly line. We have to spend money if we want security. The money we might spend on decentralization, however, would be money soundly invested. We would get something lasting for each dollar spent. In a very real sense, our investment would amortize itself and our money come back to us with interest.

From the Chinese Wall to the Maginot Line, protecting walls have provided men a refuge in time of danger. Attacked by enemies, men have sought to protect themselves in a walled place of refuge, a walled town or city; they have even tried to protect a whole nation with one vast wall. Those protecting walls became outmoded as weapons of attack changed. A defence-seeking community carried always the heavy burden of keeping its walls in repair, moving them, rebuilding them. This was always a costly undertaking.

Today that expense is no longer a burden. Indeed, the advent of the airplane and the development of atomic weapons have made obsolete, not only the city wall, but also the concentrated city that wall required. Highly concentrated centers of production, communication, and government today, instead of providing safety, invite their own destruction. An attack upon such centers might, at one and the same time, cripple production, destroy defence possibilities, and so lower morale as to make continued resistance impossible. Today we can find security only through the dispersal of cities and industries. As new weapons become more and more destructive, security can be attained only if decentralization is combined with the integration of industry and agriculture, only if there are created relatively self-sustaining regions able to provide for the needs of their people in war or in peace.

The development of atomic weapons will effect the spacing of our communities and city aggregates but not their structure itself. Donald Monson* gives a summary of the latest facts available which will effect the spacing of new cities. There are mainly two factors which have a decisive influence: the blast damage and the radioactive fall-out. For the effect of the blast

---

* Monson, Donald: Is Dispersal Obsolete?

damage of a twenty megaton bomb he refers to Knapp* who estimates that it would extend over an area of fifteen miles radius from point zero. If the bomb is increased to the limit of the chart at forty five megatons, the radius would be about twenty miles. Increasing the curve by crude projection to one hundred magatons (assuming that the scaling laws hold), the radius would be about twenty-five miles, the curve seemingly becoming asymptotic at that point.

Lapp** points out that the extent and degree of radioactivity of the fall-out depend on several factors: the power and composition of the bomb, height of explosion, velocity, and direction of the wind, and composition of the debris. The worst problems occur when bombs of high megatonnage are set off close to the earth's surface. The fall-out will, however, normally occur down-wind and will be scattered by the combined effects of the surface winds and the characteristic forty to sixty knot winds of the stratosphere. The radioactive shadow will extend over an area of fifty miles within the area of the wind direction.

In order to demonstrate, diagramatically, how these defence demands will effect the spacing and the size of cities in a given area with a given population, we take the industrial area, centered in Chicago, which extends to Milwaukee in the north, to St. Louis in the southwest, and Indianapolis in the southeast. It contains approximately 80,000 square miles and it is inhabited by thirteen million people of which nine million live in cities over ten thousand. These people as well as their industries have to be redistributed.

In our wind diagrams, to the four main directions of the compass the four between them were added making a total of eight wind directions. The wind may blow in any of these directions however, at different times. Therefore, it seems to be the most reliable solution to have around the cities an open area of fifty miles radius for the absorbtion of the possible radioactive fall-out. Then in our area we would have forty cities, each with a population of two hundred and twenty-five thousand. Cities of such a size are still an inviting target. If however we increase the number of cities and decrease their population and, by spacing them twenty miles apart, we would have two hundred cities each with a population of forty-five thousand. If one of these should be bombed, then only forty-five thousand people would be exposed to the full effects of the bomb. An additional forty-five thousand, or in some cases ninety thousand, depending on the direction of the wind, would be subject to the radio-active fall out. This means that on the average one hundred twelve thousand five hundred people, only half as many would be exposed to the effects of the bomb and

---

* Knapp, Harold A. Jr. South Woodley Look at the H-Bomb
** Lapp, Ralph E. Civil Defence Faces New Peril
  Bulletin of Atomic Scientist's, Chicago, Dec., Oct., and Nov., 1954 issues

of this number only approximately one-third would be exposed to its full effects. To bomb these two hundred cities effectively, two hundred bombs would be needed. Consequently, the smaller cities would be a less inviting target and therefore much safer. Though the danger zone of the radioactive fall-out may increase in size, decentralization remains the only way in which relative protection may be secured.

These cities do not need to be alike. They could be varied according to

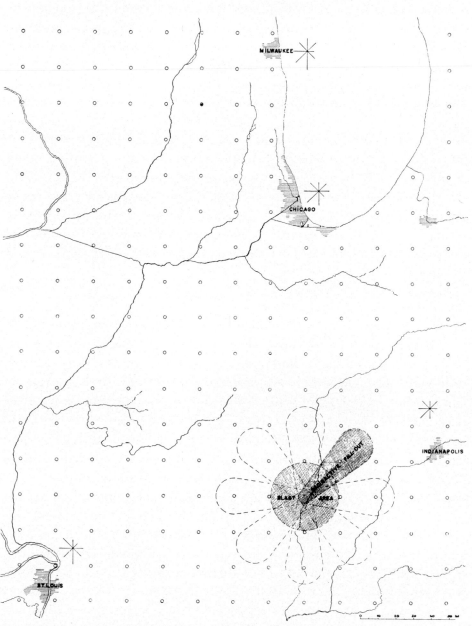

252. EFFECT OF H-BOMB *on the Size and Distribution of Cities*

their function, as for instance the decentralized city around an inlet (Ill. 241) demonstrates. Such a re-distribution of people and their industries is quite possible in the United States with its relatively low population density. However, it would be impossible in the over populated countries of Europe and Asia.

If the regional concept we propose were accepted with all its implications, all that would be needed to make the concept reality would be a comprehensive plan, with a new concept of zoning, and the determination to follow this plan. The planning problem involved is twofold. There is, as we have seen, a physical problem, the actual planning of a region and its settlements. But there is also a legislative and administrative problem. The two phases of the planning problem are, of course, closely interrelated. The most important legislative-administrative task would be the unification of the region in such a way as to maintain diversity and retain a maximum degree of local independence.

Perhaps our planning ideas could help solve these intrinsic problems. A non-partisan agency, immune to political and economic pressure, might be able to create an administrative system able to balance the divergent forces of independence and dependence. Such an agency could also create a zoning ordinance which would determine the use of land for the maintenance of a balanced regional economy with all its diversified implications, and which would also determine WHERE WHAT could or should be built.

Because of the financial problems involved, decentralizaiton seems an unrealizable, chimerical undertaking. But it only *seems* so. Decentralization is less a problem of money than it is of will. Determination can bring it to pass. Adolph A. Berle, when he was Assistant Secretary of State, once said: "In finance there are techniques which are as able to rebuild and to rehouse the United States as they are able to equip an army. They have not been used primarily because there was no compelling desire to use them." Today the compelling necessity for the use of these techniques has come. It is also a surprising fact that the money needed to make decentralization a reality is already provided for—at least in theory.

After the Second World War, plans were made and money appropriated for the construction of non-farm housing units. It was the aim of this national housing program to construct 12,600,000 units within ten years and thus to relieve the housing shortage and to eliminate vast slum areas in our cities. We do not know exactly how many of these housing units were built,—perhaps half of those originally planned. But we do know that they were built without a comprehensive plan to govern their location and without regard to future development. We can, moreover, as William

Wheaton* points out "afford to channel new growth into the decentralized pattern. The volume of such growth is prodigious: twenty-five billion dollars last year (1950) for new plants and equipment, 1,500,000 new homes, enough for five million people, with roads, water, sewers, schools, stores and other services to go with them. This annual increment of new growth, properly guided, could relocate a fifth or a third of our urban population with their factories in each decade."

We are facing the necessity of rebuilding our highway system. It has become obsolete because it was not designed for the heavy truck traffic it must now carry. In a survey made in 1949, Thomas H. MacDonald, federal Commissioner of Public Works, found that, out of the 40,000 miles of our most heavily traveled roads, only 1,900 miles are adequate for the immensely increasing motor traffic. It is estimated that we need to spend five billion dollars a year for fifteen years, a total of seventy-five billion dollars, to replace our obsolete highways and bridges. This money, too, might achieve the placing of these roads in accordance with a sound plan. Other undertakings could be added to this list. We are constantly spending large sums of money, for instance, on soil and conservation, on the preservation and control of water resources, on irrigation, on flood and erosion control, on land reclamation and reforestation. If these projects were coordinated and fitted into a comprehensive plan, they too could further decentralization. Some of these projects are, by their very nature, national or even continental in scope. Others are determined by regional or local needs.

There are two ways in which such vast undertakings may be executed. There is the piecemeal method which gives no consideration to the effects of one project upon another or to the relation of the projects to a whole. The result is the eternal perpetuation of confused and unsatisfactory conditions. But there is also another method: to do things with a clear and comprehensive aim in view, to coordinate the many diverse and necessary tasks toward the achievement of real value for the present and for the future. If such a spirit could be made to prevail, unlimited possibilities for the accomplishment of our desired ends would be opened.

Decentralization would no longer need to be considered an impractical dream. It could become practical reality. The means to accomplish it are now ready to our hands. What is needed is the will to plan their integration and their use.

It would be a wonderful thing if some magician were to perform a miracle and, with one wave of his wand, transform things as they are into things

---

* Wheaton, William L. C.: *Federal Action Toward a National Dispersal Policy* Bulletin of the Atomic Scientists. Vol. VII. No. 9. September, 1951

as they ought to be. But there are no magicians. We must ourselves perform the miracle. And we cannot hope to perform it over night. If, however, we recognize that planning is basically the interpretation of the great technical and economic forces of our time, we shall be moving toward that miracle. These forces shaped the regions and their settlements into their present form; they will eventually reshape them. It is our task to plan wisely and in harmony with nature, to use all technical means available, to the end that the region may find again a form suitable to its function in the national life and become capable of fulfilling the needs of its people. Governmental powers, technical skills, administrative abilities are abundantly available for our use. Have we the will to use them? Have we, within ourselves, the determination which is the magic agency alone capable of bringing the dream to fulfillment, of making the miracle a living reality?